The Forgotten Era

'This is the indispensable book for anyone interested in the pre-colonial history of what now constitutes Nigeria. Incredibly necessary, magnificently done, Siollun charts the characters and events that shaped the political, social, cultural and economic lives of those who inhabited Nigeria's territories centuries before colonisation. *The Forgotten Era* is as important to understanding the past as it is to comprehending the present and planning the future.'
—Remi Adekoya, author of *It's Not About Whiteness, It's About Wealth*

'Anyone who wants to understand the world, needs to understand Nigeria, a country with the largest Black population in the world. And there is no more eloquent and informed guide than Max Siollun. This is a totally essential book that you'll want to annotate, re-read and gift many times.'
—Sathnam Sanghera, author of *Empireland: How Modern Britain is Shaped by its Imperial Past*

'Max Siollun accomplishes what few dare to attempt – a revival of a time when the region now known as Nigeria was alive with vibrant kingdoms, city-states, and complex social dynamics long before European colonisers imposed their narratives. Blending the rigour of a scholar with the captivating depth of a griot, he brings history to life with a cinematic sweep and intellectual confidence. Prepare to be transported, challenged and, ultimately, changed.'

—Gimba Kakanda, writer, researcher and Co-Lead at the Presidential Initiative for Innovation, Policy Evaluation and Research (PIIPER), Nigeria

'Max Siollun is the most committed contemporary chronicler of Nigerian history. It's impossible to pick up a Siollun book and not emerge a different person, purged of popular historical falsehoods, and brimming with riveting insight into how Nigeria has come to be what it is today.'

—Tolu Ogunlesi, journalist, photographer and writer

'Without a doubt, Max Siollun is the best Nigeria-focused historian of our times. Like his other outstanding books, *The Forgotten Era* is an engaging and accessible deep-dive into the storied past of an ever-dynamic country that, by 2045, will be the third most populous in the world. An unforgettable read, Max's latest book skilfully demystifies Nigeria's pre-colonial past in ways that can help us make sense of both its knotty modern-day challenges and its disconcertingly uncertain future.'

—Matthew T. Page, former US State Department Nigeria expert and Associate Fellow, Chatham House

'Max Siollun has succeeded at a near-impossible task: making Nigeria's pre-colonial history accessible for readers without flattening the tremendous diversity of the many peoples who would eventually become one nation.'

—Alex Thurston, Associate Professor, School of Public and International Affairs, University of Cincinnati

The Forgotten Era

Nigeria Before British Rule

Max Siollun

First published 2025 by Pluto Press
New Wing, Somerset House, Strand, London WC2R 1LA
and Pluto Press, Inc.
1930 Village Center Circle, 3-834, Las Vegas, NV 89134

www.plutobooks.com

British Library Cataloguing in Publication Data
A catalogue record for this book is available from the British Library

ISBN 978 0 7453 5008 0   Hardback
ISBN 978 0 7453 5010 3   PDF
ISBN 978 0 7453 5009 7   EPUB

This book is printed on paper suitable for recycling and made from fully managed
and sustained forest sources. Logging, pulping and manufacturing processes are
expected to conform to the environmental standards of the country of origin.

Typeset by Stanford DTP Services, Northampton, England

Printed and bound by CPI Group (UK) Ltd, Croydon CR0 4YY

EU GPSR Authorised Representative
LOGOS EUROPE, 9 rue Nicolas Poussin, 17000, LA ROCHELLE, France
Email: Contact@logoseurope.eu

Contents

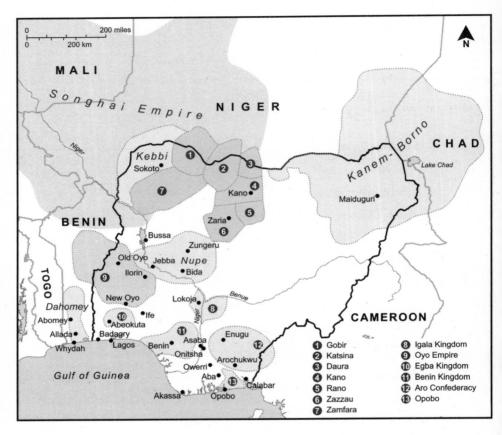

Map 1   Key pre-colonial states in the River Niger area, 1800

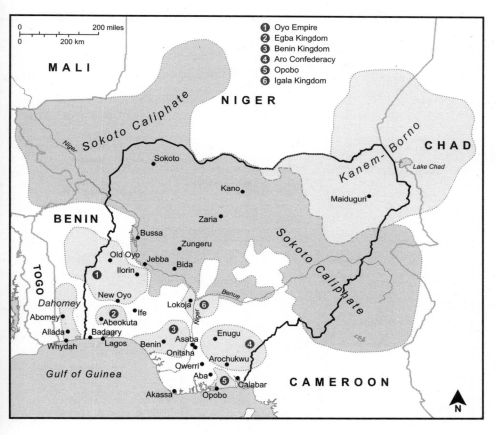

Map 2 Key pre-colonial states in the River Niger area, 1810

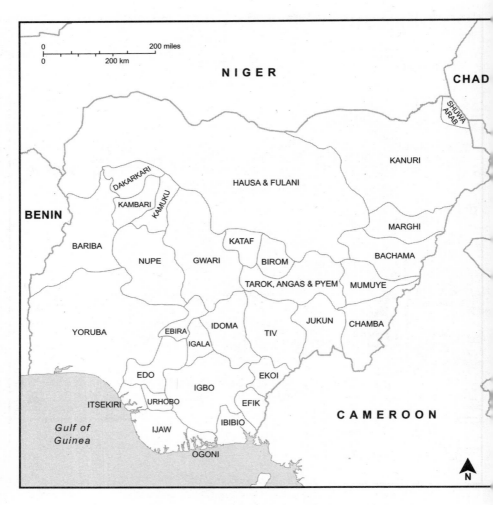

Map 3   Map of Nigeria's ethnic groups

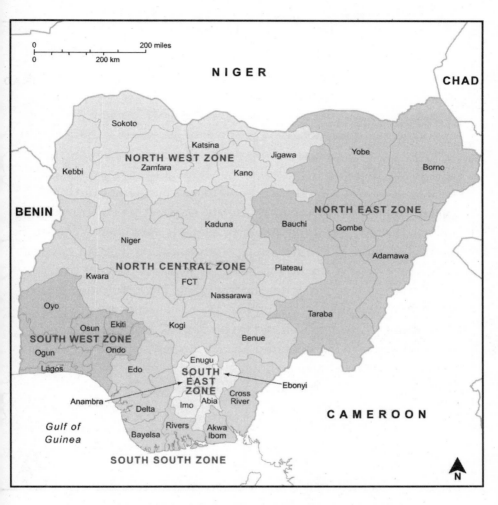

Map 4   Current map of Nigeria's 36 states and geo-political zones

Dedication

I have dedicated most of my prior books to the memory of my father. I will dedicate this book to a young woman who used to see my father in her dreams even after he died. She had recurring dreams where she would see him walking down a narrow road to an unknown destination. In those dreams she would walk towards him, but always woke up before she reached him. Then one night she chased after him as he walked down the usual narrow road, and called out to him. He turned around to see the young woman who called out to him. To the young woman's surprise, my father was not pleased that she was trying to follow him. He asked her: 'What are you doing here?' When the young woman replied that she wanted to follow him to where he was going, he instantly told her that she could not follow him to where he was going. He instead told her to go back immediately and asked her 'Who is looking after our son?' After telling the young woman that her son needed her, and that she needed to be with her son rather than him, the young woman did as my father told her. Saddened, she stopped following him along the narrow road and watched him walk away for the final time.

She returned to her son's side as my father instructed, and there she has remained ever since. She also stopped having the recurring dream of following my father down a narrow road. That young woman is my mother. Who knows what would have happened to her and I had my father not, via her dreams, communicated his desire for her to dedicate her attention to their son rather than constantly trying to follow her husband after he died.

I must apologise to my mum that it took this long for me to dedicate one of my books entirely to her. Mum – thank you for everything you have done for me. Thank you for carrying the burdens of multiple generations of an entire family, for forgiving those who wronged you, and instead returning their mistreatment with compassion, generosity, and kindness that they never showed you. Thank you setting an example for how a human being should behave, as well as putting up with a son who inadvertently extended your grief by growing up to look and sound exactly like your dead husband; thereby constantly reminding you of your loss every day. You once wrote in your grief-stricken diary: 'our son has no daddy … I still pray that our Lord will grant him good health and a long useful life so that he will live to complete those things you couldn't complete'. Given your husband's big ambitions, I probably have not done everything he would have done. Nonetheless, I hope I have at least pleased you by jumping into a few of his footsteps.

Preface

This book is a prequel to my previous book *What Britain Did to Nigeria*. Why should anyone write or read a book about Nigeria's pre-colonial history? Here are a few excellent reasons. Firstly, a book about Nigeria is not only a book about its 200 million+ citizens, or just a book about the country with the largest Black population in the world. It is also a book about a country that will soon have the third largest English-speaking population in the world (with twice as many English speakers as Britain), and also a history of one in every five people in sub-Saharan Africa, and even more people in the diaspora in North and South America, Europe, and the Caribbean.

The second reason is that existing histories of Africa are usually histories of slavery, colonialism, or of Europeans 'discovering' African cities, mountains, rivers, and other landmarks that the natives had somehow not noticed (in other words, a history of what *Europeans* did in Africa, rather than a history of Africans themselves). There is thus a *need* to tell Nigeria's pre-colonial history.

I will begin with a pre-emptive apology. Although I tried to give airtime to as many different regions of pre-colonial Nigeria as possible, given the massive ethnic, linguistic, and religious diversity of Nigeria, it was impossible to include all of its over 500 indigenous language groups.

THE LAND OF THE BLACKS

Outsiders have always called West African lands by names other than those the indigenes use. These names evolved over time. Ancient Arab chroniclers referred to it as *Bilad al-Sudan* ('The Land of the Blacks'). In the sixteenth–eighteenth centuries European writers described West Africa as 'Guinea', and in the nineteenth century 'Sudan' or 'Soudan' became the most popular European term for it. Despite Guinea and Sudan being countries today, the prior references to them were to a much larger geographic area encompassing the entire region of West Africa south of the Sahara Desert. In 1899 British colonial officers considered 'British Soudan' and 'Niger Soudan' before finally giving the name 'Nigeria' to their largest West African colony.

Foundational heroes have been critical to building national consciousness and unity in other countries; for example, George Washington in the USA, Mustafa Kemal Atatürk in Turkey, David Ben-Gurion in Israel, Charles de Gaulle in France, and Mahatma Gandhi in India. The memory of West Africa's heroes were displaced during the colonial era. Because pre-colonial histories of West Africa are so rare, it can seem like a place without history or inspirational characters. Yet on the contrary, just like the Americas, Asia, and Europe, pre-colonial Nigeria had its own cast of mesmerising protagonists including revolutionaries, intellectuals, innovators, and villainous assassins. These include the family that inspired a revolution in the lands to which their ancestors migrated, overthrew three different kingdoms that had reigned for over 1000 years, created the biggest state in pre-colonial Africa, and when not causing revolutions; found time to write over 300 different books and pamphlets. There is also the royal court official who engineered the death of four kings that he worked for, and the little slave boy who became the first Black bishop in history, a linguist, scholar, prolific writer, and who met and befriended Queen Victoria and other leading members of the British aristocracy.

Pre-colonial West Africa also had a wonderful series of magico-religious lore to rival those of ancient Greece and Rome. Yet pre-colonial Nigeria was not a land of innocence. At times its people were so committed to their religions that some of them killed in service of those religions. There is an intermediate place between the 'Dark Continent' accounts that European colonial officers wrote about West Africa, and the often romanticised accounts that indigenous West African historians wrote in the immediate post-independence era in the 1960s and 1970s in their attempts to shake off negative European stereotypes and unearth new African heroes. That intermediate place is in this book.

Prelude
In the Beginning – Nok

The earliest physical evidence of Nigeria's pre-colonial history emerged from a mysterious but skilled people in Nigeria's middle region who left no oral or written records about themselves. When tin miners accidentally dug up an over 1500 year-old terracotta head in 1944 near Jos[1] in central Nigeria, they did not realise that they had discovered traces of an unknown lost civilisation and the oldest artworks ever found in sub-Saharan Africa. The terracotta they found was remarkably similar to another terracotta head that was dug up 15 years earlier about 40 miles away in a village in Kaduna State in northern Nigeria called Nok. Archaeologists realised that the two terracottas were related and made by people from the same culture. After seeing them, a young British official named Bernard Fagg who studied archaeology at Cambridge University nicknamed these people 'Nok' – after the name of the village where the first terracotta was discovered in 1928. As word got out, more and more people came forward to present archaeologists and museum officials with similar ancient objects they had dug up, and over the next few decades, hundreds more Nok terracottas were discovered. About 75 per cent of the Nok terracottas were excavated between Nok and Jemaa, where the first two Nok terracottas were found. During a twenty-first century excavation, archaeologists found 1700 terracotta pieces in an area of only 450 square yards,[2] which indicated that the area was previously densely populated or that its sculptors were prolific. Because the Nok area is so large and excavation work by trained archaeologists is infrequent, it is likely that hundreds or thousands more terracottas remain buried underground, and that what we currently know about them is the tip of an ancient iceberg.

---

1 The sculpture was found at a village called Jemaa.
2 Atwood, 2011, p. 36.

The Nok left few clues about themselves other than their artwork. No one knows what language(s) they spoke, whether they had kings and queens, or how their society was organised. Yet the amazing variety of terracotta figurines they made and left behind gave several clues about who they were and how they lived. They are the 'ground zero' from which the reconstruction of Nigeria's pre-colonial history begins.

The Nok area covers approximately 30,000 square miles (about the same size as Portugal) and includes Nigeria's capital city Abuja, and modern-day Benue, Kaduna, Nasarawa, and Plateau States in the so-called 'Middle Belt' region of central Nigeria (see Map 4). The Nok terracottas' importance transcends archaeology and art. They are massively significant for several reasons. Firstly, the Nok terracottas are the oldest known sculptures in sub-Saharan Africa. Secondly, they represent evidence for the earliest known human civilisation in West Africa. Perhaps the most iconic of them is a sculpture of a man and woman kneeling in front of each other, with their arms wrapped around each other in a loving embrace. Another almost erotic sculpture depicts a woman cupping her breasts, while others show people singing or playing musical instruments, as well as figurines that were probably used in religious ceremonies. Excavators also found ruins of the iron furnaces used to make the terracottas. The Nok had love, artworks, music, religion, and technology. These are markers for the existence of an advanced civilisation which no one knew existed in West Africa over 700 years before the Great Wall of China was built, and before Rome became a republic.

The terracottas even show what the Nok people looked like. Their human statues usually showed people with oval-shaped eyes, men with their hairlines shaved back, and women with elaborate hairstyles or headdresses. The Nok also left fragments of their society's dark side. Some of their sculptures show prisoners bound with ropes around their necks and waists. Ornamental discoveries also include jewellery such as earrings, lip plugs, and nose rings.

Microscopic analysis of the clay that the Nok used to make their terracottas shows that the same clay was used throughout the Nok area.[3] This means either that the Nok sculptors always obtained their clay from the same place, or more intriguingly, that they had a special guild of sculptors.

It is surprising that scholars speak of a unified 'Nok culture' because in contemporary times, the Nok zone is the most multi-ethnic and multi-lingual part of Nigeria. Over 100 different indigenous languages are spoken in the two states where the first two terracottas were found in 1928 and 1944. The areas where these items were found are now inhabited by ethnic groups in Nigeria's Middle Belt such as the Birom, Gbagyi, Ham, Kataf, Tarok, and Tiv. The Nok were probably the ancestors of these ethnic groups. Revealingly, the lip plugs found among the terracottas resemble those worn by Ham women as recently as the twentieth century.[4] It is unlikely that the Nok were a mono-culture, and more likely that instead of being a single cultural zone, a similar form of art and/ or religion existed among several different language groups. The Nok remain an enigma because they abruptly disappeared, leaving behind only their artworks and the tools they used to make them. While the Nok left no oral or written history about themselves, several other ancient Nigerians left lots of lore about who they were and what they did ...

---

3   Ibid., p. 36.
4   Fagg, 1959, p. 290.

The Hausa Seven

Hausa is one of the most widely spoken languages in Africa. Over 60 million people speak Hausa in countries such as Nigeria, Chad, Niger, and Sudan. However, until around 400 years ago, the people who spoke Hausa did not call themselves Hausa, nor did they identify themselves as one group. Instead they called themselves 'Hausawa' (Hausa speakers) or by the name of the place in which they lived. For example 'Kanawa' (those who lived in Kano) and 'Katsinawa' (those who lived in Katsina). Despite its prominence, Hausaland's early history is often overlooked in favour of the tectonic changes that immigrants imposed there in the nineteenth century. Yet Hausaland's early history remains important for contextualising the changes that later arose, and because it was a confluence point for many seminal pre-colonial events.

THE KING SLAYER OF DAURA[1]

Although it is not known where the Hausa people or their language first came from, an ancient document entitled *Daura Makas Sarki* ('The King Killer of Daura') records a popular legend in Hausa tradition which claims that the first rulers of Hausaland were the descendants of an Iraqi prince named Bayajidda. According to this legend, Bayajidda was the son of Abdullahi, the King of Baghdad. Bayajidda left Baghdad and travelled to the Kanem-Borno Empire in what is now north-east Nigeria. When he arrived there he married the daughter of the *Mai* (King) of Borno and they had a son called Biram. However, after learning that the *mai* planned to kill him, Bayajidda fled Borno, and travelled west to a town in Hausaland called Daura (in current north-western Nigeria). While there, Bay-

---

1   Daura is the hometown of former Nigerian president Muhammadu Buhari.

ajidda killed a snake called Sarki (king)[2] that had been terrorising the town's residents and preventing them from drinking water from their well. When the town's Queen Daura (after whom the town was named) heard that someone had killed Sarki, she offered to reward the snake slayer by sharing her queendom with him. Several false claimants came forward until Bayajidda proved that he killed Sarki the snake by presenting its severed head as evidence. Bayajidda proposed to Queen Daura, and for the second consecutive time, he married a blue-blooded woman as Daura agreed to marry him as a gesture of gratitude for killing Sarki. As news of a snake-slaying hero spread, Bayajidda acquired the nickname '*Makas Sarki*' (King Slayer). Bayajidda and Daura had a son called Bawo who later had six sons. Some versions of the legend claim that Bawo's six sons were supposedly born in three twin births.[3]

THE SEVEN HAUSAS

Bayajidda's son Biram with the *magira* (King of Borno's daughter) and his six grandsons from his son Bawo supposedly became rulers of seven Hausa States known as *Hausa Bakwai* (the Seven Hausas). Whether or not the Bayajidda legend is true, fable, or pure fabrication, at least seven large Hausa States named Biram, Daura, Gobir, Kano, Katsina, Rano, and Zazzau definitely existed over an area of approximately 200 square miles in what is now northern Nigeria and southern Niger. Although the exact date of their formation is not known, they likely arose sometime between the seventh and ninth centuries.

The hero killed the snake, married the queen, and fathered kings happy ending elements in the Bayajidda legend has parallels with fictitious St George-type European legends regarding a dragon-slaying hero. However, even if the Bayajidda story is apocryphal or has been embellished, its deeper meaning still merits further analysis. The almost ubiquitous oral and written histories in multiple West African societies spread far apart (such as Borgu,

---

2   *Sarki* is the Hausa name for 'chief' or 'king'.
3   Kano's version of the legend claims that Bawo was the snake killer.

Borno, and Oyo), regarding a travelling hero from the Middle East make it unlikely that the Bayajidda legend has absolutely no historical basis. The mystery of 'The King Slayer of Daura' is amplified by several common misinterpretations of it. It is often presumed to be a legend that explains the origin of the Hausa people. However, Bayajidda's story does not explain where the Hausa *people* first came from. It instead explains the origin of the Hausa *monarchy* in existence at the time it was written. Bayajidda's children and grandchildren were clearly not the first rulers of Hausaland, since Bayajidda met and married a woman who was already the Queen of Daura before he arrived there.

THE QUEEN SLAYER

There are at least two hidden and often overlooked clues in the Bayajidda story that allude to its deeper meaning. The first clue is that the *Daura Makas Sarki* mentions that four other queens preceded Queen Daura. Bayajidda's marriage to the fifth consecutive queen suggests that Daura's monarchy was based on female rulership. Daura was not an outlier and female leadership was also present in other parts of Hausaland. As late as 1907, women held senior positions in the governing administrations of Zaria and Birnin Gwari. Secondly, the *Daura Makas Sarki* stated that the snake Bayajidda killed was female. The explicit gender references to five consecutive queens and a female snake are very unlikely to be coincidence. Both the gender and name of the snake that Bayajidda killed are pertinent. The document also mentions that Daura's people stopped referring to their queen's house as hers, but after Bayajidda's marriage to her, instead started referring to it as 'the house of the king slayer'. This suggests a diminution in, or repeal of, Queen Daura's authority. Bayajidda may thus have killed not just a snake, but also overthrown a pre-existing ruler. These clues make it very likely that Bayajidda's tale is at least partially a story of changing gender relations in Daura; represented by Bayajidda's displacement of Daura's lineage of female queens, and his descendants' replacement of them with kingship. Thus his honorific title of 'King

Slayer' might be mistaken, and he may be more accurately described as the 'Queen Slayer'; the man who ended matriarchy in Daura and replaced it with male leadership. It may also be reasonable to assume that Daura was the first Hausa kingdom to emerge and that the *Daura Makas Sarki*'s references to Borno explain the era during which parts of Hausaland were vassals to Borno (as exemplified by multiple loan terms and titles from Borno such as *birni* (city) and *galadima* (a fief holder or provincial governor)).

The Bayajidda legend also has ramifications beyond Daura. If Bayajidda is based on a historical figure, there are two likely contenders. The first comes from an alternate name that some sources gave to him. Borno's version of the story ends after he fled from Borno, and includes an interesting postscript: 'In later days the people of Bornu [*sic*] heard that Abu Yazid had become the Sultan of Daura.'[4] The reference to an 'Abu Yazid' becoming the King of Daura is undoubtedly a reference to Bayajidda. A Berber man named Abu Yazid led a revolt in North Africa in the tenth century. After he was defeated, his followers fled south and seemingly disappeared. It is possible that the Bayajidda legend is a corrupted rendition of this and that some of Abu Yazid's followers ended up in Borno and Hausaland. A second possibility is that the Bayajidda legend is a compressed and metaphorical rendition that coalesces several events and process such as an invasion or migration of people into Hausaland, the beginning of kingship, and/or the arrival of Islam or Middle Eastern influence there. Although the legend makes it appear that Bayajidda's insertion into the Hausa ruling dynasty was instant, it may be an allegorical explanation of political and religious changes that occurred over several years or centuries.

GARRISON STATES

Each of the Hausa States supposedly founded by Bayajidda's descendants was named after its walled capital city known as *Birni* (plural: *birane*). These capital cities were fortified and surrounded by high

---

4   Hallam, 1966, p. 48.

walls. For example, Kano's walls were 30 to 50 feet high. There were at least 247 walled towns in Hausaland prior to 1800.[5] The style and development of these walls evinced both economic and military purposes. Most of the area within the walls was uninhabited and as a city's population grew, it expanded the walls to maintain large unoccupied spaces within them. The walls were built to protect a city's residents in the event of a siege or war, and also protected arable land and resources within them. The Hausa *birane* left farming space inside the city walls; so that if they were attacked or subjected to an extended siege, their residents could grow and obtain food without leaving the city. The uninhabited spaces inside the city walls could also absorb refugees from rural areas during a siege or famine.

Although they were similar to each other, each of the Hausa States was independent and had its own *sarki* (king). The working-class commoners were referred to as *talakawa*. Each state also had a specific duty that it was responsible for. For example, Gobir was known as *sarkin yaki* (the king of war) that guarded Hausaland from Tuareg invaders. Kano and Rano were known as *sarakunan babba* (kings of indigo) as they were centres for producing and dyeing clothes. Kano had many artisans who were skilled at weaving and dyeing clothes in different beautiful and bright colours. They dyed clothing by dipping them into pits of water mixed with ash, potassium, and indigo plants. Daura and Katsina were known as *sarakunan kasuwa* (kings of the market) as they were trading states. Zazzau was known as *sarkin bayi* (king of slaves) as it was the slave-raiding state that supplied slave labour to the other Hausa States.

'A RACE OF TRADERS'

Although in contemporary times, Igbos are regarded as Nigeria's prototypical traders and micro-entrepreneurs, Hausas had that reputation in the pre-colonial era. A British traveller to Hausaland in the late nineteenth century described Hausas as 'a race of traders'.[6] Hausas were among the most prolific and successful itinerant traders

---

5   Phillips, 1992, p. 220.
6   Robinson, 1900, p. 27.

in pre-colonial Africa. They travelled hundreds of miles throughout West and North Africa to trade. Hausaland was part of a vast international and inter-continental trading network that spanned across West and North Africa, and into Europe. As late as the nineteenth century, 30,000 camel loads of salt arrived yearly in Kano for distribution as far away as Ashanti-land in modern-day Ghana. The Ashanti exchanged their gold and kola nuts for livestock, cloth, and salt from Hausa traders. This trade was so routinised that expatriate Arabs and Ghanaians lived in Kano; which then (as now) was a large trading city. Trading with North Africa and obtaining European goods was a hazardous and laborious endeavour. Traders from the Hausa States such as Katsina, Kano, Zaria, and other sub-Saharan African states such as Kanem-Borno and Timbuktu loaded goods including gold, ivory, leather, clothing fabrics, kola nuts, and ostrich feathers onto camels, and embarked on a dangerous northward 2–12-month journey across the Sahara Desert. During their journeys, traders often passed the skeletons of others who died on the same journey before them. When they arrived in North African locations in Algeria, Morocco, Libya, and Tunisia, they exchanged their goods for cowries, clothing, salt, and European goods such as French silk, glass beads from Venice in Italy, coffee from Turkey, sugar from France, and other more mundane items such as tobacco, guns, mirrors, and paper. Arab traders in North Africa acted as middlemen who obtained goods from European sellers, and resold them to traders from sub-Saharan Africa. Hausa traders in turn exported the European and North African goods they obtained further south to areas that later became south-west Nigeria, further south to the Benin kingdom, and Hausa traders even travelled as far south as Aboh and Asaba in Igboland.

'THE SEVEN BASTARDS'

The Bayajidda legend also mentions the history of other Hausa States outside the core seven, and other neighbouring non-Hausa States. According to this part of the legend, Bayajidda also had a son called Karbogari with a Gwari woman. Karbogari then had seven sons who also established seven other states: Gwari, Kebbi, Jukun (also known as Kwararafa), Nupe, Yauri, Yoruba, and Zamfara. The Hausa referred to these seven states by the impolite phrase *Banza Bakwai* ('Seven Bastards' or 'Illegitimate Seven'). Gwari and Nupe were located in the areas that are now Niger and Kwara States in north-west Nigeria. Kwararafa was located in the areas that are now Adamawa and Taraba States in north-east Nigeria, Kebbi and Yauri were in modern-day Kebbi State, Yoruba was in south-west Nigeria, and Zamfara was in the far north-west of Nigeria (see Map 4).

While the *Banza Bakwai* story cannot be taken literally, it may be a metaphor for foreign states that Hausaland had established relationships with. It also demonstrates that the people of Hausaland were aware of other people that lived in faraway lands, and that long before Nigeria's formation, the Hausa, Oyo, Gwari, Nupe, and Jukun people already knew about, and met each other. The story of the *Banza Bakwai* may also be politically motivated attempts by the Hausa to de-legitimise neighbouring enemy or rival states by portraying them as products of Bayajidda's concubine. For example, it is notable that Kebbi and Kwararafa (both of whom invaded Hausaland at different points in time) are included among the so-called illegitimate states. Oddly, Borno and Songhai were not included in the *Banza Bakwai* despite their considerable influence on, and conflicts with, Hausaland.

THE *KANO CHRONICLE*

One of the best sources for Hausaland's pre-colonial history is an anonymous and undated Arabic document that begins with the words: 'This is the history of the lords of this country called Kano ...', and itemises Kano's history during a 1000-year timespan from the tenth century to the early twentieth century. This document, popularly known as the *Kano Chronicle*, challenges the common narrative that Africans had no written pre-colonial history, and also contains a list of Kano's kings and other key events in Hausaland up to 1892.

The *Kano Chronicle* mentions the exploits of two prominent personalities. The first is a warrior queen of Zazzau (later Zaria) named

7

Aminatu (Amina). According to the *Kano Chronicle*, Amina lived in the first half of the fifteenth century and embarked upon a 34-year campaign of conquest across Hausaland that saw her conquer not only neighbouring Hausa States, but also lands as far as Kwararafa (home of the Jukun) and Nupe. However, other sources such as the *Abuja Chronicle* described her as the daughter of Zaria's king, rather than Zaria's queen (and about 100 years later than the dates given in the *Kano Chronicle*). Amina's warrior image has been embellished with accounts claiming that after conquering enemy armies in battle, she would choose a lover from one of the defeated warriors, make love to him, and then execute him the following morning.

The King of Kano Mohammed Rumfa who governed from 1463 to 1499 was probably the most famous Hausa king. The *Kano Chronicle* claims that 'He can have no equal in might, from the time of the founding of Kano, until it shall end.'[7] His reign is renowned as one of economic and religious growth, and improvement of Kano's infrastructure. Rumfa opened additional markets, ordered the destruction of an animist religious shrine and the construction of a mosque in its place, and expanded Kano's walls. His reign was also one of majestic splendour as he acquired a harem of over 1000 women, dressed opulently and wore sandals embroidered with ostrich feathers, and had trumpets to announce his arrivals and departures. Rumfa also increased the government's power in a manner that would have serious repercussions 300 years later. He acquired the right to commandeer the property of private citizens (such as cattle and horses) and the right to take first born virgins for himself. Such extravagant exercises of power at the expense of private citizens later contributed to the series of grievances that initiated the most serious revolt against the Hausa kings in the early nineteenth century.

HAUSA AND FOREIGN RELATIONS

Hausaland was ruled by foreign conquerors during much of the last 500 years. Conquest by neighbouring empires caused Hausaland

---

7   Palmer, 1908, p. 77.

to absorb influences from multiple sources such as Borno, Songhai, and the Middle East. The *Kano Chronicle* is very candid in referencing not only Kano's triumphs but also its sobering losses; such as that when Kwararafa (Jukun) invaded and sacked Kano in the late sixteenth century, 'ate up the whole country and Kano became very weak'[8] and its surviving residents fled to Daura. At different points in time during their history, some of the Hausa States were allied with, or were part of, non-Hausa empires. Hausaland was sandwiched between the two powerful states of Songhai and Borno to its west and east, respectively. Some areas in western Hausaland were part of the Songhai Empire, and some of the eastern states were vassal states to Borno. Oddly, a Hausa State was included among the so-called *Banza Bakwai*. Its reasons for categorisation as an illegitimate state are apparent from its history. Although it had a large Hausa population, Kebbi was a province of the Songhai Empire, and was located adjacent to Hausaland's western frontier with Songhai, which was the largest and most powerful pre-colonial state in Africa between the fifteenth and sixteenth centuries. By military conquest, Songhai extended across vast tracts of territory that are now included in seven African countries: Gambia, Guinea, Niger, Nigeria, Mali, Mauritania, and Senegal. Songhai was almost the size of half of Europe and travelling from one end of it to the other was a 60-day journey. Since Kebbi was sandwiched between Hausaland to its east and Songhai to its west (see Map 1), it became vital to Hausaland's security. Although many of Kebbi's people spoke Hausa, its population was multi-ethnic and included other ethnic groups such as the Lelna and Tuareg.

According to the sixteenth-century author Leo Africanus, Songhai's armies marched into Hausaland in 1513. The Hausa States resisted but after failing to mount a common defence, Songhai's forces destroyed them one after the other and killed the kings of Gobir, Katsina, and Zazzau. They also captured the King of Kano but allowed him to stay on the throne after he agreed to pay one-third of his revenue to Songhai. After this invasion Songhai's ruler

---

8   Ibid., p. 82.

Askia Mohammed (also known as 'Askia the Great') installed residents in each of the conquered Hausa States. Despite the vivid descriptions of Songhai's invasion of Hausaland, there are reasons to doubt that it actually happened. Firstly, Leo Africanus is the only source that described the invasion. Oddly, the *Kano Chronicle* (which references Hausaland being invaded by other states that were not as strong as Songhai) did not mention this seemingly pivotal event, nor did the *Timbuktu Chronicles* (which is the Songhai equivalent). It may be that Leo Africanus identified the wrong conqueror that inflicted this devastation on Hausaland. The perpetrator of this invasion was probably not Songhai, but ironically, another Hausa State.

KANTA KOTAL OF KEBBI

Kebbi's placement among the *Banza Bakwai* may be due to one or both of the facts that it eclipsed all the others in military prowess, and because it allied itself with an enemy state. Mohammed Kotal from Kebbi was pivotal to Kebbi's emergence as a mighty state. His father was a village head with the title of *magaji*, while his mother was from Katsina. Kotal was a rebellious child and when his father died, his brother was chosen to succeed their father. After being passed over, Kotal left his family, became a warrior, and joined Songhai's army. After Songhai conquered the desert area of Asben (in modern-day Niger Republic) and expelled its Tuareg inhabitants, Kotal found another reason for rebellion. He was unhappy with the amount of war booty he was given following the invasion, and sometime between 1516 and 1517 he repealed his allegiance to Songhai, declared Kebbi's independence and himself as the *Kanta* (King) of Kebbi. This was an extremely bold move as at the time Songhai was at the height of its power. In the following year (1517 or 1518) Songhai sent a force to recapture Kebbi but Kotal defeated them. Over the next 30 years he not only resisted Songhai's attempts to re-conquer Kebbi, but also confronted Borno. Kebbi acquired such a fearsome military reputation that after some time Songhai stopped trying to regain Kebbi and accepted its independence from Songhai.

Kanta Kotal was not satisfied merely with being independent from Songhai and wanted more. He built walls around Kebbi, and during the next 30 years transformed Kebbi into the most powerful of the Hausa States. He also built a new Kebbi capital at Surame (in present-day Sokoto State of north-west Nigeria) and another town called Birnin Kebbi (which is now the capital of Kebbi State in north-west Nigeria). Kebbi conquered some of the other Hausa States and lands to the south of Hausaland in the Nupe area, and carved out an empire for itself that stretched from the fringes of the Sahara Desert to its north, to the Niger River to its south. When Kotal invaded the land of Air (in what is now Niger Republic) in the sixteenth century, the powerful Borno Empire came to help Air. A great war broke out, but Kebbi won after defeating Borno at Nguru in what is now north-east Nigeria. On his way back to Kebbi from this war, Kotal died in 1556 after a poisoned arrow hit him at Katsina.

Kebbi's power and reputation at the time of these conquests may have been even greater than currently acknowledged, because even the Hausa chroniclers, who regarded it as one of the *Banza Bakwai*, admitted that Kotal was a great ruler and conqueror. A remarkable aspect of Kebbi's resilience was that it was landlocked by Songhai and encircled by enemies, yet it still managed to resist successive attempts by the three mightiest empires of its heyday (Songhai, Borno, Hausaland) to subdue it. Kebbi's contemporary population is religiously mixed and includes Muslims and Christians. Although it is no longer as large as it used to be, many of its people are still soldiers and the Zuru area of Kebbi is a plentiful source of military recruits for the Nigerian army. For example, the current *Emir* of Zuru (traditional ruler), Mohammed Sani Sami, is a retired Nigerian army officer. A former Nigerian Chief of Army Staff, Lt-General Ishaya Bamaiyi is also from Zuru.

Despite the many upheavals that Hausaland experienced over a 500-year period, its greatest challenge was still to come. Islam entered Hausaland in the second half of the fourteenth century when a group of about 40 Muslims from Mali visited Kano and convinced the King of Kano Yaji to become a Muslim. Yaji built a mosque facing east and also encouraged his people to become Muslims. In the second half of the fifteenth century, one of Yaji's successors Mohammed Rumfa spread Islam in Kano with advice from a scholar named Abdulrahman. However, not all Hausas became Muslims and some of them continued to worship their old gods. Some of those who became Muslims combined Muslim practices with their old religions. The continuing co-existence of Islam and other animist religions generated controversy and debate about whether Islam should be the exclusive religion in Hausaland, and the extent to which society should tolerate the practice of other religions. This tension placed the Hausa kings in the firing line because they were not only the heads of state, but also set the state's religious trajectory. This mixing of old and new faiths continued for hundreds of years and, as will be demonstrated in the next chapter, eventually caused a revolution.

2
Son of the Learned

Events in northern Nigeria over 220 years ago continue to influence the region's identity in the twenty-first century. Although the region has experienced multiple religious upheavals in the last 45 years, understanding its development and modern-day character requires an examination of revolutionary religious events there more than two centuries ago. The challenge of this chapter is to write about an event whose existence is known, but whose causation and context is less well known.

ORIGINS OF ISLAM IN NIGERIAN

Africans were the first people in the world to practise Islam outside the Arabian Peninsula. Islam first entered Africa with 16 early followers (twelve men and four women) of the Prophet Mohammed who left Mecca in Saudi Arabia to escape persecution. They travelled to Abyssinia (ancient Ethiopia) around 615 AD where the Christian King of Aksum allowed them to stay and protected them. Islam penetrated into the area that would later become Nigeria from two directions. Traders and migrants brought Islam into the Kanem-Borno Empire (now in north-eastern Nigeria) between the eleventh and twelfth centuries. Islam entered Hausaland (to Kanem-Borno's west) 200–300 years later in the fourteenth century. Islam spread incrementally and was helped by several factors. Some of its core tenets involve mobility and travel (such as pilgrimage). The mobility of some of its early West African adherents among nomadic people helped its spread. Malian traders who travelled around West Africa were also important vectors for propagating Islam. As they travelled, their religion travelled with them. Islam's spread was also assisted by its visual elements. Its adherents' distinctive attire such as turbans and veils, and the conspicuous elements of its adherence (such as praying multiple times a day and fasting) made Muslims and their religion easily admired and recognisable by outsiders.

However, despite the efforts of the fourteenth century King of Kano Yaji (discussed in Chapter 1), Islam did not entirely displace old animist beliefs, and the latter continued to co-exist alongside Islam. Some sources claim that Islam was an incubated religion of the city-dwelling Hausa kings and elites, while the rural peasantry remained animist. For example, the *Maguzawa* declined to adopt Islam and continued with their animist beliefs. Rather than abolish or replace pre-existing religions, Islam joined them, and was seen by many people as a new item added to the menu of religious beliefs available in Hausaland. Some Muslim converts incorporated residues of their pre-Islamic rituals into Islam and combined Muslim practices with their old religions. Islam's arrival split Hausaland's religious adherents into three broad groups: those who converted to Islam, those who converted to Islam but mixed it with animist religions, and lastly, people such as the *Maguzawa* who refused to accept Islam. This mixing of old and new religions was controversial and generated religious factionalism between those who retained the old faiths, those who mixed the old and new, and those who insisted on a complete abandonment of the old religions and strict adherence to Islam.

'BY FAR THE MOST INTERESTING PEOPLE IN CENTRAL AFRICA'

Hausaland was not mono-ethnic. It included other ethnic groups who assimilated by adopting the Hausa language, and other distinct ethnic groups such as the nomadic Tuareg (who are nicknamed the 'blue men of the desert' due to the bright blue robes they often wear). A group of light complexioned, tall, slim immigrants caused the most seismic event to ever occur in Hausaland. These immigrants were originally cattle-rearing nomads who travelled thousands of miles across West Africa as they took their cattle in search of grazing land and watering holes. Foreigners were fascinated with them and an American Christian missionary described them as 'by far the most interesting people in Central Africa'.[1] These immigrants were known by different names in the areas they travelled to. Others seemed determined to call them by names other than that which they used to describe themselves. The French called them 'Peul' or 'Pulo' (singular), the Kanuri called them 'Fellata' or 'Fulata', while they called themselves 'Fulbe'. The most popular name by which they are known is that which Hausas gave to them: 'Fulani'.

The Fulani's origins are a mystery. Their physical appearance and language (Fulfulde) are so radically different from that of their neighbouring ethnic groups that it is certain that their origins lay far away. The mystery of their origin led to outlandishly speculative theories that they originally came from Asia, southern Europe, Egypt, Kenya, or that they were one of the lost twelve tribes of Israel. Between the fifteenth and sixteenth centuries, many of them started moving to Hausaland from the area that is now modern-day Mauritania and Senegal. Fulfulde is from the same language family as the Wolof language spoken in the region they migrated from. The Fulani can be divided into three broad groups that correspond to their different lifestyles. One group of the Fulani known as *Fulbe Ladde*[2] (so-called 'Cattle Fulani') are pastoralist nomads that travel constantly with their cattle. The nomadic Fulani have a symbiotic relationship with the communities they interact with. Their cattle provide butter, meat, and milk to their sedentary hosts; who in return provide them with grazing land and water. Despite exchanging resources with their host communities, the nomadic Fulani rarely intermarried with other ethnic groups, and as a result maintained their distinctive physical features more than other Fulanis. The second group is the *Fulbe Siire* (so-called 'Town Fulani') who are settled urban dwellers (although some of them also own cattle). The third Fulani group are the *Torodbe* who are educated, religious and who brought religious books with them into Hausaland.

---

1 Bowen, 1857, p. 199.
2 Although others commonly call them *Bororo*, the *Fulbe Ladde* do not refer to themselves as such, and *Bororo* is considered impolite.

The *Torodbe* were key influencers in the development of Islam in Hausaland and other parts of West Africa. They regarded themselves as experts on the proper practice of Islam, and were employed as Islamic clerics in the royal courts of West African kings.

The Fulani's wandering lifestyle made them vectors of Islam, and they can be found across a 2500-mile belt of contemporary West Africa starting from its western-most point in Mauritania, and extending across Senegal, Mali, Burkina Faso, Niger, Nigeria, and Cameroon. In the eighteenth century, the biggest Fulani population concentration was in Hausaland. The Fulani immigration to Hausaland led a remarkable family into the Hausa State of Gobir (which was located in what is now northern Nigeria and southern Niger Republic). In the middle of the fifteenth century, the family's patriarch Musa Jokolo emigrated from Futa Toro (which is now in modern-day Senegal) and settled in Birkin Konni (now in the southern part of modern-day Niger Republic). Three hundred years and eleven generations later, one of Jokolo's descendants had a son born on Sunday 15 December 1754 at a place called Maratta, in the village of Galmi (now located in Niger Republic near its southern border with Nigeria). Since the baby boy's father Mohammed was a learned Islamic cleric of the *Torodbe* Fulani, he was known as Usman Dan Fodio ('Usman, Son of the Learned').[3] Dan Fodio's family can be regarded as the 'first family' of northern Nigeria. Rarely has one family had such a massive impact in such a short space of time.

Dan Fodio's family moved to a place called Degel (which is now in modern-day Sokoto State of north-west Nigeria). As a youngster, Dan Fodio studied the Koran firstly with his father, and then travelled to Agades (in modern-day Niger Republic) to study with a Tuareg cleric named Jibril Umar who had great influence on him. Umar was expelled from Air and Gobir for trying to start a jihad. He was also in Mecca when it was under the Wahhabis. After this tutelage, Dan Fodio began preaching and writing around 1774 when he was 20 years old. He preached a reformist message of reli-

---

3   His name is also sometimes transliterated as 'Fodiyo' or 'Fodiye'. He is also sometimes referred to as 'Othman' dan Fodio, 'Shehu', or 'Sheikh'. In this book I will use the more common 'Usman Dan Fodio'.

gious and social purification, urged people to drop their animist rituals and devote themselves exclusively to Islam. He attracted a large following as he travelled from place to place with his younger brother Abdullahi. As news of his preaching spread beyond Degel and around the surrounding countryside, people flocked to join and follow him. He became an itinerant preacher, a tri-lingual Islamic scholar who could speak and write in Arabic, Fulfulde, and Hausa, and wrote several books and poems. Dan Fodio's austere and disciplined lifestyle made him seem selfless, unworldly, and uninterested in self-aggrandisement. As a young man, he owned only one pair of trousers, one gown, and one turban, and earned a living as a rope-maker, which allowed him to multitask while reading and studying. Stories of his wisdom, prophecies, and supernatural powers are legion. He was also reputed to be astute and charismatic. An example of the stories told to demonstrate the intense devotion he inspired from others is his slave Shekara, a crippled girl who was a nanny to his children. She became so devoted to Dan Fodio that she refused to accept manumission as it would mean her being parted from him.

Dan Fodio had on again, off again relationships of friendliness, ambivalence, then finally hostility with the ruling Hausa authorities. Oral tradition states that Bawa, the *Sarkin* (King) of Gobir hired Dan Fodio to be a *mallam* (religious teacher) for the royal house, and that one of his pupils was a prince named Yunfa. Although he did not realise it at the time, Bawa ended up employing the man who would destroy his dynasty. Dan Fodio's popularity and large following was sufficient to make him confident enough to visit Bawa in 1788 at Gobir's capital Alkawala to make five demands: namely, Dan Fodio should be allowed to perform *Dawah* (proselytise and call the people to Islam), people should not be restrained from responding to his call, any man wearing a turban was to be treated with respect, prisoners should be freed, and taxes not sanctioned by the Koran should be revoked. It is a mark of Dan Fodio's popularity (or of the threat he posed) that he could make such demands from the king, and that the king acquiesced to all of them.

He not only made demands of Hausa kings like Bawa, but also gave them advice, admonitions, and prophecies.

As Dan Fodio's theological expertise increased, so did his spiritual experiences, charisma, and confidence in the righteousness of his cause. Although Dan Fodio's proselytising mission commenced peacefully, his message threatened the authority of the Hausa kings. He threw himself into the religious maelstrom in Hausaland by claiming that although Hausa society was ostensibly Muslim, the Hausa kings allowed their people to also engage in animist religious practices and to mix Islam with them. He accused them of revering spirits that inhabited inanimate structures such as trees and stones. He also opposed the absence of gender segregation at social events, women appearing unveiled in public, and women dancing at public events where men were present.

Dan Fodio's accusation that eighteenth-century Hausaland was a place of unbelief and syncretism is rarely questioned because there is little surviving information regarding the level of religious devotion in that era. However, there is evidence that both disputes and corroborates Dan Fodio's accusation. As far back as the fifteenth century, the revered *Sarkin* Kano Mohammed Rumfa was widely credited with welding Islam onto the structure of his government and ordering the building of a central mosque in Kano. Rumfa corresponded with the famous Algerian Islamic scholar Abd al-Karim al-Maghili, and when al-Maghili visited Kano, he wrote and left for Rumfa a book entitled *The Crown of Religion Concerning the Obligations of Princes*, to serve as an instructional manual for the proper functioning of an Islamic state. Dan Fodio's portrayal of Hausaland as a land of unbelievers is also challenged by his own employment by the royal house of Gobir. The fact that the *Sarkin* Gobir, Bawa took Islam seriously enough to hire Dan Fodio as a religious teacher for the royal house demonstrated that at least some of the Hausa kings prioritised Islamic education. However, syncretist practices which existed alongside Islam supported Dan Fodio's accusations. For example, there is testimony alleging that every few years, the kings of Kano sacrificed animals under a sacred tree to ward off misfortune, and that every 10–15 years a serious crisis would precipitate the sacrifice of a young man kidnapped by the king's agents.[4] As late as the early twentieth century, a British colonial administrator who lived in Hausaland alleged that 'Mahomedanism [Islam], in fact, sits very lightly on the Hausas, and is for the most part merely a thin veneer over their old pagan beliefs.'[5] If Islam and animism were still being mixed as late as the early 1900s, then it would be reasonable to assume that such mixing also existed (or was even more prevalent) a century earlier.

Neither Dan Fodio's rise or his confrontation with the Hausa kings was sudden. In my prior book *Soldiers of Fortune*, I deployed the term 'coup baiting' to describe the twentieth-century Nigerian practice of inviting a military coup by deliberately inciting civil and military political opinion against the incumbent government. Dan Fodio engaged in 'coup baiting' more than 100 years before Nigeria was created. He spent over 30 years preaching, with sometimes incendiary rhetoric against the Hausa authorities, reminding the populace of the royalty's misdeeds, and turning public opinion against them. For a movement with insurrectionist intentions, it was a brilliant public relations campaign against the Hausa authorities. His habit of touring and preaching in the countryside allowed him to acquire a large following in widespread rural areas undetected during a religious career spanning over a quarter of a century. Prophecies and millenarian beliefs had foretold that a *mahdi* (messianic religious reformer) would arise to lead the people in a struggle that would precede the end of the world. The social unrest of the times lent credence to the *mahdi* prophecies, and many identified Dan Fodio as the *mahdi*. He was surrounded by thousands of loyal supporters including his family, other Islamic scholars, and students who, like him, insisted on exclusive fidelity to Islam, and who believed that he had supernatural powers (I will refer to his supporters as the *Usmaniyya* for ease of reference). The Hausa kings did not seem to realise the danger he posed to them until it was too late.

---

4 Philips, 1992, pp. 50–1.
5 Orr, 1908, p. 283.

THE SWORD OF TRUTH

Dan Fodio often ensconced himself in meditational retreats for weeks at a time, during which he isolated himself in the bush or desert, to fast, pray, and meditate. He had several mystical experiences commencing around 1789 when he was 36 years old, and which continued for at least the next 15 years. During these mystical retreats he had visions which he regarded as prophecies (one of his wives Aisha was also a mystic). In his era, Sufism was a popular branch of Sunni Islam in West Africa. Many Sufis belonged to one of two prominent Sufi *tariqas* (brotherhoods or 'pathways') named *Qadiriyya* and *Tijaniyya*. Perhaps Dan Fodio's most influential and profound vision occurred when he was 40 years old, and involved him seeing the Prophet Mohammed and the *Qadiriyya* founder Abdul Qadir al-Jilani. During this vision, Dan Fodio said that:

> He [Jilani] sat me down, and clothed me and enturbaned me then he addressed me as 'Imam of the saints' and commanded me to do what is approved of and forbade me to do what is disapproved of; and he girded me with the Sword of Truth, to unsheathe it against the enemies of God.[6]

This vision in 1794 may have been the pivotal one that convinced Dan Fodio that he had divine sanction to carry out God's mission. After *Sarkin* Bawa was killed in battle in 1789, his brother Yakubu succeeded him, and he too was killed in battle in 1794 or 1795 while trying to avenge Bawa. Dan Fodio's relationship with subsequent Hausa kings deteriorated and the kings began to regard the *Usmaniyya* as a dangerous and radical sect. After Yakubu's death, his brother Nafata succeeded him as the *Sarkin* Gobir, but revoked the earlier concessions that Bawa had made to Dan Fodio. Instead, Nafata ordered that no one except Dan Fodio could preach to the people, no one could be a Muslim unless his father was also a Muslim, and that all Muslim converts should revert to their prior faith. Nafata

---

6   Hiskett, 1994, p. 66.

also forbade men from wearing turbans and women from veiling their faces. Wearing turbans and veils was a sensitive issue for the *Usmaniyya* because it was regarded as an outward demonstration of being a Muslim and of allegiance to Dan Fodio. Since most of what we know about this era was written by the *Usmaniyya*, we do not have more details regarding why Muslim Hausa kings suddenly took the incendiary decision to place restrictions on Muslim conversion, knowing that such measures were likely to provoke unrest and a backlash from the followers of a popular religious leader who were already on the brink of mutiny. Although no context has been provided for Nafata's edicts, they may not have been as spontaneous as previously portrayed. Some of the *Usmaniyya* had become increasingly militant and restless, and as far back as 1794 or 1795 Dan Fodio told his followers to arm themselves (around the time Nafata became the *Sarkin* Gobir). It is possible that Nafata issued these edicts as a counter-response to the *Usmaniyya's* increasing threat and their potential as a dangerous armed religious insurgent group inside his domain.

Nonetheless, Nafata did not get to see the outcome of his edicts, and instead left their consequences for his son to resolve. In the same way that Dan Fodio prophesised the death of Nafata's predecessor, Yakubu, he also prophesised Nafata's death, and that Nafata would be succeeded by his son Yunfa. Yet confrontation was not inevitable. It seemed that tension would subside when Dan Fodio's former student Yunfa succeeded his father Nafata in 1801. Yunfa's ascension offered hope for a non-violent resolution, and Yunfa even tried to mend fences by visiting Dan Fodio at his home in Degel to greet his former teacher. However, Yunfa inherited the bitterness and societal cleavages caused by Nafata's decisions.

Nafata's edicts had split loyalties within Gobir. As Dan Fodio's influence and reputation grew, his followers constituted almost an independent state within Yunfa's kingdom. Some of Dan Fodio's supporters under the leadership of a Hausa named Abdulsalam (one of Dan Fodio's students) had left Gobir in protest at Nafata's edicts and moved to the town of Gimbana near the Zamfara River in the Kebbi region, and remained there until Yunfa came to power. Yunfa tried to bring Abdulsalam back into the fold by telling him to return to Gobir. However by then the *Usmaniyya* were too aggrieved to be placated. The *Usmaniyya* alleged that when Abdulsalam ignored Yunfa's order to return and instead barricaded himself at Gimbana, Yunfa ordered him to be arrested. Yunfa's forces attacked Gimbana and arrested or killed many of Abdulsalam's followers. The fact that these attacks occurred during Ramadan aggravated their impact on the *Usmaniyya*. Although this incident was subsequently depicted as the outcome of Yunfa's and Dan Fodio's conflicting orders to their respective followers, it is not certain that either of them was directly involved in igniting it. It may instead have been a spontaneous argument that escalated after Yunfa's men took offence when Abdulsalam contemptuously declined their request to lead a prayer for them. Regardless of the conflict's origin, the impetuous elements among the *Usmaniyya* were so outraged that when they spotted Yunfa's forces close to Degel with Muslim captives they had arrested, they attacked the captors and released the captives.[7] The fact that they managed to overpower Yunfa's men shows that, by now, the *Usmaniyya* were more than a community of religious students and teachers, and were very well armed. Not only did they carry weapons, but they also believed they were backed by Dan Fodio's supernatural powers. Tales of his invocation of his supernatural talents were usually rendered in a way that further incited the *Usmaniyya* against Yunfa. In one story, Yunfa allegedly tried to murder Dan Fodio by firing a gun at him, but when he pressed the trigger the gun backfired and hurt Yunfa instead. In another story, Yunfa allegedly tried to kill Dan Fodio by summoning him to his palace and enticing him to sit down on a mat in his palace courtyard, underneath which Yunfa had concealed a booby trap consisting of a pit full of spears. When Dan Fodio's brother Abdullahi tried to sit on the mat, Dan Fodio prevented him from doing so and calmly sat on the mat himself. To Yunfa's alleged astonishment, not only did Dan Fodio fail to fall into the booby trap, but the pit

---

7 Both Dan Fodio and his son Bello were upset at the way their supporters escalated the conflict by attacking Yunfa's men. Bello called them 'hot heads' (Last, 2014, p. 27).

became miraculously filled with sand. Stories of such miracles circulated in a way that both increased the excitement regarding Dan Fodio, and the *Usmaniyya*'s animosity against Yunfa and their view of him as a tyrant.

HIJRA

On 21 February 1804 Dan Fodio (assisted by Tuaregs led by Mallam Agale who promised to defend him) and the *Usmaniyya* withdrew en masse, carried their belongings, loaded those too heavy to carry onto camels, and travelled 60 miles on a *Hijra* (migration) to a place called Gudu (in current Sokoto State of Nigeria), which was a 4–5-day journey away from Degel. They sought to emulate the Prophet Mohammed's migration away from secular society from Medina to Mecca in 622 AD. Yunfa wrote a letter to Dan Fodio in which he pleaded with him to return to Degel. However, Dan Fodio refused to return unless Yunfa repented and purified Islam. While at Gudu, the *Usmaniyya* elevated Dan Fodio's position from *imam* to *amir-al mu'minin* ('commander of the believers' in Arabic). This appointment effectively amounted to a declaration of independence, which severed the *Usmaniyya* from Yunfa's authority and made them an autonomous community in Gobir. Yunfa became alarmed when large numbers of people followed Dan Fodio into exile, and forbade further emigration. On some occasions Yunfa's forces confiscated the property of those who were leaving to join Dan Fodio. Tension escalated into near-war when Yunfa's forces attacked the *Usmaniyya* at Gudu.

JIHAD

In 1804 Dan Fodio passed the point of no return. He wrote an open letter to his supporters called the *Wathiqat Ahl al-Sudan wa man sha Allah min al-ikhwan* ('Dispatch to the folk of the Sudan and to whom so Allah wills amongst the Brethren') which was widely distributed across Hausaland. The *Wathiqat* effectively served as a 27-point manifesto for jihad and spelt out the obligations of

Muslims. It was a declaration of war, religious edict, and political manifesto all in one. It stated that 'the status of a town is the status of its ruler', and that it was obligatory for Muslims to depart from any territory that was not ruled by a Muslim. The jihadists' religious and political aims intertwined as they refused to live under the leadership of those they deemed unbelievers. Worryingly for the Hausa kings, the *Wathiqat* also declared war against, and called for the overthrow of, any government led by an apostate. It stated that: 'to make war upon the king who is an apostate ... who mingles the observances of Islam with the observances of heathendom, like the kings of Hausaland for the most part, is obligatory by assent, and that to take the government from him is obligatory by assent'. The *Wathiqat*'s content made a peaceful resolution of the stand-off between Yunfa and the *Usmaniyya* very unlikely. There was a teacher and student element to the conflict as it pitted Dan Fodio against his former student, now king, Yunfa. As the two sides tried to rally support, Dan Fodio's fourth son Mohammed Bello travelled to Kebbi to distribute letters calling for people to support his father. As more people (including the working-class Hausa *Talakawa* and the cattle Fulani) from the Hausa States defected away from Yunfa to pledge allegiance to Dan Fodio, Dan Fodio blessed their leaders and gave them green flags as symbols of authority from him with which to wage jihad.

The jihad was not spontaneous, nor did it occur in a vacuum. It was a successor to prior Fulani-led jihads in West Africa. Dan Fodio already had a template from almost 80 years earlier, when Karamokho Alfa declared a jihad in Futa Jallon (modern-day Guinea) in 1725, created a confederation of Muslim theocratic states, and declared himself commander of the believers. Subsequently, in 1776 Abd-al-Qadir overthrew the Denianke dynasty in Futa Toro and declared jihads in areas that are now in modern-day Gambia and Senegal. Although these Fulani-led jihads in the land of Dan Fodio's ancestors occurred more than 1000 miles away from Gobir, they foreshadowed events in Hausaland. The timing of Dan Fodio's jihad declaration was also iconic as the early nineteenth century was a time of revolutions around the world. The Haitian revolution occurred in the same year the jihad started (1804), the French revolution took place five years earlier, and the American revolution occurred about 20 years earlier.

Although Dan Fodio's jihad is the most seismic event ever to occur in northern Nigeria, it has many unknown or under-examined back stories. Much of the existing literature about the jihad presents it as solely a religious war. While religion was its primary driver, other secondary political and social grievances and objectives contributed to it. Some of these socio-political controversies ironically foreshadowed some conflicts in contemporary Nigeria. The twenty-first-century conflict in modern Nigeria between farmers and nomadic cattle herders is not new. It also existed in Hausaland more than 220 years ago. The difference between then and now is that the pattern of sectarianism has changed. Whereas today, farmer-herder conflicts often pit predominantly Muslim herders of Fulani or Tuareg ethnicity against farmers in other parts of the country (who are often Christians), 220 years ago, while the herders were then as now, Fulani or Tuareg, the farmers they clashed with tended to be Hausas from the same geographic area. Such clashes often arose from restrictions that Hausa authorities imposed on cattle grazing, and *jangali* (cattle tax). Examples of such restrictions included limits on grazing and watering, and punishments for grazing infractions. Fulani cattle owners regarded such restrictions and taxes as harsh and unjustified, and often tried to evade them. Their favoured evasion tactics sometimes involved subterfuge such as hiding cattle in inhospitable terrain that inhibited detection of their presence, under-counting their cattle, or making them difficult to count by dispersing the herd and keeping them moving on the pretext that the animals are difficult to control when strangers are close to them.[8] Hausa authorities were irritated by Fulani attempts to evade their regulations and taxes. When Hausa authorities seized Fulani cattle as a punishment for such evasion, it escalated the animosity between them and the Fulani. An example of the manner in which pastoralist–farmer conflicts coalesced into the jihad is

---

8   St Croix, 1945, pp. 35–6.

one of Dan Fodio's jihadists in northern Kebbi: Abubakar Luduje, who along with other cattle rearing nomads, had clashed with local farmers in the area regarding grazing rights. Dan Fodio's jihad transformed Luduje's conflicts with Hausa farmers into a jihadist war against the same people.

Slavery was another grievance. Although both the Fulani jihadists and the Hausa kings were slave owners, the former were more selective about who they enslaved. While the Hausas were less likely to discriminate about the religious background of those they enslaved, the jihadists exempted Muslims and their Fulani kin from enslavement. Since the jihadists considered it illegal to enslave a Muslim, their stance on slavery ironically gained Hausa support for them by encouraging conversion to Islam as a means of immunising themselves from enslavement.

These social grievances affected the ethnic composition of the two sides. The jihad is often described in ethnic terms as a 'Fulani jihad' against Hausas. Such vocabulary gives it the erroneous appearance of an ethnic war between Fulani invaders and Hausa kings. While the jihad was Fulani led, it was not a binary ethnic conflict between Fulanis and Hausas. Two of the primary protagonists who triggered it were Tuaregs (Dan Fodio's influential teacher Jibril Umar) and Hausa (Abdulsalam whose conflict at Gimbana was the straw that broke the camel's back). This is not to say that ethnic motives were completely absent. While the Fulani did not have overtly racial motives for the jihad, their racial view of themselves and attitudes towards other ethnic groups influenced their relations with them. Due to their light complexion and differentiated physical features, some Fulanis considered themselves to be different from, and above, their 'Black' neighbours.[9] Fulanis used the pejorative term 'Habe'[10] to refer to Hausas. The term was originally a Fulfulde word to describe non-Fulani people but evolved into a racial slur. Fulanis used it so much that centuries later, even British colonial officers started referring to Hausas as 'Habe', erroneously believing it to be interchangeable with Hausa, and not

9   Daniel, 1926, p. 279.
10 Plural of 'kado'.

realising its offensive meaning. The *Torodbe*'s learned status contributed to their sense of superiority. However, the Fulani could not fight an ethnic war against Hausas who outnumbered them by more than ten to one. Thus the jihad leaders needed to mobilise other sources of grievance.

The Hausa *Talakawa* were also aggrieved by the taxes levied by the Hausa kings, and thus they had an economic motive to join Dan Fodio's revolt. These political and social grievances that contributed to the jihad complicated and blended ethnic and religious loyalties among the combatants. For example, Hausa Muslims who believed that Dan Fodio was fighting for the sanctity of their religion also joined the jihad. Ironically, not everyone on Dan Fodio's side was a Muslim. Some of the nomadic Fulani were not Muslims and joined the jihad out of ethnic solidarity with the *Torodbe* Fulani. Despite their different lifestyles, the nomadic, town, and *Torodbe* Fulani did not live completely separate lives, and had overlapping social and family links between themselves. Thus the jihad was not an ethnic war, nor was there a clear-cut religious distinction between the two warring sides. In multiple ironies, a Fulani-led jihad against the Hausa King of Gobir featured Hausas helping Fulanis to fight against other Hausas, non-Muslim Fulanis fighting alongside Muslim jihadists, and Hausa Muslims who opposed the jihad fighting against fellow Muslims. In the heat of battle, both Dan Fodio and Yunfa's armies were heterogeneous and included Hausas, Tuaregs, Fulanis, Muslims, and non-Muslims.

The jihad was also partially a political protest. The *Usmaniyya* accused the Hausa kings of corruption and misrule. Some of their grievances included the levying of taxes not approved by Islam, judges who demanded bribes, royal intermediaries who did the same in exchange for introductions to the king, and members of the aristocracy who demanded presents, took the daughters of peasants, and lived in luxury while their subjects suffered. It is difficult to corroborate these accusations since the *Usmaniyya* presented these allegations, and there are few surviving counter-narratives from the Hausa rulers. However, the *Kano Chronicle* inadvertently provided a clue about the veracity of these allegations by admitting that the fifteenth-century *Sarkin* Kano Mohammed Rumfa sent royal attendants to a slave settlement to claim and bring for him all the first born virgin daughters there.[11] In an ancient equivalent to the modern-day government power of eminent domain, the Hausa kings could also commandeer the private property of commoners (such as their cattle and horses). If such practices occurred as far back the fifteenth century, the resentment they generated may have reached boiling point by the time Dan Fodio declared jihad over 300 years later. In the maelstrom of these social, political, and religious grievances, the jihad can also be viewed as an intellectual movement. Many of the jihad leaders were extremely erudite polyglots who could speak, write, and read in three or four different languages, and were also prolific writers who were well versed in classical Arabic and Islamic literature. They read widely about Islam's golden age, tried to revive it in Hausaland, and had a vision for a puritanical Islamic Caliphate they wanted to emerge after the jihad.

'death is our desire'

The first major military confrontation between Dan Fodio's and Yunfa's forces began on 21 June 1804 close to a lake known as Tabkin Kwatto, about 20 miles west of Gudu. The confrontation was a military mismatch and the *Usmaniyya* were in a perilous position. Yunfa's forces (the *Gobirawa*) were more numerous, more experienced, better equipped, and included over a hundred cavalrymen. The *Gobirawa* fighters also wore plumed helmets and body armour, had shields, a large entourage including women, and had plentiful baggage and provisions. As will be shown below, being so well provisioned later hurt the *Gobirawa*. In contrast to the well-kitted *Gobirawa*, the outnumbered *Usmaniyya* fighters consisted mostly of men on foot and archers, and they wore large, wide straw hats over their turbans. They had no more than 20 horses, and suffered deprivations such as food shortages, malnutrition, and

---

11   Palmer, 1908, pp. 77–8.

disease. However, the battle was not a pure numbers game. Despite being out-equipped and outnumbered, the *Usmaniyya* were better motivated, and were convinced that they were fighting for a righteous cause against unbelievers, whom they were either prepared to vanquish or die in the attempt. Their morale was also boosted by their conviction that their leader Dan Fodio had supernatural powers. The *Usmaniyya* were in a 'heads I win, tails I win' situation. If they won against the odds, it would be a divinely ordained victory against unbelievers. Conversely, if they lost and died, they would become martyrs and be rewarded in paradise. Hence, the *Usmaniyya* did not fear death. Dan Fodio's son Mohammed Bello wrote that 'death is our desire. He who found death found what he sought. The slaughter of so many of our people if it made our enemies happy, made us too look upon this martyrdom as happiness.'[12] In contrast, the consequences of losing were dire for the *Gobirawa*. If they lost, they would either be summarily executed, or if the *Usmaniyya* allowed them to live, it would be on the condition of them, their wives, and children being enslaved, with their homes and towns being plundered and destroyed.

'axes cleft his head, split asunder'

Dan Fodio's younger brother Abdullahi led the *Usmaniyya* into battle. After shouting 'Allahu Akbar!' three times, the *Usmaniyya* charged at the *Gobirawa*. The battle of Tabkin Kwatto was brutal, and descended into ugly hand-to-hand fighting with axes and swords, and tales of 'many a great man our hands flung down, and axes cleft his head, split asunder'.[13] The *Usmaniyya* archers neutralised the *Gobirawa*'s cavalry and mobility advantage by picking off their horsemen with bow and arrow shots. Despite being outnumbered and fighting against a better armed enemy, the *Usmaniyya* emerged victorious in a sensational military upset. Dan Fodio's daughter Nana later wrote verses venerating the victory and mocking Yunfa (who, it was alleged, fled with his followers in a dishevelled

---

12   Arnett, 1922, p. 84.
13   Hiskett, 1994, p. 88.

state): 'Yunfa fled from bare-legged herdsmen. Who had neither mail nor horsemen. We that had been chased like hares, can now live in houses.'[14] As the surviving panic-stricken *Gobirawa* survivors fled, they ended up equipping their enemies by leaving their provisions, weapons, and horses behind, which the *Usmaniyya* seized as war booty. The jihadists buried their dead warriors, but refused to dignify the slain *Gobirawa* by doing the same for them, and instead left their corpses to rot on the battlefield and be devoured by hyenas and vultures. In modern times the victory of Dan Fodio's forces is treated almost as a foregone conclusion, and the unlikelihood of victory at the time of the battle is rarely mentioned. The *Usmaniyya*'s victory against the odds at Tabkin Kwatto had an electrifying impact that boosted the jihad's zeal. It caused many fence sitters to jump down from their perch and join them, thereby swelling Dan Fodio's army. The victory also evened the military balance as the *Usmaniyya* footmen emerged from the battle better armed and with cavalry after capturing the *Gobirawa*'s horses. Within one year the military disparity had decreased as the two sides began to resemble each other.

Yunfa sent messages to the other Hausa kings to warn them that due to his failure to extinguish a small fire in Gobir, the fire grew until it burned him. He warned them not to allow the same fire to burn them too. However the warning came too late to save Yunfa or the other Hausa kings. A rebellion that arose from local grievances against Gobir's rulers snowballed and the 'small fire' that Yunfa warned about spread and burned across Hausaland. Since the Fulani were present throughout Hausaland and were not invaders coming from outside, they were able to trigger simultaneous uprisings in multiple Hausa States. As a result, many parts of Hausaland were too preoccupied with their own defence to come to the aid of their neighbouring Hausa States.

Dan Fodio is often presented as a warrior leader, and a British army officer described him as 'the African Napoleon'.[15] While Dan Fodio was the jihad's spiritual leader, it is unlikely that he did much

---

14 Daniel, 1926, p. 281.
15 Vandeleur, 1898, p. 235.

(if any) fighting himself due to his advanced age (50) at the time the jihad began. His younger brother Abdullahi, son Mohammed Bello, and the sometimes hot-headed *amir al-jaish* (commander of war) Aliyu Jedo were his generals who led the fighting. These three men were curiously astute battle commanders, and demonstrated a level of military expertise which made it clear that they were more than just the scholars and Islamic proselytisers they presented themselves as. The physically imposing Abdullahi was organised, a master of surprise attacks, and was well versed in battle formations and tactics. Despite being a young man in his mid-20s, Bello was militarily adroit, a good cavalry commander, and precociously used his cavalry to draw the *Gobirawa* forces out into the open and into the firing line of his archers during the battle of Gwandu in 1805.[16] How they acquired so much military knowledge is a mystery. A scholar speculated that Abdullahi and Bello's fluent command of Arabic may have led them to read Arabic military texts.[17] Even if they read such sources, that does not explain how they were so easily able to implement written theory onto the battlefield. Somehow, somewhere, Abdullahi, Bello, and Jedo must have experienced battle before the jihad.

Yet the jihadists did not have everything their own way. Two incidents changed the jihad's trajectory. Firstly, when the jihadists tried to attack Gobir's fortified capital city of Alkalawa in December 1804, the *Gobirawa* ambushed and routed them a few miles outside the city at Tsuntua. Yunfa's forces inflicted severe losses on the jihadists and killed over 2000 of them, including over 200 men who had memorised the entire Koran. It took two days to bury the 2000 corpses. The loss of so many pious men affected the way the jihadists fought subsequent battles. Their loss ironically improved the *Usmaniyya's* military prowess and simultaneously diluted the scholastic element within them. This setback also changed the *Usmaniyya's* ethnic composition and made them more reliant on Fulani fighters. Unable to rely solely on preachers, religious students, and scholars, clan leaders and those who could fight gained greater

---

16   Hiskett, 1976, p. 140.
17   Ibid., p. 140.

prominence. Thereafter, the jihad became like a franchise as people from other parts of Hausaland who were not directly connected to Dan Fodio rebelled against the Hausa kings, or came to Dan Fodio to pledge allegiance and obtain a flag from him. Being a flag bearer carried the incentive of becoming the governor of territory which the flag bearer conquered. This gave flag bearers a strong incentive to successfully prosecute the jihad.

In the adrenaline and heat of battle, some lost their discipline. Two incidents involving attacks on devout Muslim communities illustrate this. The first example was a mutiny at Kwolda; a town where half of the residents were Dan Fodio supporters. Bello admitted that:

> this town was at peace with us and half the people were our own folk. Yet our army attacked them and plundered all they had. *Waziri* Abdullahi [Dan Fodio's brother] rose up to prevent them and exhorted them to desist. They refused to obey him. Then I went and entered the town to prevent them plundering. They came near to killing me ... I was in much fear for the upshot of it.[18]

Bello and his uncle Abdullahi gave up on trying to suppress the mutiny when other *Usmaniyya* commanders ignored Abdullahi's orders to stop the attacks and withdraw. The second example emerged from Yandoto (now in Katsina State of Nigeria). Yandoto was one of several Muslim scholar communities in Hausaland and was a centre of religious learning. It was akin to a pre-colonial university town, and many Muslim scholars resided there. However, Yandoto's scholars refused to join the *Usmaniyya* and accused them of misleading the people. In late 1805, Bello travelled to Yandoto with Muhammadu Dan Ashafa (who was expelled from Yandoto after siding with Dan Fodio), and sent Ashafa inside to negotiate with its scholars. When they refused to join or negotiate with the *Usmaniyya*, Bello lost his patience, and sent his forces in to attack and destroy the town. The Yandoto incident showed that Muslims

18 Arnett, 1922, p. 107.

were not a monolithic group. As will be demonstrated in the next chapter, the treatment meted out to Yandoto also created serious controversy with other Muslims.

WOE TO THE VANQUISHED

The speed with which the jihad toppled the Hausa States was remarkable. Abdullahi captured Birnin Kebbi in 1805, and Kano and Katsina fell to the jihadists in the same year. The symbolic victory of the jihad was probably in October 1808 when Bello captured Gobir's capital Alkalawa. By 1809, the jihadists had also overthrown the kings of the other Hausa States.[19]

After the ancient Gaul Brennus defeated a Roman army in 390 BC and invaded and devastated Rome, he famously rejected Roman complaints about his severe armistice terms by throwing his sword down and exclaiming '*Vae Victis!*' (Latin for 'woe to the vanquished'). This ancient maxim affirming that those defeated in war should not expect clemency and were at the mercy of their conquerors also haunted the defeated Hausa rulers. After the *Usmaniyya* captured Alkalawa, they sacked the city and killed Yunfa. Alkalawa's ruins are now in the Sabon Birnin Local Government Area of modern-day Sokoto State in north-west Nigeria. It was not only Yunfa that paid severely for defeat. Those closest to him also lost their freedom or became spoils of war for the victors. The jihadists captured his mother Maitakalmi and one of his wives Katembale.[20] Bello took Yunfa's widow Katembale as one of his concubines. Most of the victorious jihadists also took the wives, sisters, and daughters of those they conquered as their concubines.

KING OF THE MUSLIMS

Dan Fodio replaced the Hausa States with a new Caliphate comprised of a confederation of theocratic Muslim states. This Caliphate

---

19   The King of Yauri agreed to support Dan Fodio and thus survived after Dan Fodio ratified his position.

20   Some accounts claim that Katembale was the daughter of the former *Sarkin Gobir* Yakubu. If so, then she was a first cousin of her husband Yunfa.

was Africa's largest state at the time it was established and by 1831, extended for 180,000 square miles.[21] By 1837, it had a population of approximately 10 million people. As shown in Map 2, it traversed across most of what is now northern Nigeria, into southern Niger, while its western border extended into Burkina Faso and almost as far as modern-day Mali, and its eastern border extended into modern-day Cameroon. At the time of its establishment, travelling horizontally from one end of the Caliphate to the other was a four-month journey.[22]

After the jihad, Dan Fodio retained the title of *amir-al mu'minin* ('commander of the believers' in Arabic) or alternatively *Sarkin Musulmi* ('King of the Muslims' in Hausa). Although he was the titular leader of the new Islamic Caliphate, Dan Fodio retired firstly to Sifawa, then to the nearby and newly built walled city of Sokoto (which native Hausa speakers pronounce as 'Sokwaoto') to devote himself to religious and scholarly activities. His writing during his time in Sifawa became instructional manuals for the moral, political, and religious administration of the Caliphate during and after his life. Dan Fodio delegated responsibility for governing the Caliphate to his son Mohammed Bello and his brother Abdullahi. He divided the Caliphate into eastern and western provinces and gave Bello responsibility for governing the Caliphate's larger eastern province from its capital at Sokoto, and Abdullahi responsibility for governing its western province from its capital at Gwandu. While accounts of the Caliphate justifiably focus on the talismanic figure of Dan Fodio and his family members such as Bello and Abdullahi, there were several other moving forces behind the jihad. The military flag bearers were critical to the jihad's success and Dan Fodio appointed them as *amirs* (Arabic for 'commanders' or 'chiefs') of the territories they conquered (which are now known as emirates). Each *amir* reported to Bello or Abdullahi depending on the location of his emirate. Thirteen of the original fourteen flag bearers were Fulani (a list of the original flag bearers can be found in Table 2.1). Yakubu (a Hausa) of Bauchi was the only non-Fulani

21 Smith, 1961, p. 175.
22 Last, 2013, p. 6.

flag bearer. More than 210 years after the jihad, a descendant of the original flag bearer still rules each emirate.

SULTAN OF SOKOTO

As English-speaking scholars began to research the Caliphate, British colonial influence and English appellations changed its etymology. The modern-day *sarkin musulmi* came to be referred to in English as the 'Sultan of Sokoto'. That phrase was never used to describe the Caliphate's ruler until Britain conquered the Caliphate in 1903 and appended the sultan title to him. British influence also changed the way that the *amirs* were referred to. In British transliteration, *amir* became '*emir*', to be spelled how it sounded to British ears. British influence also changed the Caliphate's name. Some British colonial officers referred to it as 'The Fulani Emirates'[23] or 'The Fulani Empire of Sokoto'.[24] However, the *emirs* and the Caliphate's residents did not refer to it by that name. They referred to it as Dar-al-Islam (Abode of Islam) or *Daular Usmaniyya* ('Usman's Empire' or 'Usman's Caliphate'). Professor Murray Last of University College London described the Caliphate as the 'Sokoto Caliphate' (after its capital at Sokoto) in his PhD thesis in 1967, and since then Sokoto Caliphate has been the standard form of reference for the Caliphate that Dan Fodio established. Despite the name now given to the Caliphate, ironically, Sokoto was not a major city before the jihad. In a parallel of the way that Nigeria's modern-day capital city of Abuja was built after the country's foundation, Sokoto was built after the foundation of the Caliphate that it became the capital of. Bello started building Sokoto for his father in autumn 1809. Dan Fodio, his family, and lieutenants resided *outside* Sokoto for most of their lives (although Dan Fodio and his sons had a house there).

The jihad had at least four important long-term consequences. Firstly, it united the Hausa States under a single political authority for the first time. Prior to the jihad, each Hausa State had

---

23 Burdon, 1904.
24 Johnston, 1967.

existed autonomously from the others, with each *sarki* governing his state independently. Although each emirate had its own *emir*, all emirates were under the Caliphate's leader the *sarkin musulmi*. The Caliphate inadvertently demonstrated the durability of the Hausa States' political institutions. Apart from tightly welding Islam onto the machinery of government, the Caliphate largely inherited and retained the governing systems of the predecessor Hausa States. These systems were so well organised and sophisticated that they were still in place when Britain arrived in northern Nigeria a century after the jihad. A British colonial officer later marvelled at 'the wonderful system of administration and taxation which we found when we took over the government of Hausa-land',[25] and alleged that:

> The whole machinery was adopted bag and baggage, lock, stock, and barrel, by the Fulani rulers from the old Habe state ... the admirable system of government which we found in Hausa-land at the beginning of the present century was not due to the Fulanis, but was a legacy from the old Habe race.[26]

Perhaps the greatest compliment that Britain paid to these systems was that instead of replacing them, Britain not only retained them, but also adopted them as tools of their governance of colonial Nigeria. Secondly, the jihad boosted conversion to Islam. The Caliphate's implementation of *Sharia* encouraged or forced Muslim conversion, discouraged the mixing of Islam with other religious beliefs and practices, and pushed non-Muslim religions to the margins of society. Slavery also provided an incentive for many to convert to Islam. Since only non-Muslims could be enslaved and slaves could regain their freedom by becoming Muslims, many people converted to Islam as a way of making themselves ineligible for enslavement by jihadists. A great irony is that the jihad was partly inspired by an objection to enslaving Muslims, yet the Caliphate that followed the jihad enslaved more people than its

25   Orr, 1908, p. 280.
26   Ibid., p. 281.

predecessor Hausa States. At one point the Caliphate had 2 million slaves[27] (more slaves than any other African state).

Thirdly, the jihad also caused an ironic cultural exchange. By the time the jihad commenced, the Fulani had lived amongst the Hausas for over 300 years, and a gradual cultural cross-assimilation had occurred during these three centuries. Conquerors frequently impose their culture and language on the conquered. Yet the jihad was not a story of mono-directional Fulani influence. While the Fulani conquerors succeeded in imposing Islam as a state religion, they adopted the language of those they conquered. Hausa became the court language of the Fulani rulers, and some Fulanis became so Hausanised from intermarriage and cultural assimilation that they could barely speak or understand Fulfulde (the nomadic Fulani remain a notable exception to this). Fourthly, since the jihad was a revolution led by religious Fulani intellectuals, it amplified education and literacy due to the vast amount of literature that the

Table 2.1 Usman Dan Fodio's flag bearers

Emirate	Name of Original Flag Bearer (*Amir*)
Adamawa	Modibbo Adama
Bauchi	Yakubu[a]
Daura	Mallam Ishaku
Gombe	Buba Yero (Abubakar)
Hadejia	Umaru
Jama'are	Muhammadu Wabi
Katagum[b]	Ibrahim Zaki
Kano	Suleimanu Dan Aba Hama
Katsina	Umaru Dallaji
Kazaure	Dan Tunku
Misau[b]	Muhammadu Manga
Nupe	Mallam Dendo
Zamfara	Abu Hamidu
Zaria	Mallam Musa

Notes:
a. A Hausa. He was the only non-Fulani flag bearer.
b. Formerly part of the Kanem-Borno Empire.

27 PBS, 2017.

jihadist leaders generated, and their consequent propagation of religious texts. As will be discussed in Chapter 11, these religiously motivated literary advancements also allowed non-religious written texts to emerge.

The story of the jihad usually ends with the victorious jihadists riding off into the sunset in a blaze of glory with no problems or opposition. However, as will be shown in the next two chapters, not everything went their way.

3
Mohammed from Kanem

Most accounts of northern Nigeria's history focus on the Sokoto Caliphate. Since most of what we now know about the jihad was written by the jihad leaders, the victors' narrative became the official history of northern Nigeria. The Caliphate looms so large in northern Nigeria that the presence of other people and states in the area is often treated as an afterthought, and counter-narratives to the jihad are exceptionally rare. One of the few exceptions to this singular narrative came from one of its neighbours. Although the Caliphate leaders presented themselves as the leading Muslim adherents in the region, one of their neighbouring empires had a longer history of practising Islam than the Caliphate and Hausaland. In fact, Hausaland modelled some of its institutions and lexicon on this neighbouring empire.

AFRICA'S OLDEST KINGDOM

The over 1000-year old Kanem-Borno Empire which encircled Lake Chad (see Map 1) is the oldest kingdom in African history. The kingdom of Kanem arose around the year 700 in the area north-east of Lake Chad (in the modern-day country of Chad). It was led by the Zaghawa (a nomadic people) but in the eleventh century immigrants (who according to Kanem's oral traditions, came from Yemen) supplanted the Zaghawa and established a new royal lineage called the *Saifawa* dynasty. Although the claim of Yemeni origin has not been proved, the ruling caste's ethnic origin seemed different from that of the common people, and also changed over time. Before the twelfth century the rulers were light skinned, which suggests a foreign origin, and progressively became darker skinned after the twelfth century; which suggests intermarriage between the ruling immigrant group and the natives.

As shown in Map 1, by the thirteenth century, Kanem encompassed the areas east, west, and north of Lake Chad (modern-day north-east Nigeria, south-west Chad, and north-west Cameroon). Kanem's population was multi-ethnic and its location close to Lake Chad generated a diverse economy. Its population included farmers and fishermen from ethnic groups such as the Kanembu and Kanuri, and cattle-rearing Fulani and Shuwa Arab nomads. Hausas referred to Kanem's people as 'Beriberi', which has sometimes (without convincing evidence) been used to claim that its original rulers were Berbers from North Africa.

THE CRADLE OF ISLAM IN NIGERIAN

Kanem's ruler had the title of *mai* and ruled through a council of twelve consisting of free-born and slave members. The *mai* usually sat on a veiled throne that obscured his appearance. Women also had important roles in Kanem's aristocracy. The *mai*'s senior wife had the title of *gumsu* and his mother (*magira*) had a lot of influence. One queen mother (Aisha) actually ruled for nearly a decade before *Mai* Idris Alooma succeeded her (in some accounts Idris is stated to be her son, or her brother in others). Another queen mother imprisoned her son for not properly enforcing Islamic law. However, Kanem's history is not just the usual elite stories of regicide and warfare. It also had a legacy as a pioneer of Islamic devotion and scholarship. *Mai* Hume (who ruled at the end of the first millennium – around 1085–97) is reputed to be the first ruler of Kanem to convert to Islam. He died in Egypt; probably while en route to pilgrimage. His son and successor *Mai* Dunama (who ruled around 1097–1150) went on pilgrimage to Mecca two times, and drowned in the Red Sea while travelling for his third pilgrimage. Subsequent *mais* also made the pilgrimage and some were devout Muslims and scholars. When the *mai* travelled on pilgrimage, he was usually accompanied by an entourage of thousands of people, including children, servants, and camels. Kanem's policies also favoured Islamic education as it gave privileges to Islamic scholars and exempted them from taxes. Muslims from Kanem established a *madrassa* (an Islamic religious school) in Cairo in the thirteenth century (some time between 1242 and 1253), which was also a hostel for Kanem visitors to Cairo (and perhaps a rest stop for Kanem indigenes en route to pilgrimage in the Middle East). Kanem-Borno also became a great centre of Islamic education in the seventeenth and eighteenth centuries, and some of West Africa's leading scholars toured there to learn and teach.

THE BULALA WARS

In the late fourteenth century, civil war erupted between the *Saifawa* and another branch of the royal family named the Bulala. In the space of only 14 years, the Bulala killed *Mai* Daud Nikalemi (1377–86) and five of his six successors. Due to the assassinations and strife, *Mai* Umar Idrismi abandoned Kanem's capital Njimi (whose modern-day location is unknown). Idrismi was the only one of six successive Kanem rulers to die a natural death and avoid assassination. After leaving Kanem, the royal dynasty moved south-west to Borno[1] in the late fourteenth century. Borno was then a province of Kanem on the south-western side of Lake Chad (see Map 1), and the kingdom never returned to its ancestral home in Kanem. The move inverted the relationship between Borno and Kanem; as Kanem became a province of Borno.

The frequent assassinations triggered more palace coups. Since the son of any *mai* was eligible to rule, there were several claimants for the throne. Each royal assassination intensified the conflict as the sons of the dead *mais* vied with each other. There were 15 different *mais* between 1400 and 1472, 9 of whom had to fight off claims from family members or other members of the royal family.[2] In the late fifteenth century, *Mai* Ali Dunamani built a new fortified capital city at Birni Gazargamu with buildings made from

---

1   In the north-east of modern-day Nigeria.
2   Brenner, 1968, p. 2.

burnt bricks. This became the monarchy's first permanent home in a century.

KANEM-BORNO'S INTERNATIONAL RELATIONS

The kingdom became reinvigorated in its new home at Borno. The geographic move was also accompanied by a change in lifestyle from nomadic to settled agriculture. Kanem-Borno established diplomatic and trade links with places as far away as Europe and North Africa, and traded in ivory and ostrich feathers. A poet from Kanem was present in southern Spain as far back as the twelfth century.[3] Borno also established diplomatic relations with other Muslim states, such as a diplomatic and trade treaty with Tripoli (Libya) in 1555, and diplomatic relations with Istanbul (Turkey) in the sixteenth century and with Egypt in the nineteenth century. Closer to home, an official in the Hausa State at Abuja (which fled there from Zaria after the Fulani jihad) held the title of *Bakon Borno* ('messenger to Borno').

Kanem's relocation to Borno also brought it closer to Hausaland (to Borno's west – see Map 1). In the late fourteenth century, *Mai* Othman Kalnama and his supporters took refuge in Kano to escape the Bulala wars. Fifty years later another *mai* also took refuge in Kano. In the sixteenth century, relations between Borno and Hausaland changed and became tributary-vassal as *Mai* Idris Alooma not only defeated his Bulala rivals in Kanem, but also extended Borno's influence by conquering Hausaland and the Tuaregs of Air (in modern-day Niger Republic). Although Borno did not annex the Hausa States into Borno, much of Hausaland became a vassal to Borno and had to give annual gifts to their Borno overlords. Kebbi and Songhai interrupted Borno's ascendancy over Hausaland, but Borno regained it and resumed extracting tribute from Hausa States such as Gobir, Kano, Katsina, Zamfara, and Zazzau in the eighteenth century. Borno's sixteenth-century conquests were due to improvements in its armaments. The British

---

3   Shaw, 1905, pp. 269–70.

historian Flora Shaw claims that at that time, Borno's musket-carrying armies were better armed than European armies. As in the late 1500s English troops were armed only with bows and arrows, and as late as 1571, Spain (which was militarily ahead of other European countries) gave muskets only to its elite forces.[4]

THE FULATA

The westward direction of Kanem-Borno's influence first from Kanem to Borno, and then from Borno into Hausaland, put it on a collision course with the Fulani conquerors of Hausaland. The clash was both political and religious. The jihad's overthrow of Hausa kings displaced rulers who paid tribute to Borno, and threatened to sever Borno's influence over its Hausa vassal states. Yet initially, the jihad leaders did not seem to have Borno in their sights. However, their Fulani brethren in Borno had other ideas. In the same way that nomadic Fulani had migrated into Hausaland, they had also wandered with their cattle into Borno and had lived there for centuries. Borno's people referred to the Fulani as 'Fulata'.

Unlike Hausaland's jihad which was triggered by the Gobir rulers' mistreatment of, and conflicts with, the Fulani, Borno's rulers did not persecute the Fulani. Yet despite there being no obvious mutual Borno–Fulani antagonism, at least three different dynamics coalesced to make the jihad a problem for Borno. Firstly, when overwhelmed by the Fulani-led jihad, some of the Hausa States such as Daura, Kano, and Katsina, appealed to Borno for help. The fact that Hausa States appealed to Borno demonstrates the fluid and different meanings ascribed to ethnic and regional cohesion in the nineteenth century. Despite their 'Hausa Bakwai' common ancestry and relationship, the Hausa States did not automatically have loyalties only to each other, nor did they always act as a cohesive bloc. Their historical relationship with Borno made Borno a natural ally to whom the eastern Hausa States would turn to in the event of a crisis. Secondly, inspired by news of the jihad's

---

4   Ibid., p. 278.

success in Hausaland, many Fulanis resident in Borno emigrated west to join their victorious brethren in Hausaland. Thirdly, one of Dan Fodio's Fulani flag bearers named Buba Yero was trying to create an Islamic caliphate in territories to Borno's south (in modern-day Adamawa and Gombe States of Nigeria). Unlike the jihad in Hausaland which targeted lax Muslims, Yero's jihad targeted non-Muslim communities. However, Yero also raided into Borno itself. The westward migration of Borno's Fulani population and Buba Yero's jihad created pressure on Borno's western and southern flanks. By 1808, two groups of Fulani in western and southern Borno (led by Ibrahim Zaki and Gwoni Mukhtar, respectively) had also commenced their own jihad inside Borno.

Since Borno was already a Muslim kingdom with a longer tradition of practising Islam than Hausaland, Borno's ruler *Mai* Ahmad was astonished by two simultaneous Fulani rebellions in his territory. He could not understand why the Fulani regarded a Muslim kingdom like Borno as a legitimate target for a jihad. Ahmad wrote to one of the Fulani leaders in Borno named Alhaji Adamu and also sent a letter to Dan Fodio himself, and asked them to explain why the Fulani were attacking a fellow Muslim state. In his letter to Dan Fodio, Ahmad also asked him why he had adopted the title *amir-al-muminin* (commander of the believers) since Ahmad was already using that title in Borno. Ahmad's protest regarding the Fulani uprising in Borno took Dan Fodio's court by surprise. Dan Fodio's son Mohammed Bello later admitted to Borno's leaders that 'As for your country [Borno] we do not know how warfare broke out there ... we have no knowledge of the state of its faith or its sultans.'[5] Based on Bello's response, it seemed that in contrast to the jihad in Hausaland, which was inspired by Dan Fodio's edict, the Fulanis in Borno took up arms and rebelled on their own initiative without the knowledge or pre-approval of the jihad leaders at Sokoto. Dan Fodio ordered Bello to write back to *Mai* Ahmad. In his reply, Bello explained the jihad's aims and asked Ahmad to support them. He also asked the Borno Fulani to cease hostilities. However, Ahmad

5 Brenner, 1968, pp. 32–3.

was absent by the time Bello's reply letter arrived. Events during Ahmad's absence are contested. In one account, Bello alleged that Ahmad threatened his messenger,[6] and in another that Ahmad actually killed the messenger[7] (although it is not clear how the blind and frail Ahmad could have done so). The Fulani leaders in Borno also protested to Dan Fodio, refused to lay down their weapons, and asked him to repeal the armistice order on the grounds that they could not observe a truce against a people that practised polytheism, and who were aiding the Hausas.

The Hausa States' appeal for Borno's help put Ahmad in a rock and hard place dilemma. If he declined to help them, he would be forsaking neighbouring kingdoms that Borno had a long history of amity with. If he intervened to help them, he risked declaring himself an enemy of Dan Fodio and his jihad leaders. What Ahmad did in response to the Hausa distress call is also contested. The Fulani account claims that feeling himself morally bound to assist Borno's Hausa allies, Ahmad sent military reinforcements to help the eastern Hausa States. Another account is that Ahmad ordered his army to counter-attack against the Fulani rebels that were attacking western Borno, and that the Fulani misinterpreted this as an attempt to aid the Hausa kings. Whichever version is true, Ahmad's attempt to suppress the Fulani revolt failed. The Fulani forces were victorious; they killed the Borno *galadima* (senior military and political commander) and other senior Borno officials, and drove Ahmad out of his capital at Birni Gazargamu. They also looted Ahmad's palace, and seized his treasures and some of the princesses of the royal house as booties of war. At this point, the Caliphate leaders became involved and Dan Fodio sent his emissary Gidado Dan Laima to Birni Gazargamu to collect Dan Fodio's share of the loot.

Much of Borno's population fled in panic and became homeless refugees as the Fulani forces under Buba Yero, Ibrahim Zaki, and Gwoni Mukhtar were 'spreading terror and destruction'.[8] *Mai*

---

6 Arnett, 1922, p. 101.
7 Ibid., p. 106.
8 Brenner, 1968, p. 34.

Ahmad evacuated his capital and escaped with his family and the surviving members of his court to a location near to Lake Chad. The 800-year-old kingdom was on the brink of collapse and being taken over by the Fulani. The elderly and blind Ahmad met with his senior surviving officials to discuss how to respond to the crisis. After this meeting he decided to abdicate and that his son Dunama would succeed him. Dunama scoured the kingdom to try and muster fighting men for a counter-attack against the Fulani. As he did so, he heard stories about a young and brilliant scholar who had moved to Borno after being born, raised, and educated in Arab lands. The scholar that Dunama heard about was living in the town of Ngala (close to Nigeria's modern-day north-eastern border with Cameroon) earning a living as a religious teacher and by selling religious charms. The scholar was famed for his alleged mystical powers and proficiency in making supernatural charms. He had also proved his martial quality by standing up to Fulanis in his neighbourhood and defeating them with a small force of religious students and teachers. Dunama summoned this revered scholar and asked him to come to Borno's aid against the Fulani. He agreed. Unfortunately for Dan Fodio and his followers, they could not easily dismiss their new adversary as a pagan as they had done to the Hausa kings and the people who had fled uphill in fear during the jihad. He was very similar to the Caliphate leaders: erudite, and well versed in Islamic law and theology. A Briton who later met him said that he had 'a most singular manner of delivery, and I scarcely ever met with any person who expressed himself so clearly, and with so few words'.[9] The man *Mai* Dunama summoned was the bi-racial child of a Kanembu father and an Arab mother. His name was Mohammed al-Kanemi (literally 'Mohammed from Kanem').

MOHAMMED FROM KANEM

Although Borno's rulers did not realise it at the time, recruiting Kanemi to their cause simultaneously gained the greatest challenge

9 Denham et al., 1826, pp. 251–2.

to the Fulani and also unwittingly prepared the path for their own replacement. Kanemi was born in 1775 near Murzuk in what is now modern-day Libya. He was remarkably similar to Dan Fodio. Both of them were literate in Arabic, and both of their fathers were also renowned scholars. Kanemi's mother was the daughter of a wealthy Arab merchant. His scholarly credentials and Islamic knowledge were impeccable, perhaps even more impressive than those of Dan Fodio and his lieutenants. Whereas Dan Fodio and his immediate family lived their entire lives in a small area of Hausaland, Kanemi spent the first three decades of his life in Libya, Egypt, and Saudi Arabia. He studied under the most revered Islamic scholars of his era, and also did something Dan Fodio never managed to do: he made a pilgrimage to the Middle East (as a young man Dan Fodio tried to make the pilgrimage, but returned after his father forbade him to do so). After his pilgrimage, Kanemi left his son behind in the Middle East for another decade so that he could further his religious education. By the time the Fulani jihad commenced in 1804, Kanemi was already a charismatic and famous scholar, even though he was not yet 30 years old. Kanemi's dual Arab-Kanembu ethnic background and the fact that two of his best friends were Shuwa Arabs gave him influence with two of Borno's primary ethnic constituencies, the Kanembu and Shuwa Arabs. He was also astute and level-headed. His initial response after coming into *Mai* Dunama's service demonstrated to the Fulani jihadists that he was not like the others they had encountered and defeated. Kanemi presented not only a military challenge, but also the most serious theological challenge to the Caliphate's leaders. He confronted the Fulani jihadists not only with weapons, but also with words.

THE PEN AND SWORD

Kanemi's introduction into the conflict brought in three crucial new dynamics: military acumen, mysticism, and most importantly, an important theological debate about the jihad. Kanemi was willing to fight the Fulani on the battlefield with weapons, and also challenged the theological ground they stood on. He wrote a letter to the Fulani leaders in Borno (including Gwoni Mukhtar – who led the raid that destroyed Borno's capital) and asked them to explain their reasons for waging jihad against Borno. When he did not receive a reply, he persisted and wrote to them again on Saturday 14 May 1808, to tell them:

> the reason for the composition of this letter is that when destiny drove me to this province as a seeker of the favour of Allah, I found the fire of discord between you and the people of this country, whose sparks were scattered, and calamity was manifested ... What is the cause of this discord? What do you demand from the people? About what matter did a conflict occur between you and them?[10]

Kanemi was careful not to attack Dan Fodio personally, given the massive charisma and influence he had with the Fulani. He instead asked them: 'Let us know whether you have contact with ... the Shaikh Usman Dan Fodio. Know that information regarding his praiseworthy state and graceful comportment has reached us.'[11] When the Borno Fulani eventually replied, Kanemi was not impressed. In fact he could barely conceal his intellectual disdain for them. He later said that the Borno Fulani:

> returned me a weak answer, not such as comes from an intelligent man, much less a learned one, let alone from one who is reforming religion. They wrote me a list of titles of books and said that in these books they saw the reason for the war. Now we have examined these books and we do not see in them what they have seen.[12]

Kanemi combined his diplomatic correspondence with military efforts on the battlefield. Borno's forces regrouped and Kanemi's Kanembu and Shuwa Arab followers reinforced them. Kanemi's

---

10   Kota, 2020, pp. 85–6.
11   Ibid., p. 86.
12   Based on translation in Arnett, 1922, p. 102, with slight modifications by the author.

repute for writing supernatural charms raised morale. Accounts of Borno's counter-attack to regain its capital are noted not for recounting the order of battle or its strategies, but rather for Kanemi's allegedly decisive supernatural intervention. Oral traditions in Borno claim that prior to engaging the Fulani on the battlefield, Kanemi isolated himself for several days in meditation and prayer, and that after emerging from his spiritual isolation, he wrote several Arabic formulae on a calabash. He then gave the calabash to Borno's army and instructed them to smash it to the ground just before they made contact with the Fulani forces on the battlefield.[13] They did exactly as Kanemi instructed, defeated the Fulani, and killed their leader Gwoni Mukhtar. Whether or not Kanemi's supernatural prowess was the decisive factor, he was helped by the fact that prior to battle, Mukhtar had lost several of his fighting men who departed for the usual seasonal migration with their cattle. However, such logistical factors were not given much airtime in the avalanche of electrifying news about Kanemi's mystical powers. Kanemi's entry changed the direction of the conflict, and helped Borno to recover its capital from the Fulani in less than one year.

After expelling the Fulani from Borno's capital, Kanemi returned home (like his adversary Dan Fodio did after the jihad), and resumed his scholarly career at Ngala. However, controversy in Borno and further Fulani attacks did not allow him to rest for long. Only one year after Borno regained its capital, the Fulani returned again in 1810 to resume raiding Borno's territory under their leaders such as Muhammadu Manga (the son of Gwoni Mukhtar who was killed when Borno recaptured its capital) and Ibrahim Zaki. The renewed Fulani attacks forced *Mai* Dunama to flee and to once again call on Kanemi for help. However, Dunama's escapes from the Fulani and inability to suppress their attacks without Kanemi's help led his court to depose him in 1810 and install his uncle Muhammad Ngileruma (his father's brother) to replace him. In 1813, Kanemi reversed the palace coup that deposed Dunama, and restored Dunama to the throne. However, Dunama now owed Kanemi

13 Brenner, 1968, pp. 37–8.

thrice; for helping him fight and push back the Fulani (twice), and for allowing him to become Borno's ruler for the second time. Kanemi cashed in the debt. As a reward, Dunama ceded a part of Borno's territory to Kanemi as his own fiefdom, agreed to pay him a percentage of the kingdom's revenues, and gave him treasures and servants. Kanemi's interference in royal succession also gave him influence within the royal court, and the loyalty he inspired from Kanembu and Shuwa Arab warriors enabled him to act as Borno's de facto minister of defence. The momentum of Kanemi's fame was now irresistible. News of how he helped Borno defeat the Fulani and his mystical powers had spread far and wide. Kanemi took the title of *shehu* (Borno's equivalent to the honorific Arab title of Sheikh), and in 1814 he built a new town called Kukawa, which later became Borno's capital.

THE WAR OF WORDS

However, Kanemi remained appalled that the Fulani had declared jihad against people who shared the same faith as them. He did not give up his determination to extract an explanation from the Fulani for waging jihad. Being dissatisfied with the Borno Fulani's response, he decided to write to Dan Fodio himself. Kanemi's letter to the jihad's spiritual leader was important because it challenged the Fulani justification for the jihad and presented the most significant theological 'other side of the story' against the Fulani. Kanemi's astute and precise theological arguments jolted the Fulani jihadists' assumption of theological supremacy and made them reflect on whether their actions were justified. Remarkably, this written theological debate went on as the two sides were fighting a war.

'Tell us therefore why you are fighting us and enslaving our free people'

Kanemi composed an articulate and dignified letter to the jihad leaders in Sokoto in which he informed them that:

... We believe in writing; even if it makes no impression on you, it is better than silence ... Tell us therefore why you are fighting us and enslaving our free people. If you say that you have done this to us because of our paganism, then I say that we are innocent of paganism, and it is far from our compound. If praying and the giving of alms, knowledge of God, fasting in Ramadan and the building of mosques is paganism, what is Islam? These buildings in which you have been standing on a Friday, are they churches or synagogues or fire temples? If they were other than Muslim places of worship, then you would not pray in them when you capture them. Is this not a contradiction?[14]

Kanemi's accusation about the jihadists enslaving Muslims hit a raw nerve and made it seem that the jihadists were applying double standards. The enslavement of Muslims was one of the grievances that enraged the jihadists and which they used to justify their jihad against the Hausa kings. Kanemi's letter had such a profound effect on the Caliphate leaders that Mohammed Bello admitted, 'There was nothing which caused us so much anxiety as a letter from Alhaji Aminu' (Kanemi).[15] Kanemi's letter caused so much soul searching among Dan Fodio and his lieutenants that they replied to refute its accusations, and to issue their own rationalisations for the jihad. Had Kanemi's challenge not elicited replies from the Caliphate leaders, we probably would not know as much about the jihad as we currently do. Dan Fodio's brother Abdullahi and his son Bello replied on his behalf. The correspondence brought to the fore two influential protagonists in Borno and Sokoto who were not the rulers of their respective states, but who were kings-in-waiting. Bello especially took up the mantle of refuting Kanemi's accusations and wrote a bristling reply in which he justified his Fulani brethren's actions in Borno by informing Kanemi that:

The first cause of our fighting against your people is that they are helping the heathen Hausas against us. You must in truth

---

14   Hodgkin, 1960, pp. 199–200.
15   Arnett, 1922, p. 102.

know that whoever helps infidels is no better than they[16]... your Amir [*Mai* Ahmad] rose up in order to harm your Fulbe neighbors who were emulating; the Shaikh. He forced them to take flight thus siding with the kings of Hausa and helping them. It is known that Unbelievers help only one another, while Believers do likewise.[17]

Kanemi goaded Bello into a lengthy riposte that served as a historical A–Z guide to the jihad. In his response to Kanemi, Bello revealed not only the Fulani justifications for attacking Borno, but also their grievances against the Hausa kings and their society, reasons for declaring jihad, and the deprivations and discriminatory treatment that the Hausa kings subjected the Fulani to. Yet when it came to Kanemi's pointed theological challenge, Bello was on shaky ground. While the Fulani could theologically rationalise their attacks against non-Muslims, and against the Hausa on the basis that they were syncretists, they would have to find a more compelling theological argument to explain why a jihad against Muslims in Borno was necessary. Thus Bello interestingly combined non-religious reasons (Borno siding with the Hausa) with religious justifications. The Fulani adopted a 'the friend of my enemy is my enemy' doctrine against Borno. According to Bello's rationale, Borno placed itself in the jihad's crosshairs via guilt by association, by rendering aid to the Hausa kings whom the Fulani had declared *persona non grata*. Dan Fodio retroactively validated a previously unsanctioned jihad in Borno and accused Borno of similar offences that the jihad leaders had levelled against the Hausa. He claimed that Borno residents had engaged in idolatry and that he had heard reports 'that they make sacrifices to rocks and trees, [and] that they practice certain observances in the river similar to those of the Egyptians on the banks of the Nile'.[18]

Yet the Fulanis' messianic conviction of being right was matched by Kanemi's insistence that their jihad was illegal. The Fulani could

16 Johnston, 1967, p. 108.
17 Brenner, 1968, p. 33.
18 Johnston, 1967, p. 110.

not accuse him of being slack in enforcing religious edicts. Those in his domain who flouted Ramadan by, for example, succumbing to the temptation to drink water or visit their wives between sunrise and sunset, were punished by being flogged 400 times with a whip made from hippopotamus hide.[19] Kanemi also raised the sensitive topic of the jihadists' behaviour when they invaded and destroyed the Muslim town of Yandoto in Hausaland. He repeated accusations that the jihadists scattered and destroyed Muslim holy books as they ransacked Yandoto:

> Moreover we see among you a thing which every Mallam rejects. You are destroying books; you are scattering them in the roads; you are throwing them in the dirt. But the name of God is on these books and you know that he who throws the name of God in the dirt is a heathen.[20]

This was a serious accusation (for it is sacrilege for a Muslim to desecrate holy books in this way). Bello did not deny the accusation but instead tried to explain it away by claiming that the wind scattered the books, and that he personally walked around to pick up the pages himself 'till I was weary for they were very many'.[21] Kanemi not only dismissed the Fulani justification for the jihad, but also accused the jihadists of waging a political war for power and material gain, and camouflaging their true intentions under the guise of religion. He told the Fulani leaders that:

> The only result of your policy is to bring tribulation and suffering on your fellow Muslims, for your followers have been killing our men and capturing our women and children. We are astonished that you should permit such things when you claim to be reforming our religion and we perceive that your true object is the power to rule over others. Though you may conceal this aim, even in your own hearts, it is, we believe, your real ambition.[22]

---

19   Denham et al., 1826, p. 255.
20   Arnett, 1922, p.103.
21   Ibid., p. 107.
22   Johnston, 1967, p. 106.

The accusation of unjustly shedding Muslim blood and of waging war for material gain and power shook Dan Fodio deeply. Yet as usual, Kanemi was careful to avoid personally criticising him. He wrote of Dan Fodio: 'We have heard of the conduct of Shaikh Uthman ibn Fudi [Dan Fodio], and we know his writings are contrary to your deeds. If this affair stems from his opinion then ... we must say we thought better of him.'[23] Yet Kanemi also made it clear that his admiration for Dan Fodio was not unconditional. He said, 'we are on [Dan Fodio's] side if [Dan Fodio] is for the truth. If he is departing from truth, then we [will] leave him and follow the truth.'[24]

Kanemi's intervention and letters to the jihad leaders remains seminal for at least three reasons. Firstly, Kanemi shook the theoretical foundations of the jihadists and made them ponder on who was a true Muslim and whom it was legal to wage jihad against. Secondly, the correspondence between Bello and Kanemi established international diplomatic relations between two warring pre-colonial African states. After the relationship between Borno and the Hausa States, Bello and Kanemi's letters established new relations between Borno and the new Sokoto Caliphate. Given the political and religious enormity of what was at stake, the civilised and moderate tone of the letters is remarkable. Thirdly, Kanemi demonstrated that the Fulani were not invincible. He was not only their match on the battlefield, but also forced them into a political compromise. Although Bello and Kanemi never met each other, a grudging mutual respect developed during the course of their correspondence and was evident in the increasingly diplomatic and almost complimentary tone of their letters. Kanemi maintained his policy of criticising the Fulani in Borno but not directing personal criticism at Bello or his family by saying: 'You know that your kinsmen who live among us are ignorant people. Their ambition is to conquer and rule this country ... Had they been as you are, then we would not have fought them.'[25]

---

23 Brenner, 1968, p. 45.
24 Arnett, 1922, p. 103.
25 Johnston, 1967, p. 109.

COLD PEACE

Dan Fodio sent his son-in-law Gidado Dan Laima to Borno and asked Kanemi to send an emissary to meet Gidado in order to discuss a truce. Relations cooled sufficiently for Kanemi to write to Bello in 1820 to propose not only a truce, but armistice lines:

> We profess the same religion, and it is not fitting that our subjects should make war on one another. Between our two realms lie the pagan Bedde people, on whom it is permissible to levy tribute; let us respect this limit. What lies to the east of their country shall be ours, and what lives of the west shall be yours. As for Muniyo, Damagaram, and Daura, they will continue to be vassals of the Sultan of Borno, who in return will surrender to you all his pretentions to Gobir and Katsina.[26]

As the conflict on the battlefield drew to a stalemate, so did the correspondence. The inconclusive war and letters allowed a 'cold peace' to emerge between Borno and the Caliphate. Although neither side officially declared the war over and skirmishes sometimes occurred, the two sides did not return to the all-out war of 1808–10. The two sides agreed to disagree, each side refused to admit defeat and could claim victory, and Kanemi's letter provided an unofficial armistice border between the two states. Getting the Fulani to concede territory for the first time was a significant political achievement. It was also an illuminating precedent of African pre-colonial mediation and conflict resolution. Although Borno regained its capital and most of its territory, it lost some parts of its territory in places such as Hadejia, Katagum, and Misau (in modern-day Jigawa and Bauchi States of Nigeria) which became part of the Caliphate. Two interesting open questions are what Borno's leaders and people thought about the jihad before it arrived on their doorstep, and how they would have reacted to it had the Fulani not declared war against them. The fact that Dan Fodio did not immediately declare

---

26 Low, 1967, p. 165.

jihad against Borno, and consented to it almost as a retroactive afterthought, suggests that war between Borno and Sokoto was not inevitable. Did Borno support the jihad until it became a victim of it? Another interesting alternate history is whether the two states could have co-existed without bloodshed as neighbouring Islamic empires. This would have required either or both of Dan Fodio and the *Mai* of Borno to accept each other as the leaders of sibling Muslim states and the other addressing himself as the commander of the believers. The impetuousness of the Fulani in Borno prevented us from finding out which of these alternative outcomes would have unfolded.

The fact that Kanemi corresponded with a foreign monarch on Borno's behalf and made peace proposals on his own initiative demonstrates how much power he had accumulated. Most prior accounts make it seem as if Kanemi became Borno's de facto ruler as soon as he helped repel the Fulani from Borno's capital in 1809. However, for a period of about 27 years between 1810 and 1837, Kanemi and the *mai* were in nebulous co-existence, and it was not clear which of them held the ascendancy. During this time, Kanemi was at least the power behind the throne. Around 1819–20 he also developed and started using his own seal. By the 1820s, Kanemi had become so powerful that even outsiders treated him as a sovereign in his own right. Although the *mai* was still Borno's titular ruler, Kanemi was perceived as the man who could make things happen.

When the first European visitors to Borno arrived in February 1823, they knew where de facto power lay and went straight to Kanemi rather than the *mai*. They were his guests for almost a year. The Europeans were the British explorers Captain Hugh Clapperton (a Scotsman and Royal Navy officer), Major Dixon Denham of the British army (who later served as superintendent of liberated slaves in Sierra Leone), and a young Scottish doctor from Edinburgh named Walter Oudney. Although Kanemi was friendly and hospitable towards them and ordered his people to build houses to accommodate them, he was initially wary about the motives of his uninvited British guests. He wondered why they had travelled so far and risked their lives on a hazardous journey merely to sightsee (as they claimed). Their inquisitive nature and desire to observe and write about everyone they met and everything they did and saw made Kanemi even more curious about their motives. Major Denham's insistence on accompanying a Borno slave-raiding party into the Mandara region did not allay Kanemi's concerns. Despite Kanemi's refusal to consent to Denham's presence on the raid, and protest that although Denham was a soldier, he (Kanemi) could not guarantee Denham's safety in such a mission, and did not want him to come to any harm while he was in Kanemi's jurisdiction, Denham insisted and accompanied the raid anyway because the British government had instructed him to take advantage of any opportunity to observe the military tactics of the natives.

'What could induce you to go so far from home – to find it out, and fight with [its] people?'

Kanemi was concerned about Britain's prior history of conquering Muslim countries, and hence probed the Britons with questions about their dealings with other countries with large Muslim populations. Kanemi's concerns led him to constantly engage the Britons in conversations which both foreshadowed events that would occur 85 years later and demonstrated how astute and articulate he was. During one of the Britons' visits to Kanemi's residence, he barely allowed them to sit down following their arrival, before going straight to business by asking them how far Britain was from India. When they replied that India was a four-month sea journey away from Britain, Kanemi asked them: 'What could induce you to go so far from home – to find it out, and fight with [its] people?'[27] When Clapperton and his companions explained that the British were great adventurers who loved exploration, and were jealous of the exploits of Dutch and French explorers, Kanemi coolly replied: 'and you went [to India] at first with only a few ships, as friends?'.[28] The British kept trying to reassure Kanemi by telling him that they had treated India benevolently, made it rich, and that Muslims there

---

27 Denham et al., 1826, p. 279.
28 Ibid., p. 279.

preferred English law to their own. However, a Moroccan native who was present during the dialogue interjected: 'By God! ... they eat the whole country – they are no friends.'[29]

'I fear they wish to overthrow the Muslim power altogether'

To assess the veracity of the Britons' self-professed benevolent intent, Kanemi summoned a member of their entourage; a bi-racial, multi-lingual man from the Caribbean island of St Vincent named 'Columbus'. His real name was Adolphus Simpkins but he acquired the name Columbus as he had travelled halfway across the world on a merchant ship, and spoke three European languages and Arabic. His multi-lingual skills earned him employment as an interpreter in the British mission. Kanemi asked Columbus to give his verdict on the Britons' intentions and asked him: 'I have sent to speak to you, and I think you will tell me the truth ... I think the English are my friends; but a man's head is always his best friend. I fear they wish to overthrow the Mussulman [Muslim] power altogether.' Columbus vouched for his British employers by replying: 'As far as I know they want to do no such thing: they wish to see, and to describe the country, with its inhabitants; and if the English are the first to do so, they will pride themselves greatly in consequence.'[30] Columbus' testimony caused Kanemi to let his guard down and ease his concerns about his uninvited British guests.

'true Muslims have always avoided shedding the blood of Christians, and assisted and protected them with their own honour'

The wandering spirit of Kanemi's British guests tested the strength of the 'cold peace' between Borno and Sokoto. After their long stay in Borno, Clapperton and Dr Oudney decided to visit the Sokoto Caliphate to Borno's west. Even though the bitterness of the recent wars between Borno and the Caliphate was still fresh in the memory, in January 1824, Kanemi wrote two similar letters to the *Emir* of Kano

29   Ibid., p. 279.
30   Ibid., p. 252.

Mohammed Dabo, and to Mohammed Bello, in which he asked them to grant the Britons safe passage, protect them, and to provide guards to escort them. In his letter to Bello, Kanemi reminded Bello that although the Britons were Christians, their people had 'maintained with the Muslims uninterrupted treaties of religious amity and friendship, established since ancient periods'. He cited Koranic principles about honour and reminded Bello 'that the true Mussulmans [Muslims] have always avoided shedding the blood of Christians, and assisted and protected them with their own honour'. He therefore charged Bello to be 'attentive to these travellers, and cast them not into the corners of neglect; let no one hurt them, either by words or deeds, nor interrupt them with any injurious behaviour: but let them return to us, safe, content, and satisfied, as they went from us to you'.[31] Given that the letter writer and recipient had sent their armies into battle against each other only a few years earlier, the honourable and sedate tone of the letter is remarkable.

Kanemi also responded to a request that his British guests persistently made to him. Denham and Clapperton had for some time pestered him to give them information about the course and location of Lake Chad. To satisfy their curiosity, Kanemi wrote a letter to the British Consul at Tripoli in late October 1824. In this letter Kanemi gave information about the location and size of Lake Chad, and by doing so innocently provided vital geographic intelligence that would aid future British invaders several decades later. He concluded his letter by signing off with 'Send our salutation to the great King of the English, and to everyone who inquires after us amicably.'[32] About 85 years later, agents of the British monarchy (using information provided by Kanemi, and maps and descriptions given by explorers such as Clapperton) conquered Kanemi's descendants.

THE RISE OF THE *SHEHU*

Kanemi's pivotal role in facing down the Fulani threat to Borno and the consequent fame he acquired meant that he could not quietly

---

31   Ibid., p. 427.
32   Ibid., p. 435.

retire and become a private citizen. Although the *mais* remained Borno's titular leaders, their lineage was living on borrowed time. *Mai* Dunama was killed in battle in 1817. As the *mai* was treated as a divine monarch, he fell victim to a Borno tradition whereby it was beneath his dignity to carry weapons. When surrounded by the enemy, he accepted his fate as did his aides who tried to protect him to the death and died with him. Dunama's younger brother Ibrahim succeeded him as *mai*. Kanemi himself later died in 1837, in the same year as his rival Bello at Sokoto. Kanemi's son Umar succeeded him as *shehu*. Dunama's death and succession by his young and inexperienced brother made the *Saifawa* dynasty vulnerable, and exposed the tensions between the *mai* and *shehu*. After Kanemi's death *Mai* Ibrahim summoned *Shehu* Umar to come to him to pay allegiance. Umar replied with a counter-demand for Ibrahim to come to him. The stand-off was broken when Umar's courtiers replied with an ultimatum and unveiled threat to *Mai* Ibrahim: 'When we buried Shehu Laminu [Kanemi] we buried only him. All the courtiers, horses, and weapons are still with his son Umar. If you refuse to come here, will see you at Birni Kafela' [Ibrahim's residence].[33] Ibrahim got the message and went to Umar. In 1846, Ibrahim's alleged attempts to regain power for his dynasty cost him his life. Umar ordered Ibrahim's arrest, detention, and execution on alleged charges of engineering Borno's invasion by a foreign state, and thus eliminated the most significant source of rival power to him. With that, the over 800-year-old *Saifawa* dynasty ended. After about 30 years of contested leadership of Borno between the *mai* and *shehu*, Umar became Borno's ruler, and caused a third transition in Borno's ruling dynasty as the title of *shehu* succeeded the *mais* and Zaghawa. Since then, Kanemi's descendants have ruled Borno with the title of *shehu* (with one brief interruption between 1893 and 1901).

Borno's rulers saved Borno from the Fulani jihad, but at the expense of losing control to the Kanemis.

---

33 Brenner, 1968, p. 95.

4
Northern Nigeria's First Family

The history of northern Nigeria during the past 250 years is syn-onymous with one family. Because the Dan Fodio family were such prolific writers, most of our knowledge regarding the Sokoto Cali-phate comes from them. Their domination of the literature regarding the Caliphate means that northern Nigeria's history consists largely of the victor's version of events.

One of the most mysterious elements of the Sokoto Caliphate's history is the lack of anti-Caliphate accounts. Given the large number of enemies the Caliphate had, one would expect to find lots of opposing accounts. Yet there are very few. Most of what we know about the Caliphate's opponents was written by the Caliphate's leaders (especially Dan Fodio's son Mohammed Bello). There is a controversial potential reason for the absence of pre-jihad or anti-Caliphate accounts. The Caliphate's great rival Mohammed al-Kanemi hinted at it in his famous letter to the Caliphate's leaders in which he accused them of destroying the conquered Hausa leaders' books. Although Kanemi's accusation is an incendiary one, it has validity and was even later corroborated by a Fulani. In 1989 Maitama Sule (a former government minister and official of the Kano Emirate) claimed that:

When they [the Fulani] came they found al-Wali [the last Hausawa ruler, Muhammadu Alwali dan Yaji, 1781–1807] a very learned person. Some people thought that he was a saint. And he wrote so many books and they dumped all his publications into a well, so that people coming afterwards might not challenge them and ask for the justification of waging such a jihad against such a religious man ... I think [the books of other Hausa *malamai*] they must have met the same fate.[1]

The deliberate destruction of their predecessor's books is so emotionally and religiously charged that it is rarely discussed. The Caliphate officials' writing also suppressed surviving pre-jihad texts and knowledge about the Hausa States. This preoccupation with accounts written by the Caliphate's officials made it seem as if everything before the jihad belonged to an irrelevant dark age.

Even when outsiders have researched or written about the Caliphate, their accounts are based largely on English translations of what the Dan Fodios wrote.[2] When outsiders did not simply translate primary material written by the Dan Fodios, they relied on accounts provided by their descendants or other Caliphate officials. For example, when British colonial authorities took an interest in the Caliphate's history, they commissioned the *waziris* of Sokoto and Gwandu (Muhammad al-Bukhari and Ahmad Sa'ad, respectively) to write the histories of their respective regions. Even as late as the 1960s when interest in the Caliphate was renewed in the post-independence era, the professors and PhD students who wrote about the Caliphate relied on the Dan Fodio family's accounts or consulted oral histories provided by their descendants and officials. The nostalgic veneration for the Dan Fodios and the Caliphate means that rejecting Caliphate-produced accounts is almost tantamount to heresy.

The Dan Fodios' control of the narrative has left two long-standing legacies. The first is that the history of the Caliphate has been, to a large extent, a series of Caliphate-sanctioned productions. Secondly, most accounts about the Caliphate focus on its triumphs in a way that makes it appear as an unbroken golden age without setbacks. However the Caliphate was beset with crises and rebellions from its early days. Yet these rarely get attention due to the focus on the jihad that preceded it. Ironically, the Caliphate's first crisis arose from rivalry within Dan Fodio's family.

---

1   Starratt, 1993, p. 62.
2   For example, Arnett (1922), Last (1967), and Hiskett (1994).

THE TEMPTATIONS OF VICTORY

Dan Fodio's movement successfully transitioned from a fringe religious reform group, to a popular armed insurgent group, to a government. Having won the war, the Caliphate's leaders were faced with two new challenges of resisting the worldly temptations that victory brought, and keeping the peace. The casualties that the jihadists suffered at the battles of Tsuntua in 1804 and Alwasa in 1805 diluted the jihad's reformist religious zeal and brought in new recruits who were attracted to, and distracted by, the spoils of war, and were not as ascetic as Dan Fodio and the original jihad leaders. After the battle of Alwasa during which some of the jihadist forces were so busy looting that they did not notice the enemy approaching and got ambushed as a result, Dan Fodio's brother Abdullahi complained:

> Me they left among a crowd of laggards, who find prayer a burden to them, who have given their hearts to seeking pleasure. Most of them have desisted from their religion. They buy the pleasures of the world, they choose the things which please their hearts. Their courage is broken. They do not obey orders. They dispute the command of their leaders. They curse him who rises up to prevent their evil doing.[3]

Abdullahi became so disillusioned about the decadence of his colleagues that he resigned during the jihad and headed east – ostensibly for Mecca. He got as far as Kano before being persuaded to return and rejoin his family and comrades. Yet after his return he remained unhappy after being sent back to the field to continue the military campaign while many of the jihadist leaders refused to join him on the battlefield and instead moved to Sifawa to be with his brother Dan Fodio.

---

3   Arnett, 1922, p. 84.

CONCUBINES

Victory also brought other temptations. Abdullahi criticised his colleagues who preoccupied themselves with 'the collecting of concubines, and fine clothes'.[4] Abdullahi's complaints had merit and were not simply due to his ascetic character. Since Muslim men are permitted to have up to four wives and the Koran does not explicitly restrict the number of concubines a man can have, many of the victorious jihadists captured the pretty wives, daughters, and sisters of the defeated Hausas and made them their concubines. Abdullahi's nephew Mohammed Bello had several concubines, including the slain King of Gobir's widow Katembale; who later bore two sons[5] for Bello, and Ladi, who was captured at Rabah in the early days of the jihad. After learning that she would have to become a concubine for the man who led her husband's killers, Katembale stoically accepted her fate by saying, 'if there is no milk, I shall have to drink water'.[6] Ladi gave birth to another one of Bello's sons (Aliyu) who later became the leader of the Caliphate. Although Dan Fodio's son-in-law Gidado Dan Laima had five sons with his wife Nana Asma'u (Dan Fodio's daughter), he also had 42 other children (21 sons and 21 daughters) with his other wives and concubines.[7] When the Scottish explorer Hugh Clapperton visited Sokoto in 1824, he was Gidado's guest and also wrote in his diaries about: 'gadado's [*sic*] harem having paid me repeated visits, I was much struck with the beauty of some of the female slaves'.[8] The practice of capturing women from the conquered side became so widespread that a historian later claimed that: 'After 1808 there was scarcely a victor's house without a Gobir concubine.'[9] In contrast, Dan Fodio was comparatively restrained as he had only one concubine: Mariya (who later bore him a posthumous son). Concubinage

---

4   Hiskett, 1994, p. 105.
5   Fodio and Mu'aledi.
6   Boyd, 1989, p. 25.
7   Ibid., p. 45.
8   Denham et al., 1826, p. 107.
9   Boyd, 2001, p. 10.

led to a private joke that while the Fulani won on the battlefield, the Hausa won in the bedroom.

WALLAHI WALLAHI

Not only did Abdullahi criticise the indiscipline of some of his colleagues, but in a thinly veiled criticism of his older brother, he also criticised 'the appointing of ignorant persons to the highest offices'.[10] He also wrote of his disdain for those 'whose purpose is the ruling of the countries and their people, in order to obtain delight and acquire rank'.[11] He indirectly corroborated Borno's *Shehu* al-Kanemi who made similar accusations against the jihadists and alleged that 'your true object is the power to rule over others'.[12] Criticism agitated Dan Fodio enough for him to compose a poem in Hausa called *Wallahi Wallahi* ('I Swear by God') in which he vehemently denied being motivated by a quest for power, or seeking material benefits and rank:

I swear by God, I did not accept temporal office in any way. I have accepted nothing from the rule of temporal office … whoever accepts office in order to exploit the country for worldly ends, I swear by God, he eats carrion! Whoever accepts office in this way, I swear by God, it is the knife of Satan [that] cuts him down. As for me, I have not sent anyone to do forced labour for me, but it is the governors of the towns who have sent you, for their own ends, I swear by God.[13]

This was not Dan Fodio's only tribulation. It also remained to be seen whether the Caliphate could make a leadership transition and survive without his inspirational presence. His family disagreed about how the Caliphate should be governed and leadership transitioned after him. Possibly suspecting that Dan Fodio was grooming

---

10   Hiskett, 1994, p. 105.
11   Ibid., p. 105.
12   Johnston, 1967, p. 106.
13   Hiskett, 1994, p. 107.

his son Bello to succeed him, while in Kano Abdullahi wrote *Diya al-Hukkam* ('The Light of the Rulers'), a template for Islamic Caliphate governance, which argued that a Muslim ruler should not be succeeded by his son. Dan Fodio wrote a rejoinder entitled *Siraj al-Ikhwan* ('Path of the Brethren'), in which he counter-argued that hereditary succession was not forbidden. These ideological differences between the brothers were also accentuated by geography as Dan Fodio and his son Bello resided at Sokoto, while Abdullahi lived 75 miles away at Gwandu. Written ideological differences finally came to the fore and caused the Caliphate's first major crisis when after a year-long illness, Usman Dan Fodio died aged 63 on 17 April 1817, less than a decade after the jihad.

THE SUCCESSION CRISIS

Abdullahi was in Bodinga (just under 20 miles south-west of Sokoto) when his brother died. He was an exceptionally qualified candidate to succeed his brother as *sarkin musulmi*. Although he was twelve years younger than Dan Fodio, he was just as erudite and pious, had excellent military credentials, and was the Caliphate's *waziri* (a high-ranking position akin to prime minister or secretary). When he heard that his brother had died he rode to Sokoto to present his candidacy, but by the time he arrived he was stunned by two developments. Firstly, he found the city gates closed and that he and his supporters were barred from entering the city. Secondly, his nephew Bello had already been appointed as the new *sarkin musulmi* in his absence without consulting him. Bitterly disappointed and hurt that he had been passed over in such a brusque manner, Abdullahi left and returned first to Bodinga, and then to Gwandu. Three weeks after being passed over, Abdullahi wrote that if there were two suitable candidates to lead the Caliphate, preference should be given to the elder candidate.[14] Abdullahi maintained a cold and dejected silence in Gwandu as he and Bello became estranged for three years.

---

14   Naylor, 2018, p. 48.

Bello's ascension also meant that Abdullahi lost his position as the Caliphate's *waziri*. Bello appointed his best friend and brother-in-law Gidado Dan Laima ('Gidado, son of Laima') as the new *waziri*. Gidado was a *Torodbe* Fulani and had been married to Bello's sister Nana Asma'u for ten years. He and Bello had studied together as children and also fought alongside each other during the jihad.

'Were he Sultan ... heads would fly about'

Bello became the Caliphate's second *sarkin musulmi* on 23 April 1817, six days after his father died. Despite being Dan Fodio's most famous son, Bello was not the oldest child. He was the son of Dan Fodio's third wife Hauwa and his position became elevated because his oldest brother Sa'ad died just before the jihad and another one of his older brothers Sambo was very well learned but was also an introverted loner who, according to Bello, 'was not given to social intercourse and kept himself much apart'.[15] Abdullahi was not the only rival contender that Bello had to overcome. He also won over competition from another brother: Abubakar Atiku. Some were relieved at Bello's appointment instead of the stern Atiku. One observer claimed that a common perception about Atiku in the Caliphate was that 'Were he Sultan ... heads would fly about.'[16]

Drawings or physical descriptions of the early Caliphate leaders are almost non-existent. While courtesy of Hugh Clapperton, we have a hand-drawn portrait of the Caliphate's rival, al-Kanemi of Borno, for unexplained reasons Clapperton did not similarly draw a portrait of Bello (despite meeting him several times). Clapperton, however, described Bello's physical appearance in 1825 as follows:

> The sultan is a noble-looking man, forty-four years of age, although much younger in appearance, five feet ten inches high, portly in person, with a short curling black beard, a small mouth, a fine forehead, a Grecian nose, and large black eyes.[17]

---

15   Arnett, 1922, p. 127.
16   Denham et al., 1826, p. 103.
17   Ibid., p. 83.

Bello also liked to use his turban to cover his nose and mouth, leaving only his eyes visible. The traits of a 'grecian nose', 'fine forehead', and 'tufted beard', have been detected in Bello's most famous descendants. Perhaps the most accurate clues regarding Bello's appearance come from his great-grandsons, the future *Sarkin Musulmi* Siddiq Abubakar III and the first Premier of the Northern Region of post-independence Nigeria, Ahmadu Bello, of whom we have plenty of photos.

Whatever his appearance, Bello did not enjoy a tranquil reign and faced multiple rebellions. Dissent followed his father's death, and some of his followers were not willing to extend to Bello the same unqualified allegiance they gave to his father. In the same way that the Dan Fodios took power by force, those they deposed also tried to retake power through similar means. The one-sided accounts of the Caliphate discussed above portrayed the pre-jihad Hausa rulers as autocratic, belligerent, and unreasonable. In their official written histories the Fulani got to explain their reasons for launching the jihad, but the Hausa kings did not get the reciprocal opportunity to explain their reasons for their actions, or to rebut the jihadists' accounts. Nor did they confirm or refute the accusation that they were idolaters. Yet even if the deposed Hausa rulers did not leave behind as large a historical library as the Fulani did, their actions spoke very loudly in the absence of their words.

ABDULSALAM'S REBELLION

Prior accounts have often completely omitted or understated the extent of Hausa counter-rebellion against the Caliphate's leaders. The jihad's aftermath is often glossed over as if all of Hausaland immediately fell in line after the jihad and supported its leaders. The surviving members of the deposed Hausa leadership did not simply vanish, as was often presented. Rather, many of them either fled outside the Caliphate to live and fight another day, or even mounted intense insurgencies from within the Caliphate itself. Ironically, the first serious rebellion that Bello faced came not from outsiders, but from within the ranks of the *Usmaniyya*.

Abdulsalam was a Hausa student of Dan Fodio and one of his prominent followers. His migration away from Gobir and refusal to return on the orders of King of Gobir Yunfa was one of the stand-offs that precipitated the jihad. Having fought alongside the Dan Fodio family during the jihad and helped them to establish a Caliphate, Abdulsalam became disillusioned after it. The first signs of discordance between Abdulsalam and the Caliphate leaders emerged shortly after Bello succeeded his father as *sarkin musulmi*. Abdulsalam sent condolences to Bello on the death of his father, but crucially, did not come to pledge allegiance to Bello in person. Bello noted his absence. Abdulsalam eventually pledged allegiance in public after Bello ordered him to come to Sokoto in person. However, Abdulsalam's belated recognition planted seeds of doubt in Bello's mind about his loyalty. Bello's courtiers encouraged and amplified those doubts by feeding him on a steady diet of incendiary intelligence reports claiming that Abdulsalam had repealed his allegiance to the Caliphate and was consorting with its enemies. Thereafter, it became easy for Bello and other Caliphate leaders to interpret everything Abdulsalam did as an act of disloyalty, or even worse, as treasonable interaction with the enemy. In the atmosphere of suspicion regarding him, Abdulsalam did not help himself. Although Dan Fodio had appointed him as a deputy district leader in the Gwandu region of the Caliphate under Bello's uncle Abdullahi, Abdulsalam did not regard the posting as commensurate with his contribution to the jihad. He wrote to Bello to complain that the best and most senior post-jihad leadership posts in the Caliphate hierarchy were allocated to Dan Fodio's family: Bello and Abdullahi governed the Caliphate's eastern and western provinces, respectively, Dan Fodio's sons Atiku and Buhari held senior positions in its south, as did Dan Fodio's son-in-law the *amir al-jaish* (commander of war) Aliyu Jedo in the Caliphate's northern region. Jedo was married to Bello's full sister Fatima. The Dan Fodios and their extended family also appropriated the captured symbols of power from the ousted Hausa monarchies. Bello received the ceremonial trumpet of the Gobir kingdom (the trumpet is now part of the *sarkin musulmi*'s official paraphernalia), Aliyu Jedo received

Yunfa's sword (and it remains with his descendants), while Gidado received an instrument that was used to notify Yunfa's arrival (it is now in the Sokoto State Museum). Such sharing of political positions and largesse between members of the Dan Fodio clan may have created resentment in Abdulsalam, and given him the impression that the Caliphate was a private family enterprise. Abdulsalam asked Bello: 'And where is the region of mine, me, Abdulsalam? It is what I possessed in the time of unbelief that I still possess in the time of Islam; it is nothing but a place to reside and a place [to farm].'[18] Abdulsalam's grumbling that what he now had was no greater than what he had before the jihad heightened the suspicions about him.

Disloyalty by Abdulsalam had the potential to be incendiary and destabilising. At a time when the Caliphate was insecure, fending off attacks from the deposed Hausa leadership, and tensely divided between Gwandu and Sokoto due to the rift between Bello and his uncle, Abdulsalam's complaints about nepotism in the awarding of leadership positions, and his increasing popularity among the Hausa had the potential to create an ethnic schism. The ethnic undertones of his identity as a Hausa, and popularity among Hausa Muslims, also carried the even more dangerous possibility to incite a Hausa revolt against the Fulani leadership. He also had legitimacy as he was one of the *Usmaniyya* and could claim to be the man whose stand was the final straw that triggered the jihad. The Caliphate leaders could not ignore him.

'He who refuses will suffer public humiliation and demotion'

More inciting reports about Abdulsalam filtered through to Bello, alleging that Abdulsalam's Hausa supporters travelled to, and traded with, Hausa provinces that were rebelling against Bello. These reports also alleged that people from 'the land of the enemy' came to Kware (the village where Abdulsalam resided) to trade. One report went further and alleged that Abdulsalam sent 'a gift to the enemy

---

18   Kota, 2018, p. 295 (I edited Kota's text to replace 'of some gardens' with the more contextually appropriate 'to farm').

to notify them that he was on their side'.[19] Although a lot of the suspicion against Abdulsalam arose from circumstantial evidence and uncorroborated allegations, Bello became convinced that Abdulsalam was colluding with the Hausa rebels. Bello demanded and expected unqualified loyalty from his subjects and said that: 'The populace must unite under one leader to whom they must give their unconditional loyalty.'[20] His sister Nana corroborated him by saying: 'Obedience to the Caliph is obligatory, it is the command of Allah … He who refuses will suffer public humiliation and demotion.'[21] As such, in Bello's Caliphate, the fence was a dangerous place to sit.

Bello's demand for unconditional loyalty sealed Abdulsalam's fate. Bello declared Abdulsalam and his group to be apostates and in September 1817, sent his forces to attack and eliminate them. After four months of fighting, Bello's forces wounded Abdulsalam in January 1818. Abdulsalam fled, but died from his wounds in Bakura (now in Zamfara State). After Abdulsalam's death, the rump of his supporters (led by his son Buhari) fled south to a town called Kalambaina about 3 miles south-west of Gwandu and continued to resist the Caliphate from there. Their move to Kalambaina made them a headache for Bello's estranged uncle Abdullahi as Kalambaina was within his domain.

With Abdullahi unable to dislodge Abdulsalam's surviving forces from Kalambaina, one of Abdullahi's wives appealed to Bello to go and help his uncle. In 1820, Bello rode out with reinforcements and unexpectedly appeared on the battlefield at Kalambaina to help Abdullahi defeat Abdulsalam's remnant forces. Although Abdullahi and Bello did not know it at the time, Abdulsalam's rebellion helped them to heal a family rift. Oral tradition claims that after the battle, Abdullahi and Bello met in front of Kalambaina's gates. As the younger man, Bello prepared to dismount from his horse to greet his uncle. As he did so, Abdullahi motioned to him to remain on his horse, and Abdullahi himself dismounted to symbolically signify that he had recognised Bello as the new

19 Ibid., p. 299.
20 Boyd, 1989, pp. 31–2.
21 Ibid., p. 32.

sarkin musulmi. However, Abdullahi had not forgotten the painful memory of being overlooked and shut out of Sokoto three years earlier. He turned to Gidado and asked him why the gates of Sokoto had been closed against him. Gidado replied that had Abdullahi been allowed to enter Sokoto, they could not have appointed anyone other than him as *sarkin musulmi.* Abdullahi's appointment would have meant that his descendants (rather than Dan Fodio's) would have inherited leadership of the Caliphate in future generations, and this may have split loyalties in the Caliphate. Gidado apologised for the hurt they caused Abdullahi, after which Abdullahi removed his cloak and gave it to Gidado – again using the gesture to symbolise that he had abdicated to Gidado the office of *waziri.* This gesture started a custom whereby when future *emirs* of Gwandu (Abdullahi's descendants) visited the *waziri* of Sokoto (Gidado's descendants), the *emir* traditionally presented the *waziri* with the cloak he wore on arrival. Thus, the rift between Dan Fodio's brother and son was finally healed three years after his death. Although as the *Emir* of Gwandu, Abdullahi still had responsibility for governing the Caliphate's western province, after the battle of Kalambaina, he went into political retirement, delegated responsibility for governing Gwandu to his son Muhammad, and much like his brother Dan Fodio did after the jihad, devoted himself to teaching and writing.

However, healing the rift in the Dan Fodio family did not immediately lead to peace in the Caliphate. Abdulsalam's was not the only instance of Hausa revolt against the Caliphate's leadership. In most prior accounts the Hausa monarchies simply disappear from the pages of history immediately after the jihad. Some of the Hausa States were displaced rather than destroyed. In response to the jihad, some of the Hausa States relocated further north and continued their dynasties from exile. For example, Gobir's surviving leaders fled to a new capital at Tibiri, and Katsina's survivors fled to Maradi (both Tibiri and Maradi are now located in Niger Republic).

The displaced Hausa leaders did not accept the jihadists' presentation of themselves as reformers, but rather viewed them as usurpers. From exile, they mounted intense counter-rebellions and raids into Caliphate territory that made some of its frontier areas so dangerous that the Caliphate's residents dared not venture out into outlying areas without armed escorts. When Hugh Clapperton travelled to Sokoto in 1824, resistance by the deposed Hausas was so substantial that Bello sent 150 armed horsemen to escort and protect Clapperton over a 300-mile stretch of land all the way from Kano to Sokoto 'through the provinces of Goober [Gobir] and Zamfra [Zamfara], which were in a state of insurrection'.[22] Such resistance led Bello to build ribats (military forts) on the Caliphate's frontiers to guard against Hausa raids. Ironically, Bello placed his half-Gobirawa son Fodio in charge of a ribat (Fodio's mother Katembale was Bello's concubine, and the widow of former *Sarkin* Gobir Yunfa). Since he was facing multiple insurgencies from the ousted Hausa leadership and his brother Atiku was watching him and coveting his position, Bello was understandably jumpy. When trying to demonstrate a sextant to Bello, Clapperton tried to open a stiff sextant case with a dagger, which Bello mistook for an assassination attempt and drew his sword in response.[23]

THE WALL OF CORPSES

It is common to describe the jihad using superlative words such as 'battle' and 'war'. However, some of the early fights involved less than 1000 people on both sides. Ironically, some of the Caliphate's biggest wars occurred after the jihad, not during it. Although he was erudite, intellectually brilliant, and a prolific writer, there were other sides to Bello the ruler-scholar. At times he and Abdullahi showed mercy, such as subjecting captured prisoners of war to a religious test and freeing those who could accurately recite the *fatiha* (the Koran's opening verses) and make ablutions (those who failed the test were enslaved). Bello could also be a ruthless and severe man. Before becoming *sarkin musulmi* he had already demonstrated this during the jihad by summarily destroying the Muslim scholars of Yandoto who refused to join the jihadists. In an effort to crush the

---

22   Denham et al., 1826, p. 74.
23   Ibid., p. 86.

Hausa rebellion, Bello exacted extreme retribution after defeating the Gobirawa at the battle of Gawakuke in March 1836. After the battle, Bello ordered the summary execution of every male over the age of 15. The Caliphate's forces killed over 25,000 Gobirawa at Gawakuke.[24] When the British army officer Major-General Foulkes travelled through Gawakuke 66 years later, he saw a 20-foot-high mound by the side of the road, and was told that the mound was created from the pile of corpses that Bello's forces left at the battle there 66 years earlier.

Despite the great slaughter at Gawakuke, revolts against the Caliphate continued. In the Caliphate's early days, Gobir, Katsina, and Zamfara were the main sources of resistance. However, other sources of resistance arose after Bello's death in 1837. In protest at the Kano Emirate's introduction of new taxes that did not exist before the jihad, a group of Hausa *mallams* led by a renowned Muslim scholar named Mallam Hamza left Kano in 1846 and emigrated to a mountainous area in Ningi (in current-day Bauchi State of Nigeria). Their grievance was that the new taxes were not sanctioned by the Koran and that *mallams* had previously been exempt from taxes. This ironically replicated complaints that Dan Fodio himself had made against the pre-jihad Hausa kings. From their new mountain residence, Hamza and his allies joined forces with non-Muslim ethnic groups such as the Butawa and Warjawa, took up arms, and launched attacks against Kano.

The jihad was only one of several outbursts of religious dissidence in northern Nigeria during the last three centuries. In the mid-1850s, millenarian movements about the second coming of the prophet Isa (Jesus) arose in Kano. The most prominent of these ironically arose from within the *Emir* of Kano's palace.

Mallam Ibrahim was a learned Muslim scholar attached to the court of *Emir* Ibrahim Dabo of Kano in the mid-nineteenth century. He was a deep thinker with a glowing reputation for his expertise in *Tafsir* (studying Koranic exegesis). Ibrahim became fascinated by the Koran's constant references to Jesus. He and his

24 Boyd, 1989, p. 62.

followers began to believe in the second coming of Jesus and that Islam had not given him the veneration he deserved. Although Ibrahim's followers referred to themselves as *Banisra'ila* (Children of the Israelites), outsiders referred to them as the 'Isawa' (followers of the prophet Isa (Jesus)). The Isawa were not Christians, had never met any Christians, yet while they ostensibly remained Muslims, their beliefs which placed Jesus on par with the Prophet Mohammed deviated from orthodox Islam sufficiently to place them in a religious grey area outside the Muslim mainstream. As the Isawa movement grew, their views (which were dangerously heretical to the Caliphate) caught the attention of *Emir* Dabo's court. The *emir* summoned Ibrahim to his palace and gave him a chance to retract his views (which Ibrahim refused to do). For his heresy, Ibrahim was publicly executed in a Kano market by having a stake impaled vertically from one end of his body to the other. This agonisingly slow method of execution gave Ibrahim time to give his followers a coded message to flee before he died, and to await the second coming of Jesus and a future messianic revelation about Jesus' true nature. His followers fled and dispersed to the outlying provinces of Kano, Bauchi, Ningi, and Zaria. It is not a coincidence that significant Christian communities still exist in most of those places today.

In some respects, the Isawa resembled subsequent religious dissidents in northern Nigeria who came 40–120 years after them, such as the Mahdists of Satiru who routed a British military expedition in 1906, the Maitatsine sect whose rebellion left over 5000 people dead in the 1980s, and *Jama'atu Ahl-ul Sunna Lidda'awati wal-Jihad* (commonly known as 'Boko Haram') of the present era. Although the Isawa were not violent like these subsequent movements, they shared other characteristics with them. All professed to be Muslims yet had idiosyncratic interpretations of the Koran and Islamic religious practice, they had millenarian beliefs, retreated to rural areas, were hostile to communities that refused to join them or share their beliefs, and all of them had confrontations with the state security forces of their era. The Isawa were more widespread and posed a much greater threat than has been previously acknowledged. Traces of their beliefs arose among the Mahdists of Satiru village (about 14 miles south of Sokoto) who rebelled against British and Caliphate authorities in 1906.[25] Two years before the rebellion, Satiru's chief had declared himself to be the *mahdi* (a religious reformer who would arise to lead the people in an apocalyptic struggle) and named his son Isa. The *sarkin musulmi* summoned him to Sokoto but he mysteriously died while awaiting trial. Caliphate authorities released the self-proclaimed *mahdi*'s followers only after they swore an oath on the Koran not to repeat their heresy.

These prophecies and Mallam Ibrahim's fate inadvertently assisted British Christian missionaries when they arrived in northern Nigeria over 40 years after his execution. Despite being hunted, persecuted, and killed, some of the Isawa and their descendants survived long enough to propagate a prophecy that white people would one day arrive to deliver more revelations about Jesus, whom they identified as the *mahdi*. When Dr Walter Miller of the CMS arrived in northern Nigeria, it confirmed the Isawa's prophecy, and their pre-existing receptiveness to messages about Jesus made Miller's job easier. Some of the Isawa's descendants came to Miller in 1912 to hear the message of Jesus, and Isawa Muslims and their children were among his first Christian converts. Among them were Russell Aliyu Barau Dikko, the first Western trained medical doctor from northern Nigeria, and Professor Ishaya Audu, who later became the personal doctor of the Premier of the Northern Region Ahmadu Bello and President Shagari. The Isawa practised their faith in a heterodox way. Some of them preached with a Bible in one hand and a Koran in the other. The Isawa were also multi-ethnic. Some of them were Hausas from *Maguzawa* communities, while others such as Audu were Kataf. Had they not been simultaneously persecuted by Muslim authorities and absorbed into mainstream Christianity, they may have formed a bridge between Islam and Christianity, and evolved into a cosmopolitan multi-ethnic vector of co-existence between the two religions.

---

25   I am grateful to Professor Garba Ibrahim for this observation.

VENGEANCE OF THE KEBBAWA

Perhaps the most enduring resistance against the Caliphate arose from people to whom rebellion against powerful empires was second nature.

During the jihad, the Fulani invaded Kebbi, sacked its capital, expelled its rulers, and installed Fulani officials to replace them. However, Kebbi's people (the Kebbawa), who had resisted the mighty Songhai Empire and secured independence from it, were not likely to accept conquest quietly. Their martial spirit had not dimmed in the 300 years since the rebellion of *Kanta* Kotal (whom their kings were descended from). The Kebbawa considered themselves to have never been conquered, and rejected incorporation into the Caliphate. Even though Kebbi was a landlocked territory surrounded by the Caliphate (which killed three successive Kebbi kings), the Kebbawa continued resisting. After the Caliphate killed Kebbi's King Karari in 1831, they tried to disincentivise Kebbi rebellions by capturing and taking Karari's son Yakubu Nabame as a hostage (similar to how Oyo took the King of Dahomey's son Avisu as a hostage in 1730, as part of the armistice terms between Oyo and Dahomey). Nabame became a Moses-like figure, taken by his people's enemies then raised by them. After living in Sokoto for 16 years and saving the life of the son of *Sarkin Musulmi* Aliyu (Bello's son with his concubine Ladi), Aliyu allowed Nabame to return home to Kebbi. However, once back home, Nabame was stung after being taunted for fighting alongside his father's killers during his exile at Sokoto. Nabame resumed Kebbi's revolt against the Caliphate and recovered much of Kebbi's territory from it (just as Kebbi had done to Songhai over 300 years earlier), but he too was also killed and became the fourth successive King of Kebbi to die while resisting the Caliphate.

'I was much impressed by the devastation wrought by the Kebbawa'

After five decades of war, in 1867 *Sarkin Musulmi* Ahmadu Rufai (a son of Usman Dan Fodio) entered into a peace treaty with Kebbi's leader Abdullahi Toga (a son of the former King Karari). The treaty recognised Kebbi's independence and allowed it to keep all the territory it recovered from the Caliphate. Apart from the armistice agreement with Borno under al-Kanemi over 45 years earlier, this was the only time the Caliphate agreed to recognise the independence of people it invaded. However, Kebbi proved to be an irrepressible rival. The peace treaty broke down eight years later in 1875 and hostilities resumed. This time, Kebbi not only defended its territory, but also took the fight to the Caliphate and captured 90 Caliphate towns and villages in the 20 years between 1883 and 1903.[26] Rather than considering these conflicts as a Kebbi resistance, they may conversely be viewed as Kebbi counter-attacks and attempts to overrun Gwandu. The intensity and obduracy of Kebbi's determination to avoid being ruled by the Caliphate was remarkable. Kebbi was at war or at odds with the Caliphate for almost 80 of the 100 years following the jihad. The Kebbawa were still fighting against the Caliphate by the time Britain arrived and conquered northern Nigeria in 1903. British officials saw signs of the great destruction that the Kebbawa wreaked during their conflicts with the Caliphate. The first British Resident of Sokoto Province Major Alder Burdon noted:

> Throughout the whole distance from Shagari to Ambursa, all round Gando [Gwandu] and northeast to within 20 miles of Sokoto, I was much impressed by the devastation wrought by the Kebbawa, much of it within the last 8 years. The country is strewn with the ruins of towns.[27]

Britain's conquest of the Caliphate may have saved the Caliphate's Gwandu region from the Kebbawa's vengeance. Burdon went so far as to say: 'I can't help thinking that, had we [Britain] not appeared, Gwandu itself would have ceased to exist in a few years' time.'[28]

---

26 Johnston, 1967, p. 195.
27 Colonial Report – Annual Report of Northern Nigeria, 1903, p. 6.
28 Ibid., pp. 6–7.

Three prominent themes emerge from this chapter. Firstly, the Caliphate was not an impervious political behemoth. It was unstable and even vulnerable during the first 50 years of its existence, and many of its neighbours resisted it. The Caliphate's territory was not geographically contiguous and it had non-Muslim enclaves within it (such as Zuru, parts of Gwariland, and the mountain regions of Jos and Bauchi) which resisted and refused to be incorporated into the Caliphate. It also did not exercise full control of its outlying areas, and similar pockets of resistance also arose there. Secondly, the Dan Fodios can be regarded as the 'first family' of northern Nigerian politics. Five members of the family in particular can be regarded as the Caliphate's architects. Each of these five family members played a different role in the Caliphate's emergence and consolidation. Usman Dan Fodio was the Caliphate's spiritual leader and inspiration, and his son Bello was its political leader who consolidated it. Bello proved himself to be a decisive, firm, and at times totally ruthless leader. He seemed to be a writer by night and a warrior by day. In retrospect, Abdulsalam's rebellion became a blessing in disguise for Bello. Without Abdulsalam's rebellion Bello may never have reconciled with his uncle Abdullahi, and the Caliphate may have split into two rival (or even warring) provinces led by the descendants of Abdullahi and his brother Dan Fodio. Instead, Bello oversaw the Caliphate's intellectual and political development, suppressed rebellions by the deposed Hausa leadership, and prevented a family rift with his uncle from deteriorating into a civil war between Gwandu and Sokoto. Abdullahi was the Caliphate's ideological conscience, and the 'first couple' Nana and her husband Gidado were its curators. Over 200 years following Dan Fodio's death, the Caliphate he established still exists. Although the Caliphate does not officially practise gerontocratic or hereditary succession, in practice the *sarkin musulmi* is a direct descendant of Dan Fodio. Three of his sons became *sarkin musulmi*, as did six of his grandsons. In post-independence Nigeria, his great-great-grandson Ahmadu Bello became the first Premier of the Northern Region after Nigeria's independence in 1960. Two branches of the Dan Fodio family still rule at Sokoto and Gwandu, with the former led by Dan Fodio's descendants and the latter by his brother Abdullahi's descendants. The third and final theme is that contrary to the impression often given in other texts, the Caliphate did not entirely destroy the Hausa States. In some cases they went their separate ways, and in others they actually fused with the Caliphate. Concubinage massively influenced the emergence of Hausa-Fulani identity and the Caliphate's ruling class. The jihadists' habit of capturing women and keeping them as concubines amplified inter-ethnic assimilation between the Fulani, Hausas, and other non-Hausa and Fulani ethnic groups in the area that later became northern Nigeria. In the jihad's early days, many concubines (such as Katembale, wife of the *Sarkin* Gobir) were aristocratic Hausa women captured from Hausa royal families. However, after the Caliphate's establishment, and the jihadists started raiding areas on the edge of, and beyond, its frontiers, they captured concubines from areas in southern Zaria, the Jos Plateau, and Adamawa. This caused non-Muslim and non-Hausa and Fulani women to be assimilated into Hausa-Fulani ethnicity. For example, as late as 1905–06, court records regarding 403 female slaves in northern Nigeria showed that they came from at least 88 different ethnic groups, most of them from non-Muslim communities outside Hausaland.[29] Hausa-Fulani concubinage and intermarriage produced several children of mixed ethnicity who went on to rule the Caliphate and its emirates. The fourth *sarkin musulmi* (Aliyu Babba) was the son of a concubine, as were at least three *emirs* of Kano. The much heralded twenty-first-century *Emir* of Kano and former Governor of the Central Bank of Nigeria Sanusi Lamido Sanusi is also the grandson of a concubine. A strange offshoot of the jihad is that while the Fulani won on the battlefield, Hausa society culturally and linguistically 'won' against the conquerors. The Fulani became Hausanised, and absorbed into Hausa society to such an extent that many of them speak Hausa as a first language and can no longer speak Fulfulde.

The Caliphate can also claim indirect credit for the establishment of Nigeria's capital city. After the jihad, the Hausa leaders of the

---

29 Lovejoy, 1990, p. 166.

ancient Hausa State of Zaria fled approximately 140 miles south to Zuba (in the present Nigerian Federal Capital Territory) which was populated by the Gbagyi ethnic group. From exile here, Zaria's King Muhammadu Makau continued to be addressed as '*Sarkin Zaria*'. Makau's brother and successor Abubakar Jatau was nick-named 'Abu Ja' ('Abu the fair skinned' or 'Abu the red') due to his light complexion. In 1828, Jatau built and declared himself the king of a walled town which was named after him: 'Abuja'.

5
Oduduwa's Children

The town of Ife in what is now Osun State in south-west Nigeria was central to the emergence of several kingdoms in south-west Nigeria, Benin, and Togo. These kingdoms regard Ife as their Garden of Eden-type cradle of civilisation where life originated.

THE ODUDUWA LEGEND

In the same way that the Bayajidda legend tries to explain the emergence of Hausa kingdoms north of the River Niger, the people of the area that is now south-west Nigeria, central and eastern Benin Republic, and eastern Togo also have their own Genesis-like legend to explain their royalty's descent from an Adam-like progenitor called Oduduwa. Although there are several different versions of the Oduduwa legend, I will detail only two of its most popular versions. The first version is supernatural and claims that Olorun (the supreme god) sent Oduduwa down to earth where he established several kingdoms. The second version claims that Oduduwa was a human being, a prince of Mecca in the Middle East who was driven out of his kingdom. After wandering for a long time he arrived at, and conquered, the town of Ife, settled there, and became its ruler, known as *ooni* (pronounced 'auh-nee'). Oduduwa had seven children; who left Ife and dispersed, with six of them becoming the six rulers of related but politically independent kingdoms, and the seventh became the King of Benin[1] to the east of the others. This second version of the Oduduwa legend with references to a conquering Middle Eastern hero with seven children, all of whom became kings, has similarities with the Hausa Bayajidda legend and the Kisra legend (popular among the Borgu people to the north

---

1 Not the same as Benin Republic.

82

of the Oduduwa kingdoms). Additionally, some versions of the legend claim that Oduduwa was Kisra's grandson. Archaeological evidence suggests continuous human presence in the Ife region for thousands of years. Thus people were already living in Ife before Oduduwa arrived there, and like its Bayajidda Hausa counterpart, the Oduduwa legend explains the origin of multiple *royal families*, not the origin of a *people*.

There is a rational explanation for why the Oduduwa legend has both secular and supernatural renditions. The supernatural lore of the Oduduwa area claims that although Olorun created the universe and life, he delegated to his deputy Obatala the task of moulding the shape of humans and God's creations. However, in some versions of this legend, Obatala is said to have failed to perform the work that Olorun delegated to him. After discovering Obatala drunk and asleep, Oduduwa usurped Obatala's role by taking the materials that Olorun gave to Obatala, and completed the creation work himself instead of Obatala. As a result, different competing versions of the legend give Oduduwa credit for finishing the job of creation, while others insist that it was Obatala. It is pertinent that while Obatala is usually presented as a supernatural being, Oduduwa is mostly presented as a mortal human being who lived, had children and grandchildren whose names are known, and then died. The depiction of Obatala as supernatural and Oduduwa as a human who migrated from elsewhere might mean that Obatala's legend is older, and that Oduduwa's legend represents his invasion and conquest (probably in Ife) of societies who believed in Obatala. The alternate depictions of Oduduwa which give him roles traditionally ascribed to Obatala strongly suggest that after this conquest, Oduduwa was retrospectively inserted into, and replaced, Obatala's role in creation legends as a way of delegitimising the previous pro-Obatala rulers. There are at least two strands of strong evidence to support this displacement theory. Firstly, oral tradition states that after waking from his drunken slumber, Obatala discovered what Oduduwa had done and quarrelled with him. Oduduwa prevailed in this conflict. This rivalry between Obatala and Oduduwa is commemorated in cultural re-enactments during the *Itapa* festivals (which commemorate Obatala) in Ife which depict Oduduwa defeating Obatala and Obatala's exile from Ife. Secondly, evidence for a pre-Oduduwa royalty is provided by the fact that less than 50 years ago, there were people in Ife who possessed crowns but were not allowed to wear them.[2] These crown holders are probably descendants of the pre-Oduduwa royal families. Oduduwa's legend may thus symbolise a transition in Ife's ruling dynasty in which Oduduwa's family overthrew the town's prior rulers.

Nonetheless, the common belief of descent from Ife had two contrasting effects. Firstly, Oduduwa's descendants accepted the primacy of Ife and its ruler as a spiritual leader. The conflation of the *Ooni* of Ife's role as a political and spiritual leader was such that a Briton described him as a 'priest king'.[3] Secondly, the people who claimed common descent from Oduduwa did not identify themselves as one people. Although they had similar cultures and languages, they regarded themselves as independent of each other. They did not use one name to describe themselves, but instead referred to themselves by local identities denoting the name of their clans or hometowns (such as Egba, Ekiti, Ijebu, Ijesha, Ketu. Ondo, and Oyo). Outsiders used several different names to refer to them. In Sierra Leone they were called 'Aku', while the people of Dahomey to their southwest called them 'Anago'. For ease of reference, I will refer to them as 'Oduduwan'.

Some customs were similar or identical to all or most Oduduwan kingdoms, while others were different from one kingdom to the next. Like the Hausa States to their north, the Oduduwan kingdoms were not united under one government or ruler, and each of them was politically independent and had its own king. There was also an element of sibling rivalry among them. They had slight variations of the Oduduwa legend, with each asserting self-aggrandising differences in fact, and embellishments to emphasise their primacy and direct descent from Ife and Oduduwa. Recognition as one of the original kingdoms established by Oduduwa's children was impor-

---

2   Agiri, 1975, p. 7.
3   Dennett, 1916, p. 17.

tant because it conferred legitimacy and prestige. Being regarded as an offshoot of someone other than Oduduwa tainted the authenticity of a group. Due to the desire to establish a direct nexus with Oduduwa, there is disagreement about the original number of Oduduwan kingdoms at inception. Depending on whose version of the Oduduwa legend one believes, the number of original kingdoms varies between seven and sixteen.[4] Then in Ketu's version of the legend, Oduduwa was a woman rather than a man.

Despite these differences, the Oduduwan kingdoms regarded their kings as sacred persons who were *ekeji orisa* ('next to the gods'). The Oduduwan kings spent most of their time in their palaces, and rarely appeared in public or allowed themselves to be seen by their subjects. For example, Ketu's king, the *alaketu* (literally 'owner of Ketu') rarely left his palace except on special designated state occasions. Even when he visited other chiefs he never entered the host's house as it was forbidden for him to be under anyone's roof except his own. Leaving their domain was so unprecedented for the Oduduwan kings that as late as 1903, when the *Ooni* of Ife travelled to Lagos to give testimony to a British colonial inquiry, the other Oduduwan kings also left their palaces as a mark of respect to, and solidarity with, the *ooni*, and vowed not to resume residence in their palaces until the *ooni*'s safe return. Some of the *ooni*'s people also accompanied him to a river crossing, and promised to wait there until he returned.

The Oduduwan kings were given the special privilege of wearing sacred crowns that were embroidered with long strings of coral beads attached to the front. Since it was taboo to look directly at the king's face, these beads were symmetrically arranged to act as a visor that concealed his face from others. The crown was specially consecrated and the king was forbidden to look inside it. Instead, he had attendants that placed it on his head and removed it. Some of the

---

4   Apart from Oduduwa, the most frequently accepted original kings are the *Oba* of Benin, *Alaafin* of Oyo, *Alaketu* of Ketu, *Oluwa* of Owu, *Onisabe* of Sabe, and *Orangun* of Ila. By the early 1900s the number of Oduduwan kings had increased to 16, including the *Alake* of Egbaland, *Awujale* of Ijebu, and Owa of Ilesha.

Oduduwan kings such as the *Alake* of Egbaland, *Awujale* of Ijebu, and *Olowo* of Owo also used giant multi-coloured, royal umbrellas as one of their insignias of office. These specially made umbrellas became such an important part of their royal paraphernalia that it was illegal for non-royal persons to use umbrellas. The kings also had esoteric coronation ceremonies. Prior to installing a new king, it was common practice for the royal kingmakers in some Oduduwan kingdoms to subject the heir apparent to the throne to a practice akin to coronation by ordeal. The kingmakers would seize and flog the king to be with whips. If he flinched or cried out in pain while being flogged, they would reject him as unworthy, and instead select another candidate who was able to withstand the ordeal.

'they tell a thousand strange things of them'

Despite supposedly being siblings, it was common for an Oduduwan kingdom to claim to be a 'senior brother' of the others. Some of these claims had a factual basis. By the seventeenth century, there were rumours that one of the Oduduwan kingdoms had become more powerful than all of the others. The Dutch merchant Willem Bosman reported that in 1698, an unnamed inland nation retaliated for the murder of one of its emissaries in Allada (in the modern-day country of Benin Republic) by despatching a huge army on horseback for a revenge mission. 100,000[5] of these cavalrymen devastated Allada, and inflicted heavy casualties. Bosman wrote that 'the slaughter was prodigious great' with 'the number of the dead being innumerable ... They were like the grains of corn in a field.'[6] Although Bosman admitted that he knew nothing about the people that inflicted this terrible revenge, he noticed that 'This nation strikes such a terror into all the circumjacent Negroes, that they can scarce hear them mentioned without trembling. And they tell a thousand strange things of them.'[7]

---

5   Likely an exaggerated number.
6   Bosman, 1705, p. 397.
7   Ibid., p. 398.

THE MEN ON HORSEBACK

The stories of mysterious armed horsemen riding from inland areas to sack neighbouring kingdoms gave a clue about who was responsible for inspiring so much dread. One of the Oduduwan kingdoms had an equestrian tradition, was renowned for its mighty cavalry, and its people were fond of making sculptures of people riding horses. Although they had not seen it, Europeans who travelled to West Africa had heard stories about a mysterious and powerful inland empire that was 'a fine, fertile and extensive country, inhabited by a great, and warlike people ... the scourge and terror of all their neighbours'.[8] Stories also claimed that the people of this powerful inland kingdom had a culture of ritual facial scarification. The symmetrical patterns they carved into their faces using blades left permanent scars from the corner of their mouths, across their cheeks, and sometimes all the way to their ears and temples. These scars acted as an unofficial national identity card which let others know their origin upon seeing them, and also made them appear even more terrifying to their enemies. Europeans could not agree on the name of this kingdom or its people, and at various times referred to them as 'Eyo', 'Eyeo', 'Eyoe', 'Hio', 'I-oe', and even 'Yahoo'. In the nineteenth century, Europeans finally learned that its capital city was called 'Katunga' and that its people were known as 'Yariba' people.

THE OYO EMPIRE

Katunga was the name that outsiders gave to the capital city of the Oyo (pronounced 'Auh-Yuh') Empire, and 'Yariba' was a loose mis-transliteration of the name by which the Empire's people later became known. It was the most northern of the Oduduwan kingdoms, with its capital city (which its people called Oyo) lying almost 200 miles north of the Atlantic Ocean, in an area that is now in Kwara State of modern-day Nigeria. Despite the stories about

---

8 Norris, 1789, p. 11.

it that occasionally filtered out, Oyo's mysteries did not become apparent to outsiders until Europeans finally set foot there in the nineteenth century. However, by the seventeenth–eighteenth centuries, Oyo had established itself as the most powerful of the Oduduwan kingdoms. At its peak Oyo's territory stretched across large swathes of land that is now in south-west and central Nigeria (such as Kwara, Oyo, and Niger States) and into the neighbouring country of Benin to Nigeria's west (see Maps 1 and 4).

OWNER OF THE PALACE

The Oduduwa legend also has a segue that explains the Oyo Empire's formation. According to this part of the legend, a brave warrior prince of Ife named Oranmiyan (who was either Odudu-wa's youngest son or grandson) went north from Ife on a mission against his northern neighbours to avenge the death of one his ancestors. While travelling he stopped on the way, settled, and established a city known as Oyo. This city became the capital of the Oyo Empire. Although Oyo's people shared cultural affinities, they did not regard themselves as one people. Oyo's people were mul-ti-ethnic and multi-lingual, and its indigenes included the Bariba, Ebira, and Nupe ethnic groups.

A king known as the *alaafin* (literally 'owner of the palace') ruled the Oyo Empire. Great ceremony surrounded the *alaafin*. He doubled as a political and spiritual leader and those who spoke to him had to be extremely careful with their vocabulary, as it was for-bidden to use any word capable of having more than one meaning in his presence. A Briton who met a reigning *alaafin* in the 1800s described him as:

richly dressed in a scarlet damask tobe, ornamented with coral beads, and short trousers of the same colour with a light blue stripe, made of country cloth; his legs, as far as the knees, were stained red with hennah, and on his feet he wore sandals of red leather. A cap of blue damask, thickly studded with handsome coral beads, was on his head; and his neck, arms, and legs, were decorated with large silver rings.[9]

The *alaafin*'s crown looked 'something like a bishop's mitre, profusely ornamented with strings of coral'.[10] Despite having a near mythical persona and being the leader of a divine monarchy, the *alaafin* was not an autocrat with absolute dictatorial powers, nor was Oyo a single contiguous territory. While the *alaafin* resided in its capital city, Oyo also had subsidiary provinces which were governed by chiefs. It also had vassal states beyond its borders which paid tribute to it by giving presents and treasure. Oyo operated a confederal system of government with its provinces having a different status according to their proximity to the capital city, and how they were incorporated into the Empire. There were broadly three categories of people within Oyo's lands. These were firstly, those who resided inside Oyo itself, secondly, other Oduduwan kingdoms whom Oyo had either conquered or who were vassals to Oyo (such as the Egba), and thirdly non-Oduduwan states that were vassals to Oyo. An array of royal officials administered Oyo's many subsidiary towns and provinces, and other aspects of its administration.

HALF HEADS

The *alaafin* appointed royal prefects known as *ajele* or *asoju oba* ('the king's eyes') to keep watch over the provinces and their rulers. They acted as the *alaafin*'s high commissioners in conquered and foreign territories. The neighbouring kingdom of Nupe (which was not an Oduduwan kingdom but whose language was similar to those spoken in Oyo) also appointed and used *ajele*. The *alaafin* also had other colourful and conspicuous staff named *ilari*. Whereas the *ajele* were permanently stationed in Oyo's provinces, the *ilari* acted as temporary messengers to states outside Oyo. Europeans nicknamed the *ilari* 'half heads' due to their custom of shaving one side of their heads while allowing the hair on the unshaven side to grow

---

9   Lander, 1830, p. 195.
10   Ibid., p. 165.

long. Small incisions were made on the shaven side of the head, into which a special potion was rubbed (which supposedly had supernatural properties). The *ilari* were often slaves, reprieved prisoners of war, or eunuchs. There were hundreds of the *ilari* (both male and female) and they carried red and green embroidered fans as their insignia of office. They usually worked in mixed gender pairs to enhance the accuracy of the identical messages which both had to memorise and convey. Despite being paired as a mixed gender tandem and being regarded as each other's companion, male and female *ilari* were forbidden from having intimate relations with each other. The *ilari's* other duties included acting as tax collectors and collecting tributes from vassal states. Oyo's neighbours also employed *ilari*, where they were known by different names such as *emese* (Ekiti, Ife, and Ijesha), *wensangun* (Dahomey), or *agunren* (Ijebu-Ode).

THE YEARS OF EXILE

Oyo was not just a big fish in a little pond. It was surrounded by other powerful states, notably Borgu to its north-west, Nupe to its north-east, and Dahomey to its south-west. The Sokoto Caliphate lay to Oyo's far north beyond Borgu and Nupe. The constellation of powerful states around it meant that Oyo did not enjoy uninterrupted ascendancy. In the sixteenth century, the Nupe kingdom invaded and overran Oyo. The then reigning *Alaafin* Onigbogi fled from Oyo and sought refuge in the neighbouring kingdom of Borgu (where his wife came from). Oyo's monarchy operated from exile for several decades and was forced to move the kingdom's capital to a place called Igboho; which was about 40 miles west of Oyo. Four different *alaafin* ruled from exile at Igboho. Despite such setbacks, Oyo finally recaptured its old capital from the Nupe and moved back there in the late sixteenth century during the reign of *Alaafin* Ajiboyede. The triumph of regaining its capital city seemed to make Oyo a nation reborn. It returned to its capital with a more militaristic attitude, and retooled its army. It deployed trained archers and acquired cavalry, which 300–400 years ago, conferred a military advantage akin to fielding a mechanised division in a modern army. From the seventeenth century onwards, Oyo's neighbours held bogeyman stereotypes of Oyo as an aggressive and imperialistic state that was easily provoked to war. For example, one source claimed that 'The military are despotic in Hio [Oyo]',[11] while the Scottish slave trader and former Governor of Whydah and the Gold Coast Archibald Dalzel (who had resided near the kingdom of Dahomey to Oyo's south-west) had heard that Oyo's:

> people are numerous and warlike … their armies totally consist of cavalry; and as every savage nation has some cruel method of rendering themselves dreadful to their enemies, this people were said to have a custom of cutting off the privitiee of those they have slain in battle: and that no one dared, on pain of death, to take an enemy prisoner, that was not furnished with 100 of these trophies.[12]

Although their reputation for not taking prisoners and for allegedly cutting off the genitalia of slain enemies was probably exaggerated, Oyo's military was critical to its power. It built a mighty cavalry force by importing horses from its northern neighbours such as the Hausa and Nupe. Horses simultaneously accelerated Oyo's transportation ability and its military strength. *Alaafin* Orompoto (a female *alaafin* who reigned in the sixteenth century) is synonymous with cavalry.[13] Orompoto's father, grandfather, and brother had been *alaafin* before her, and she was reputed to be a skilled horse rider and mighty warrior. The frequent association of her name with horse riding and mounted military forces may indicate that she was the ruler that initiated Oyo's mounted cavalry regiment. She had 2000 guards, half of whom rode on horses, and the other half of whom patrolled on foot. She also gave large leaves to her soldiers which they tied to their horses' tails to obscure their footprints and to prevent their enemies from using footprints to track them. Oyo's

---

11 Bowdich, 1819, p. 209.
12 Dalzel, 1793, p. 12.
13 Johnson (1921, p. 161) presented Orompoto as a man.

cavalry allowed it to project its influence beyond its territory, and to also use its military to amplify its economic power. Oyo's recovery and restoration to its capital, combined with a military reinforced with cavalry, led it into a period of imperial expansion. *Alaafin* Ajagbo commenced this era of expansion and it continued under *Alaafin* Ojigi in the eighteenth century. Oyo's military and political strength led it to claim that it was an overlord over the other Oduduwan and non-Oduduwan kingdoms around it. However, some of its neighbours refuted or diminished Oyo's alleged control or influence over them. Ife in particular claimed primacy since it was the epicentre from which the other Oduduwan kingdoms dispersed. In order to conceptually reconcile Oyo and Ife's conflicting claims of pre-eminence over each other and their Oduduwan sibling kingdoms, a British trader who wrote about them claimed that the position of 'the Alafin and Oni [*sic*] are equivalent to those of our King and the Archbishop of Canterbury'.[14] Such positioning of the *alaafin* and *ooni* as the respective political and religious leaders of the Oduduwan area were creative ways to reconcile their competing claims. The tiered relationships between Oyo and its neighbours, and Oyo's ambitions of being a regional superpower generated a century of spectacular drama.

OYO AND DAHOMEY

The kingdom of Dahomey was located to Oyo's south-west in the southern area of what is now Benin Republic, and was an economic and military rival to Oyo. Many Europeans had and have an exotic fascination with Dahomey – especially because of its corps of female 'Amazon' warriors.

King Agaja (who reigned from 1718 to 1740) is considered to be one of Dahomey's greatest warrior kings, and expanded Dahomey by conquering its neighbouring kingdoms. Dahomey seemed to be able to overpower all of its neighbours except one: Oyo. Dahomey and Oyo's respective economic and imperial ambitions put them

---

14   Dennett, 1910, p. 91.

on a collision course with each other. Dahomey's location close to West Africa's Atlantic Coast made it strategic to the Trans-Atlantic slave trade. Meanwhile, Oyo was a middleman slave-trading state. It captured slaves from its neighbouring territories and then sent them to slave-trading ports on the Atlantic Coast to its south. Since Dahomey lay between Oyo and the coastal slaving ports (see Map 1), Dahomey's actions could block or disrupt Oyo's ability to trade slaves at those ports. Such interconnecting economic interests inevitably led to a test of strength. Dahomey fired the first salvo; not at Oyo, but at the coastal kingdoms of Allada and Whydah to Dahomey's south. King Agaja ordered Dahomey's invasion of Allada and Whydah in 1724 and 1727, respectively. Agaja's motivation for these invasions is unclear. One interpretation is that the decrease in slave trading following the invasions means that Agaja invaded in order to disrupt the slave trade. Another possible interpretation is that he intended to gain control of key slave-trading ports. Whatever his motivation was, the consequences of Agaja's decision to invade Allada and Whydah hung like a curse over Dahomey for almost a century.

Allada and Whydah sent messengers to the *Alaafin* of Oyo appealing for help. There are two rational explanations for what Oyo did next. Either Allada was a vassal state to Oyo (after Oyo invaded it in 1698) or Oyo regarded Dahomey's invasion of two key trading ports as a serious threat to Oyo's economic interests. Even though Dahomey was approximately 300 miles away, Oyo subjected Dahomey to a torrent of military assaults during the six-year period between 1724 and 1730. Oyo invaded Dahomey on four separate occasions in those six years. Year after year, Oyo's army poured into Dahomey and wreaked havoc by burning its towns, destroying crops in harvest, inflicting fatal casualties, and taking hostages. Although the sound of Dahomey gunfire frightened the Oyo horses, Dahomey was unfortunate to be located in open areas where horses could run free and their riders armed with javelins, swords, bows, and arrows were more mobile and could get to Dahomey's riflemen before they could reload and fire. Oyo's invasions became so routinised that for over half a decade, Dahomey and Oyo played a deadly game of military hide and seek. Dahomey would prepare for the inevitable Oyo invasion in the dry season by burying their treasures, evacuating their homes, and fleeing into the woods, then return to rebuild their homes and towns after Oyo's soldiers departed.

During its 1729 invasion, Oyo's army prepared for a long stay instead of the brief seek, destroy, and withdraw operations that Oyo had deployed before and that Dahomey had become accustomed to. Rather than withdrawing after their invasion, Oyo's soldiers garrisoned, built houses to accommodate themselves, and refused to leave until May 1729 (two months after they arrived) when their supplies started to run low. Withdrawing its army, and missing out on the opportunity to eliminate a powerful rival state may appear to be a grave tactical mistake by Oyo. However, the decision may have been due to environmental factors outside Oyo's control. While Oyo proved its logistical prowess and that it could feed and equip its army during months'-long journeys over vast distances, the weather proved an insurmountable hurdle. This 1729 battle seemed to make each side aware that while Oyo's military was powerful, and could overrun and make life miserable for Dahomey, ecology prevented Oyo from permanently occupying Dahomey. Oyo timed its invasions of Dahomey to coincide with the dry season because its cavalry would be depleted if its horses were exposed to the wet climate during the rainy season. The deadly tsetse fly (which killed horses) was more prevalent during the rainy season. Hence, Dahomey was secure in the knowledge that the annual rains would eventually force Oyo's soldiers to depart. Yet the cyclical near-annual destruction of its people's homes and towns was also too steep a price for Dahomey to keep paying. Both parties had good reasons to agree to an armistice.

King Agaja enlisted a senior Portuguese trader to act as a mediator in negotiations with Oyo. In 1730, Dahomey and Oyo agreed terms for a peace treaty. The peace terms allowed Agaja to remain on the throne – but at a price. Dahomey's invasion of Whydah incentivised Oyo to demand economic concessions from Dahomey as Oyo saw Whydah as a source of great wealth from which Dahomey could pay Oyo. The armistice terms forced Dahomey to become a vassal state to Oyo, and to pay Oyo an annual tribute in the form of coral, cowries, textiles, and by sending some of its citizens to Oyo. The peace treaty also demonstrated how contracts were enforced in pre-colonial West Africa. While it was customary for contracts to be entered into via verbal oaths in front of witnesses, the Dahomey–Oyo treaty provided an example of how contracting parties tried to discourage default. As a surety for the agreements reached, Agaja gave his youngest son Avisu to Oyo as a hostage. Dahomey and Oyo also sealed the deal with royal marriages. *Alaafin* Ojigi married one of Agaja's daughters, while Agaja reciprocated the gesture and married one of Ojigi's daughters. Such cross-marriages not only disincentivised a breach of the treaty, but were also designed to encourage fair treatment of the wives, since each side knew that his daughter was in the other side's care.

However, the peace treaty broke down in the late 1730s. Dahomey tried to rescind the treaty after *Alaafin* Ojigi died. Considering itself no longer bound by a treaty agreed by a dead king, and arguing that it could not comply with the treaty's exorbitant demands, Dahomey stopped paying tribute to Oyo. However, Oyo saw things very differently and demanded full enforcement of the treaty. To prove that it meant business, in 1738 Oyo once again descended on Dahomey 'with an irresistible army and laid the country waste with fire and sword to the gates of Abomey'[15] (Dahomey's capital city). Oyo's army began their attack in the morning, and Dahomey's troops (who were battle hardened from their kingdom's frequent wars) resisted all day with guns which they acquired from trading with Europeans on the Atlantic Coast. Despite its brave resistance, and inflicting heavy casualties on the Oyo invaders, Dahomey's army had to retreat at night to relieve its exhausted soldiers after a day-long battle against an enemy that kept on pouring reinforcements onto the battlefield to replace casualties. Dahomey's soldiers used the night-time respite to evacuate their king and his family to a secret safehouse, then also evacuated their wounded warriors, women, and

---

15   Norris, 1789, p. 12.

children. The Dahomey survivors escaped and left their unguarded capital to Oyo's forces who pillaged and burned it as they usually did, before staying for a few months and going home.

Oyo kept harassing Dahomey with military assaults and demanding the reimposition of the 1730 treaty. Dahomey's King Tegbesu (who succeeded Agaja) tried to ward off Oyo's attacks by periodically giving presents to the *alaafin*. However, Tegbesu's sporadic gifts merely delayed the inevitable, as Oyo insisted that the only way for Dahomey to stop the invasions was for it to resume paying the annual tribute to Oyo. Tegbesu knew first-hand what Oyo was capable of as he had resided in Oyo for a decade. Before becoming king, he was known as Avisu: the son of former King Agaja who had been sent to Oyo as a hostage surety for the 1730 treaty. He took the name Tegbesu upon becoming king. Tegbesu decided that it was better to pay Oyo for peace than to leave Dahomey at the mercy of constant Oyo invasions. In 1747, he agreed to reinstate the 'payment for peace' formula that his father Agaja had implemented with Oyo. Not only did Oyo reimpose the 1730 treaty terms, but it also demanded arrears for the prior missed tribute payments, and levied interest indirectly by increasing the amount of tribute to be paid. The new tribute terms required Dahomey to give Oyo 400 bags of cowries, 400 corals, 41 guns, 41 men, and 41 young women every November.[16]

The renewed treaty terms enabled Oyo to establish a predatory relationship with Dahomey and feed off it. Oyo enforced the enhanced treaty with a zeal that bordered on extortion. It kept emissaries in Dahomey to keep the *alaafin* apprised of events there. Apart from extracting the tribute, Oyo garrisoned soldiers in Dahomey, and interfered in Dahomey's internal policies, down to mundane matters such as forbidding Dahomey's people from wearing silk. Oyo also made other ad hoc demands of Dahomey. For example, when one of Dahomey's senior government officials (the *mehu*) died around 1781, *Alaafin* Abiodun's *ilari* demanded to inherit the deceased *mehu*'s property and 100 of his wives on Oyo's

16 Dalzel, 1793, p. 74 (41 seems to have been a number of symbolic significance to the royalty).

behalf, and refused to leave without them. The King of Dahomey did not wish to part with so many women and so sent only some of them. Three months later, Abiodun sent another *ilari* with a demand for the rest of the *mehu*'s wives and an ultimatum that if they were not sent, he would send his army to come and fetch them. The King of Dahomey complied with the demand – sort of. He raided a neighbouring territory to capture women to make up the number for Oyo.[17]

Feeling that they were being fleeced and that the tribute was a humiliation for a kingdom as powerful as Dahomey, Dahomey's leaders paid the tribute to Oyo grudgingly, and were constantly on the look-out for an excuse to avoid or reduce it. Dahomey was not above using subterfuge to evade the tribute. For example, on one occasion, Dahomey withheld coral from its annual tribute payments to Oyo and explained it away by claiming that no coral was available. Oyo's people treasured coral which they used to make jewellery, and which also formed part of the materials in the *alaafin*'s crown. *Alaafin* Abiodun was incensed by Dahomey's deception when he learned that some people from Oyo bought coral from Dahomey. Abiodun again sent *ilari* to Dahomey with the coral to show Dahomey's king what had been purchased from his own land despite being supposedly unavailable. The *ilari* also delivered a stern message from Abiodun to remind the King of Dahomey that the independence of his kingdom was conditional on paying the tribute, and that Oyo would conquer Dahomey if he did not pay the tribute in full.[18] Although it was a frequent source of friction between Dahomey and Oyo, the reimposed 1730 treaty lasted for 70 years until 1827.

Despite Oyo being strong enough to project its power beyond its borders, its greatest weakness was its internal *Game of Thrones*-style cut-throat politics. As will be shown in the next chapter, its attempt to avoid tyranny by implementing an intricate separation of powers ironically came to haunt it and generated a succession of crises.

---

17 Ibid., pp.175–6.
18 Ibid., p. 209.

6

The Men on Horseback

A seven-member council known as the *Oyo Mesi* had the duty to appoint each *alaafin* and acted as his council of advisers. A prime minister-style official known as the *bashorun* led the *Oyo Mesi*. The *bashorun* was more than a consigliere. He was Oyo's second most powerful person after the *alaafin*, and ruled as regent during an interregnum, or if an *alaafin*-elect was a minor and too young to rule. Despite the power bestowed on him, becoming *alaafin* was akin to being initiated into a suicide cult. Ancient Oyo did not recognise positions of 'former' or 'retired' *alaafin*, and only death could separate the *alaafin* from his position. The *Oyo Mesi* had the power to impeach the *alaafin* in dramatic fashion if they lost confidence in him. Oyo had a code of ritual suicide similar to the Samurai in ancient Japan. The *bashorun* could symbolically inform the *alaafin* of the *Oyo Mesi*'s decision to depose him by giving him an empty bowl or parrot's eggs and telling him: 'The gods reject you, the people reject you, the earth rejects you.' After receiving this 'gift', the *alaafin* had to honourably abdicate by committing suicide. The *alaafin* rarely resisted the order to kill himself, because in ancient Oyo, suicide was considered a brave or honourable death to avoid shame. Bishop Crowther later said that:

It is not uncommon among the [Oyo people], under some injury, vexation, or disappointment, to commit suicide, either by taking some poisonous draught, sticking themselves with a poisoned arrow, or cutting their throats or bellies with a sword or razor. Such are generally looked upon as acts of bravery.[1]

---

1   Crowther, 1843, introductory remarks, p. vi.

Ketu's *Oloye* (its equivalent of the *Oyo Mesi*) could also sentence Ketu's king (*alaketu*) to death by demanding his suicide. The *Oyo Mesi* was discouraged from abusing its power to sentence the *alaafin* to death because one of them had to die with him. Oyo's original tradition was that the *alaafin's* oldest son (the *aremo*) succeeded his father as *alaafin*, but this tradition was abolished and the *aremo* became ineligible to succeed his father. Although the *aremo* exercised huge powers while his father was alive, he was expected to kill himself when his father died.[2] Yet the professed reason for the amendment (avoiding patricide) did not happen often. Tellingly, the *aremo's* inegibility empowered the *Oyo Mesi* since they got to choose the new successor *alaafin* rather than the choice being automatic. It also elevated other members of the royal family as more claimants became eligible to become *alaafin*.

Although Oyo's royal succession seemingly caused a needless waste of several lives, it was also a system of political checks and balances. The *Oyo Mesi* were discouraged from abusing their power since regime change could be initiated only by the death of multiple people, and at least one of the people that sentenced the king to death had to die with him.

Althugh Oyo's separation of powers was intended to discourage tyranny, it also inadvertently caused instability. The conflicting powers of the *alaafin*, *bashorun*, and *Oyo Mesi* created a tectonic series of crises that saw Oyo rise to the zenith of its glory and into the abyss in the space of 35 years.

GAHA THE KINGSLAYER

Oyo's oral traditions record the exploits of the most infamous *bashorun*. For 20 years between 1754 and 1774, this *bashorun* eclipsed the power of every *alaafin* he worked with, and he acquired an almost cartoonish level of villainy. As *Alaafin*-elect Labisi was preparing to be coronated as *alaafin*, a new *bashorun* named Gaha came to office. The coronation of a new *alaafin* is a lengthy process

---

2   The tradition was abolished in 1859 after *Aremo* Adelu refused to kill himself as was expected of him, and instead succeeded his father Atiba.

that involves much ceremony and revelry lasting three months. After the *Oyo Mesi* selected a new *alaafin*, other rival claimants were usually exiled from Oyo as two potential kings could not be simultaneously resident in the same place. Before being coronated, the *alaafin*-elect walks approximately 1 mile from the *Afin* (royal palace) to visit the *Bara* (royal mausoleum where deceased *alaafin* are buried) for the first and only time in his life. While at the *Bara* he prostrates and pays homage at the tombs of his ancestors, and gives and seeks blessings from them. After visiting the *Bara* prior to his coronation, he is forbidden from ever setting eyes on it again. The widows of deceased *alaafin* instead live in the *Bara* along with a high priestess who was the *Bara's* official custodian. Although Oyo claimed primacy among the Oduduwan kingdoms, its coronation ceremonies acknowledged its descent from Ife. Before installing a new *alaafin*, the Sword of Oranmiyan was consecrated at Ife and then taken to Oyo where it was ceremonially placed in the new *alaafin's* hands during his coronation ceremony. A new *alaafin* is required to make his own entrance into the palace through a new hole cut into the wall for him. The length of these traditional ceremonies gave lots of opportunity for something to go wrong.

Alaafin-elect Labisi never got the chance to enter the palace. Gaha pre-empted Labisi's succession by forcing him to commit suicide before his coronation ceremonies had been completed. Labisi's successor Awonbioju at least got to reign. He lasted for 130 days but Gaha despatched him too after he refused to be subservient to him. Awonbioju's successor *Alaafin* Agboluaje also committed suicide, and was succeeded by his brother Majeogbe who tried to get rid of Gaha by poisoning him. However the poison did not kill Gaha but succeeded only in paralysing him. After Majeogbe died, perhaps the most famous *alaafin* of all succeeded him.

The *alaafin* who succeeded Majeogbe was described as 'a tall and slender prince, of a very dark complexion, a comely person, of dignified manners, and altogether fit to wear a crown ... wise and prudent'.[3] The new *alaafin* was named Abiodun. He learned from

3   Johnson, 1921, p. 182.

the fate of his predecessors, and shrewdly tried to avoid overtly antagonising or challenging Gaha. Instead, he outwardly submitted to Gaha and visited him every morning to pay him respects. Abiodun was simply biding his time. He conspired with provincial leaders to plot against Gaha. The popular narrative of what happened is that Abiodun convinced provincial leaders and the army to rise up against Gaha. The result was brutal and ugly. In 1774, Abiodun engineered a revolt not just against Gaha but also the mass murder of his family including his sons and their wives. Even Gaha's pregnant family members were not spared as their stomachs were cut open and the unborn babies killed. Abiodun saved a special fate for Gaha. Even though Gaha was by now old, infirm, and crippled, Abiodun ordered him to be burned alive.

LET THE TRUTH BE TOLD

At least three key matters for consideration arise from the tales of Gaha's exploits. The first is whether such gory events really happened. The alleged events of Gaha's era were so extraordinary that it is tempting to dismiss them as allegory or embellished folk tales. Although it seems implausible that one *bashorun* could successfully implement a reign of terror for 20 consecutive years under which four consecutive *alaafin* died under his watch, there is corroboration for both the occurrence and timing of Gaha's implausibly eventful tenure. In October 1754, the Governor of the British fort at Whydah (in modern-day Benin Republic) wrote to his superiors and mentioned that 'The king of Io [Oyo] is dead, and they are wrangling and fighting who shall have the stool. *Two that have been seated on it within these two months are both killed*'[4] (italics added). The letter's timing and its mention of two kings being killed 'within these two months' is a reference to the death of *Alaafin* Labisi and his successor Awonbioju in quick succession (the first two *alaafin* that Gaha worked with).

---

4   Akinjogbin, 1963, p. 214.

Johnson's 1921 book[5] portrayed Gaha's demise as the product of a retributive plot hatched by Abiodun. However, 128 years before Johnson's book was published, the Scottish slave trader Archibald Dalzel (who spent considerable time in West Africa) provided both corroboration that the Abiodun–Gaha conflict really occurred and evidence of a different cause for it. Dalzel wrote about a controversial incident in 1774 during which:

> the ministers of the King of Eyeo [Oyo], being tired of his government, had attempted, as had been their usual practice, to depose their monarch ... But this Prince had the good sense to despise, and the fortitude to resist, such a ridiculous custom. He, therefore, peremptorily refused the parrot's eggs, which had been offered for his acceptance: telling his ministers that he had as yet no inclination to take a nap ... The ministers were extremely disappointed and ... they endeavoured, therefore, to effect by force, what they could not accomplish by this stale trick. Ochenoo, the prime minister, put himself at the head of the rebel party, which, though formidable, was soon defeated by the adherents of the Sovereign, with great slaughter. Ochenoo himself, with all his numerous family, were put to death by the victors; who did not even spare the pregnant women, but ripped open their bellies, and cut to pieces the immature fruit of their womb.[6]

The timing of Dalzel's account (written just under 20 years after the Abiodun–Gaha stand-off) and his description of a conflict between Oyo's king and 'prime minister', including gory details of pregnant women being disembowelled, leave no doubt that the king and prime minister he described were Abiodun and Gaha, respectively. The 'ministers of the King' he referred to are the *Oyo Mesi*. Although Dalzel named the prime minister as 'Ochenoo', this was probably a corrupted Anglicised transliteration of *Osorun* (abbreviation of *bashorun*). Dalzel's account also included additional details that were not in Johnson's account. According to Dalzel, Gaha and

5 Johnson, 1921.
6 Dalzel, 1793, pp. 156–7.

the *Oyo Mesi* had tried to force Abiodun's abdication by suicide. However, Abiodun refused to commit suicide, and instead ordered the pre-emptive slaughter of Gaha, his family, and followers in order to prevent himself from having the same fate as his four immediate predecessors. News of the Abiodun–Gaha conflict was so explosive that it travelled far beyond Oyo. When the King of Dahomey (approximately 300 miles away) heard that Abiodun had prevailed over Gaha, he sent a congratulatory message to Abiodun.[7]

The second group of issues for consideration are the broader meanings and repercussions of the Abiodun–Gaha conflict. Most prior accounts have presented Oyo's eighteenth-century conflicts between Gaha and multiple *alaafin* as an outcome of Gaha's greed and personal ambition, and as personality conflicts between rival political leaders. Most accounts make it sound as if Gaha was acting alone. If so, a pertinent question is why the *Oyo Mesi* and population stood by while Gaha sentenced several kings to death? Placing the blame exclusively on Gaha's cruelty and venality may be an outcome of the pro-Abiodun propaganda that arose in the aftermath of his victory over Gaha. An alternative explanation is that several people and events were compressed into Gaha's story. While personal rivalries may have been part of the calculus, it does not entirely explain such frequent bloodshed and the cruelty of the violence deployed. Abiodun could have justified Gaha's murder as an act of pre-emptive self-defence. However, including Gaha's extended family in the violence suggests that this was about more than retributive justice. The slaughter of his children and pregnant daughters-in-law seemed to be an attempt to wipe out Gaha's bloodline, and suggests that some or all of them were a threat to Abiodun in some way, or that there were rival throne claimants to Abiodun in Gaha's family.

These events can also be interpreted as an economic contest, and as a battle for control of Oyo's constitutional powers. It is pertinent that regicide became common when Oyo was at the peak of its economic and military power in the eighteenth century. Gaha

---

7   Ibid., p. 157.

became *bashorun* 6–7 years after Oyo reimposed the peace treaty that allowed it to levy tribute from Dahomey. At this time, Oyo was extracting presents, treasures, and slaves from Dahomey and other vassal states that it conquered. As in modern Nigeria, the concentration of economic and political power in the same source placed a great premium on political leadership. Control of Oyo's government offered not only political power, but also the opportunity to receive and enjoy the kingdom's economic benefits. Johnson claimed that Gaha appointed his sons to positions of authority around the kingdom, from where they collected tributes from vassals, instead of the tributes being paid to the *alaafin*. Thus the battles between Gaha and successive *alaafin* may be interpreted as a competition for control of Oyo's state treasury. It was also a constitutional crisis about the separation of powers between the *alaafin*, *bashorun*, and *Oyo Mesi* that saw them jostling for supremacy in the bewildering maze of their conflicting powers.

The Gaha-era crises had a long-term legacy. As heralded as he was, Abiodun unintentionally endangered Oyo's unity and the lives of his successors. If it is true that Abiodun rejected the *Oyo Mesi's* death sentence on him, then he may have set a precedent for violating Oyo's constitutional and theological traditions. If he refused to abide by ancient conventions and yet lived and prospered to an old age, then he demonstrated that such customs could be ignored and that the sky would not fall down on the transgressor. Abiodun's example came back to haunt his successors. By using the provincial army and provincial political leaders to overcome Gaha, Abiodun also inadvertently allowed the provinces to see how powerful they were and how much the *alaafin* relied on them in times of crisis. It raised a question of which of the *alaafin* and provinces needed each other more. Abiodun's elimination of Gaha did not resolve the battle for supremacy between the *alaafin* and his officials. The battle resumed as soon as Abiodun died but took on a different form. After Abiodun, the pattern of conflict changed from one between the *alaafin* and *bashorun* to one between the *alaafin* and his provincial officials.

THE FIRST MILITARY COUP

History often repeats itself in Nigeria. The causal factors of the country's first military coup in January 1966 included a political crisis in the country's south-west caused by an alliance between the south-western politician Samuel Akintola and Hausa and Fulani northerners. The coup was considered unprecedented at the time. However, this was not the first time that such an alliance arose or that a military coup emerged from it. A very similar chain of events occurred in the same geographic area about 150 years earlier.

In south-western Nigeria, one man's name is as synonymous with treachery. He is accused of betraying his own people by acting as a Trojan Horse that enabled their enemies to infiltrate and conquer them. To many people in south-west Nigeria, he is what Judas Iscariot is to Christians. For about 25 years between the late eighteenth century and early nineteenth century in Oyo, a remarkable web of intrigue and back-stabbing swirled with one man at the centre of it. This man's actions and decisions set in motion a complex chain of events that caused the downfall of an empire, and also advanced the cause of both Christianity and Islam in Nigeria. More than 200 years later, the consequences of what he did still reverberate in Nigeria. The man at the centre of this volatile storm was named Afonja.

AFONJA

Afonja was the governor of the provincial city of Ilorin; which was to the south-west of Oyo's capital city. He was descended from a bloodline of warriors that opposed the notorious *Bashorun* Gaha. Both Afonja's grandfather and father had fought against Gaha's men (who killed Afonja's grandfather). Afonja even had to repel an attack by one of the late *Bashorun* Gaha's surviving sons Ojo, who tried to gain vengeance against Afonja for the role of the latter's family in the death of Gaha.

Afonja was initially on good terms with the ruling administration of *Alaafin* Abiodun (who was Afonja's relative), but for opaque reasons, after Abiodun died he withdrew his support for Oyo's rulers and transformed from a pro-regime supporter into an anti-regime insurrectionist. After Abiodun died, the usual unproven rumours that he was a victim of patricide emerged. If the rumours were true, then there were a large number of potential suspects since Abiodun allegedly had over 600 children. Awole (also known as 'Arogangan') succeeded Abiodun. According to Johnson, Awole was Abiodun's cousin.[8] Crowther, whose account was more proximate in time (written 45 years before Johnson), claimed that Awole was Abiodun's brother (which if true meant that Afonja was also Abiodun's nephew).[9] Crowther's use of 'brother' may have been a common Africanised term in which many Africans often do not acknowledge distances in blood relations with different terms, and verbally conflate all near relatives as siblings (many African languages also do not have a word for 'cousin').

Awole appointed his nephew Afonja as *aare-ona-kakanfo* (the commander-in-chief of Oyo's provincial army). The modern-day equivalent of Afonja's position is the chief of army staff. Afonja's relation to two consecutive *alaafin* makes what happened next very puzzling. Appointment as *kakanfo* made Afonja the de facto third most powerful person in Oyo's political hierarchy, behind only *Alaafin* Awole and the *bashorun*. Awole and Afonja co-existed for about seven years and then something went terribly wrong sometime between 1796 and 1807. While the broad factual outline of what happened is known, the causation of the events, and the motivation of the people involved, is not. Crowther claimed that Afonja became rebellious after not being appointed as *alaafin* to succeed Abiodun and began plotting to destabilise or overthrow Awole.[10]

Upon the installation of a new *alaafin*, it was traditional to ask the *alaafin* to nominate an enemy whom his army should vanquish. Awole initially declined to nominate an enemy, but after much

8   Johnson, 1921, p. 188.
9   Crowther, 1852, p. v.
10   Ibid., p. v.

prompting he nominated a fortified town called Iwere,[11] which was built on top of a hill and regarded as impregnable. Being *kakanfo* was a dangerous occupation. The position's terms of service required its holder to die if he could not complete a mission within three months. Thus, Awole's order for the army to crack a nut as tough as Iwere placed Afonja's life in great peril. Upon reaching Iwere, Afonja's troops complained that Awole must have intended their death; otherwise, he would not have sent them on a mission to capture a town that was considered impossible to overcome. They also protested that attacking Iwere would be sacrilege as it was the hometown of former *Alaafin* Abiodun's mother. Their resistance to the order was amplified by the fact that Abiodun had appointed many of the officers that Awole ordered to attack Iwere. They refused to carry out Awole's order, but instead mutinied and killed the royal officials accompanying them (including Awole's brother). After massacring the royal party, the army then turned and marched to Oyo and staged what was in effect a military *coup d'état*. They placed Awole under siege and demanded his suicide. Awole refused to comply with their demand, and the army in turn refused to leave until he did. After a stand-off lasting 42 days, Awole received the *Oyo Mesi's* ominous empty calabash and knew what he had to do next. The *Oyo Mesi* had either decided to side with Afonja and the army, or disapproved of how Awole was handling the crisis.

AWOLE'S CURSE

Awole did not resist his fate but made a defiant last gesture. He walked out to his palace courtyard carrying a sacred calabash and three arrows. He fired the arrows north, south, and west – and cursed those who disobeyed him as follows:

> my curse be on ye for your disloyalty and disobedience, so let your children disobey you. If you send them on an errand, let them never return to bring you word again. To all the points I shot my arrows will ye be carried as slaves. My curse will carry you to the

---

11 Now located in present-day Oyo State in south-west Nigeria.

sea and the beyond the seas, slaves will rule over you, and you their masters will become slaves.[12]

After firing the arrows, he raised the calabash in the air then dropped it. As it smashed into pieces on the floor, he again cursed that a broken calabash cannot be mended, 'so let my words be irrevocable'.[13] It might have been one of the most devastatingly effective curses of all time. Oyo never saw long-term peace again after Awole. He committed suicide by taking poison as demanded of him, after which the army raided and pillaged his palace. Chaos and devastation followed Awole's death. Those who disobeyed him were later themselves disobeyed by their subordinates, and those whom they once enslaved rebelled against them. The Oyo Empire never recovered from Afonja's coup against Awole.

News of what the army did to Awole travelled far. In the early nineteenth century a British traveller in Ashanti-land (modern-day Ghana) wrote of a memorable event in Oyo some years earlier whereby Oyo's king sent his 'army against a northern neighbour' and on their return from the expedition, the army 'sent deputies to enjoin his [the king's] abdication'.[14] Although some of the facts are different from Johnson's account, the story of the army mutinying against their king and demanding his abdication was his narration of Afonja's coup against Awole many years earlier.

After Awole's death, Afonja declared Ilorin to be independent of Oyo. Other provinces followed suit and also seceded from Oyo, and its vassals stopped paying tribute. Awole's brother Adebo succeeded him as *alaafin*. Afonja declined to attack Adebo or Oyo itself, but contented himself with rejecting any *alaafin* after Abiodun and rejecting Oyo's political authority over Ilorin. Nonetheless Adebo did not last long. He was on the throne for only 120–130 days[15] and died in murky circumstances.

---

12   Johnson, 1921, p. 192.
13   Ibid., p. 192.
14   Bowdich, 1819, p. 209.
15   Johnson says 130 days (1921, p. 193), while Crowther says 120 days (1852, p. v).

'THE NEW MOON HAS APPEARED'

When messengers told Afonja that Maku had succeeded Adebo as *alaafin* by metaphorically stating that 'The new moon has appeared', Afonja defiantly replied 'let that new moon speedily set'.[16] These are the only known words of Afonja that have ever been recorded in writing. Maku did not last long either. After he lost a war, the *Oyo Mesi* politely informed him that the *alaafin* could not continue ruling after losing a war. He committed suicide by poison after reigning for only three months. Remarkably, the constant regicide was legal under Oyo's constitution. The only unusual aspect of it was that it suddenly became frequent. An unanswered question is why the kingdom did not modify its traditions when it became apparent that they were being abused. After Maku died, the position of *alaafin* was declared vacant for several years (either because no one wanted the position or in order to restore stability). The length of the interregnum is uncertain but during it, *Bashorun* Ojo ruled as regent.

Several prior accounts allege that Afonja's actions were motivated primarily by his ambition to become the *alaafin* and that he became aggrieved after the position was repeatedly given to others rather than him.[17] If overall leadership of Oyo was Afonja's motive, then he went about achieving it in a very strange way. His refusal to force his way to kingship after he led the army to besiege the capital and forced *Alaafin* Awole's suicide is inexplicable if he wanted to become *alaafin*. With the *alaafin* position vacant after Awole's death and the army behind him in the capital, he had the kingdom at his mercy. Yet instead of forcefully seizing power, he simply departed and returned to Ilorin. He did not try to overthrow Awole's successors either, but he was instead content to merely withhold recognition of them. Afonja must have wanted something else. His subsequent actions and alliances suggest a very different motive.

---

16 Johnson, 1921, p. 196.
17 Ellis, 1894, p. 11 and Crowther, 1852, p. v.

SMOKE AND MIRRORS

In the complicated dynamic and multiple conflicting stories, it is difficult to outline a linear narrative of what happened. However, for about 25–30 years between the late eighteenth century and 1823 five different cataclysmic events occurred around Afonja:

1. A military coup led by Afonja against Awole;
2. The secession of Ilorin – also led by Afonja;
3. A slave rebellion;
4. A 'coup within a coup', whereby different factions amongst the conspirators turned against each other; and
5. A religious war.

In the rush to assign responsibility for these crises to betrayals and conspiracies by individual actors, wider regional and religious factors are often omitted. By the time Afonja struck, Ilorin was a multi-ethnic city and included people of Oyo, Bariba, Hausa, Fulani, and Nupe ethnicity. Ilorin required more than ethnic solidarity to secede. The causes of Ilorin's opposition evolved and changed over a period of several years in the early nineteenth century. Initially, Ilorin's goal was secession, then it became a sanctuary for escaped slaves, before morphing into a jihadist force.

By the mid-eighteenth-century Islam had penetrated into the northern part of Oyo, and was originally known as *Esin Imale* (the 'Malian religion'), which gives a clue about the people who introduced it. By the 1800s, Oyo's population included a substantial Muslim minority comprised of indigenous Muslim converts and Muslim immigrants from elsewhere such as pastoral Fulanis, as well as Hausas and Nupes. In Oyo's cut-throat *Game of Thrones*-style politics, making good decisions was not enough to ensure one's safety and survival. Supernatural intervention was big business. Those who were deemed to have supernatural powers or who paraded themselves as diviners were in high demand. In this regard, Oyo's people welcomed and patronised Muslim *mallams* as they were reputed to be skilled at divination and at making charms.

These were important services for clients who wanted protection in an era of insecurity, or to negate the prowess of enemies who had themselves engaged their own supernatural assistance. The *mallams'* client base also included those who wanted to increase their power.

ALIMI

Muslim immigration to Ilorin radically altered the Oyo–Ilorin conflict. Around 1817, Afonja invited an itinerant Muslim Fulani preacher named Shaikh al-Salih Janta to move to Ilorin 'to act as his priest'.[18] Despite the awkward terminology of a Muslim being a 'priest', it is likely that this was a synonym for Afonja engaging al-Salih to manufacture supernatural devices for him. Not only was al-Salih respected as a scholar, but he was also regarded as a mystic. Oyo's people called him 'Alimi' by turning his vocation of *alim* (learned Islamic scholar) into a descriptive personal name. Alimi was born in Tankara,[19] and prior to coming to Ilorin, he moved from place to place within the Sokoto Caliphate (including Kebbi, Sokoto, and Gwando Gaje) before touring locations in Oyo such as Ogbomosho, Kuwo, and Ikoyi.[20] Most of the prior accounts portray Afonja and Alimi as allies in a devious scheme to infiltrate Ilorin and overthrow the *alaafin*. According to this traditional narrative, Afonja and/or Alimi incited Hausa slaves to rebel against their masters and recruited them to act as a mutinous anti-Oyo army.

OYO'S HAUSAS

However, not all Hausas resident in Oyo were slaves, nor did all of them act on orders from Afonja and/or Alimi. On the contrary, Oyo's Hausa community was a diverse group, and Afonja and Alimi did not orchestrate all of their actions. Many of Oyo's Hausa res-

---

18 Johnson, 1921, p. 193.
19 It is not certain whether this refers to Tungan Tankara in Kebbi State in the north-west of present-day Nigeria or to Tangara in the southwest of present-day Niger Republic.
20 Danmole, 1984, p. 60.

idents were economic migrants and worked in a diverse range of vocations as barbers, cattle rearers, nurses, rope-makers, and traders. It was also typical for expatriate Hausa workers to appoint a leader in their host community. In Oyo, they appointed a Hausa immigrant named Ibrahim Bako to be their *Sarkin Gambari* ('King of the Hausas' – since Oyo's people referred to Hausas as 'Gambari'). The *sarkin Gambari* acted as a liaison and mediator between the Hausa immigrants and their host communities, and also arbitrated disputes between them. Bako thus wielded great influence over Oyo's Hausa community that was quite independent from Afonja and Alimi.

The tendency to portray all negative events of the era as part of an Afonja–Alimi conspiracy overlooks the rebellion's economic and military causes and consequences. Afonja's revolt also inspired a slave rebellion among Hausas, many of whom left their masters and flocked to join Afonja. This endangered Oyo's economic and military security. Although it was not only (as widely believed) Hausa 'slaves' who rebelled, the defection of these Hausas had more serious repercussions than losing a source of labour. Oyo's military security was vulnerable to their shifting loyalties. Oyo relied on immigrants from communities with an equestrian culture (such as Hausas and other immigrants from Borno) to rear and ride horses. Many Hausas in Oyo had lived there for so long that they spoke Oyo's language more fluently than Hausa. The defection of such linguistically indigenised Oyo Hausas struck right at the source of Oyo's military and economic power. Some of them were soldiers or cavalrymen, and when they rebelled, they fled with their horses. Their defection to Afonja's side also meant the loss of much of Oyo's labour force, and of people who had experience of rearing, handling, and feeding horses, and of fighting on horseback.

THE *JAMAA*

Ilorin became a refuge for escaped Hausa Muslim slaves who fled there for the promise of liberation. These Hausas called themselves the *Jamaa* (the 'association' or 'community') and acted as a rebel army.

From 1817 and continuing for the next decade, the 20,000-strong[21] *Jamaa* frequently raided and devastated Oyo's countryside. Some of the *Jamaa* exacted vengeance by returning to, and pillaging, the homes of former masters who mistreated them. They also wreaked havoc as they destroyed the towns and villages they raided, and kidnapped and sold their residents into slavery. The insecurity they caused also resulted in the deterioration of Oyo's economy. Since Ilorin was located between Oyo and northern trade routes, their roving disrupted Oyo's import of goods from its northern neighbours.

Not long after Alimi's arrival, Afonja also invited a rich and powerful Muslim scholar and friend of his named Solagberu to move to Ilorin. Solagberu's ethnic origin is obscure. While he was widely reputed to be an indigene of Oyo, there is contradictory evidence that his real name was Mohammed Mukhtar, and that he was an itinerant Kanuri preacher from Bama in Borno (in present-day north-east Nigeria).[22] Muslims flocked to Solagberu's side from neighbouring provinces and he and they quartered themselves in Ilorin's outskirts. This was an ironic reversal of the practice in modern-day Nigeria whereby Christian and other immigrant communities to Muslim cities usually live in neighbourhoods on the city's outskirts known in Hausa as *Sabon Gari* ('New Town' or 'Stranger's Quarters'). Johnson claimed that Solagberu's followers isolated themselves away from non-Muslims and lived in a separate part of Ilorin they renamed *Oke Sunna* (the quarter of the faithful).[23] However, since Ilorin already had an indigenous Muslim population before Solagberu's arrival, it is possible that *Oke Sunna* pre-dated him and that he and his supporters supplemented its existing Muslim population.

Although Afonja usually gets the blame for inviting Alimi and Solagberu into Ilorin, thereby allowing an alien religion to infiltrate into Oyo, Oyo already had an indigenous Muslim population prior to their arrival. Ilorin was a safe place for Muslims, and Alimi and Solagberu would have been comfortable moving there with

---

21   Page, 1908, p. 9.
22   Sa'ad, 2015, p. 294.
23   Johnson, 1921, p. 194.

or without Afonja's invitation. Oyo also could not insulate itself from outside events. Oyo's territory had two different ecological zones. Its south included dense forests, while its northern region was a dry savannah area. To protect its horses from illnesses such as trypanosomiasis ('sleeping sickness'), a parasitic disease transmitted by tsetse flies in the forest belt, Oyo located its horses mostly in its northern savannah region. However, Oyo's need to distance its cavalry from the southern forest belt was a security risk. The concentration of Oyo's strength in dry savannah inland areas placed it within striking distance of another powerful state with an even more formidable cavalry tradition: the Sokoto Caliphate. The shockwaves of Usman Dan Fodio's jihad and its spill-over into Nupeland in 1810 brought the jihad to Oyo's doorstep. A Muslim Fulani preacher from Kebbi named Mallam Dendo tried to extend the jihad into Nupeland. When the Nupe repelled Dendo, he fled to Ilorin to take refuge with Alimi (and perhaps brought into Ilorin, inciting tales of events in Nupeland).

RELIGIOUS UNREST

By 1820, Ilorin had multiple Muslim factions under Afonja and Fulani scholars such as Alimi and Dendo, Hausas loyal to the *Sarkin Gambari* Ibrahim Bako, other Muslims loyal to Solagberu in *Oke Sunna*, as well as the other indigenous Muslim and animist populations. The multi-ethnic and multi-religious dynamic at Ilorin also split the loyalties of Oyo's population with some of the Muslims siding with the Muslim immigrants and others retaining their loyalty to the *alaafin*. Although the different Muslim communities converged under the banner of religion to confront the *alaafin*, they had different motivations. While Muslim clerics such as *Mallam* Dendo and Alimi's sons wanted to extend Dan Fodio's jihad and create a Muslim emirate in Ilorin, some of the *Jamaa* saw for themselves a chance to engage in banditry, plunder, and gain revenge against their former masters. This was not an isolated problem for Afonja alone. Even the revered Dan Fodio could not control the excesses of his troops when they got over-excited in battle and committed abuses when acting on the exhilaration of having sanctioned access to, and use of, weapons.

Ilorin also had dormant ingredients for a jihad. An objection to enslaving Muslims was one of the triggers for Dan Fodio's jihad. Oyo's enslavement of Muslim Hausas who were then shipped to the Americas in the Trans-Atlantic slave trade was a topic sensitive enough for Mohammed Bello to complain in 1812 that Oyo sold Muslim slaves to Christians, and to appeal for such sales to stop. Despite Bello's grievance, ironically the jihad he and his family waged contributed to the enslavement of Muslims in Oyo. For example, when the jihadists invaded Borno in the early 1800s, they captured, enslaved, and sold a Borno indigene named Ali Eisami. An Oyo indigene later bought Eisami and kept him until the time of Afonja's rebellion decades later. The same grievance contributed to Oyo's slave rebellion. The seclusion of Solagberu's followers was also reminiscent of the manner in which Dan Fodio and his followers separated themselves before declaring their jihad in 1804. It is very likely that the Muslim immigrants at Ilorin found it difficult to reconcile their emotional support for Dan Fodio's jihad with living in a kingdom ruled by an infidel king (as Muslims would have regarded the *alaafin*). Yet these similarities with Dan Fodio's jihad do not mean that Dan Fodio orchestrated the unrest at Ilorin. It is very unlikely that he ordered, or was even aware of, events at Ilorin. He was ill and in the last year of his life when the religious tumult at Ilorin intensified. However, his jihad was an emotional accelerant that motivated Muslims elsewhere to rebel and declare jihads in the areas where they resided.

When the *Jamaa* raided and destroyed the town of Osogun in 1821, they captured their most famous victim of all time. The *Jamaa* attacked Osogun first thing in the morning while its residents were making breakfast, and set their houses ablaze. During this attack they kidnapped a young boy of around 10–12 years old named Ajayi, and sold him into slavery. As will be demonstrated in chapter 12, the *Jamaa's* kidnap of this young boy later triggered consequences beyond the wildest imagination of the attackers and their victims. Since the victors wrote most accounts of the jihads, one rarely hears about what it was like to be on the receiving end of them. Young Ajayi survived the ordeal and later provided a very vivid description of the terror that the *Jamaa* sowed when they attacked:

> For some years war had been carried on in my Eyo [Oyo] country, which was always attended with much devastation and bloodshed, the women, such men as had surrendered or were caught, with the children, were taken captive. The enemies who carried on these wars were principally the Eyo Mohammedans, with whom my country abounds, who with the Foulahs [Fulani] and such foreign slaves as had escaped from their owners, joined together ... and annoyed the whole country.[24]

Ajayi's account makes it clear that the raiders were multi-ethnic and included Muslim Fulanis and others from Oyo. The 'foreign slaves ... escaped from their owners' that he referred to were the Hausa slaves who had joined Afonja.

While not everything Afonja did was an act of treachery (as often perceived), he had a knack of inadvertently setting traps for himself. For example, he convinced Alimi to bring his sons to Ilorin. Alimi's two oldest sons, Abdulsalami and Shitta, were more bellicose than their scholarly father and their presence amplified the religious unrest within Oyo. In the space of a few years, Afonja's alliances and decisions suddenly escalated a conflict about regional autonomy and the secession of Oyo's provinces into a slave rebellion, and finally into a jihadi war against Oyo.

Afonja's alliance with the Fulani and Hausa immigrants came back to haunt him. Although it is not clear how much control Afonja exercised over the *Jamaa*'s actions, he was unable to simultaneously cope with opposition from the *alaafin* at Oyo and the *Jamaa* who were running amok at Ilorin and neighbouring areas. In trying to confront both, he sharpened his own execution blade. Most accounts claim that Afonja was not a Muslim. However, it

---

24 Page, 1908, p. 9.

is difficult to explain why Muslims such as Alimi and Solagberu would move to Ilorin at the invitation of a non-Muslim and ally with him. To accept the prior accounts requires us to accept the bizarre logic that jihadist Muslim Hausa slaves would follow and fight for the cause of a non-Muslim leader, regard the *alaafin* as a pagan, but treat Afonja differently. It is likely that Afonja became a Muslim at some point in time before or during his alliance with the *Jamaa*, Alimi, and Solagberu. One source claimed that 'Afonja even destroys his own [animist] shrine at their [*Jamaa*] request in order to erect a Friday Mosque in its place and finally becomes a praying Muslim himself'.[25]

Afonja's relationship with the *Jamaa* and Alimi's son Abdulsalami broke down. As the *Jamaa* were getting out of hand, Afonja either tried to restrain them from their increasingly unruly behaviour, or they reacted badly when Afonja tried to disband them after using them for his bidding. Either way, the *Jamaa* mutinied and descended on him in 1823. Afonja went down fighting but died under a hail of arrow and javelin shots, after which the *Jamaa* burned his body.[26] Oyo's chiefs refused to come to Afonja's rescue as they were alienated by his alliance with immigrants. The behaviour of Alimi after Afonja's death suggests that his murder was not premeditated and may have been a spontaneous act after a disagreement. For example, after Afonja's murder, Alimi rebuilt Afonja's house and protected his children and family.[27]

The fact that the conflict escalated after Afonja's violent death suggests that he was not its sole orchestrator, and again provides evidence that it emerged from an overriding religious motive. After his death, the Oyo-Ilorin conflict transcended Afonja's initial secessionist ambition, and became a jihadi war to extend the Sokoto Caliphate's frontiers into Oyo. Some sources claim that Dan Fodio's

25   Reichmuth, 1993, p. 159.
26   Accounts of Afonja being burned to ashes are given credence by the fact that his descendants still consider using ashes in the preparation of food to be taboo (Danmole, 1984, pp. 61–2).
27   Johnson, 1921, p. 199. An Arabic source claimed that Afonja was killed while fighting against Abdulsalami's forces (Danmole, 1984, p. 61).

younger brother Abdullahi gave Alimi a flag and authorised him to extend the jihad into Oyo.[28] However, as will be discussed below, it is very unlikely that Alimi (who died soon after Afonja) was acting in concert with the Sokoto Caliphate. The deaths of Afonja and Alimi did not bring peace. Instead, conflict escalated as Alimi's sons Abdulsalami and Shitta came to the fore. Free of the restraining influence of their father, Alimi's sons sequentially eliminated the other Muslim factions at Ilorin until they had leadership. Abdulsalami's forces killed Solagberu after a long siege. Around 1823, the jihadist Fulani armies under Alimi's son Abdulsalami invaded and captured Ilorin. Alimi's son Abdulsalami declared himself the first *Emir* of Ilorin, and established an Islamic emirate there. Some accounts claim that *Emir* Abdulsalami forced Oyo to become a vassal to Ilorin and the *alaafin* to convert to Islam. However, the Fulani conquest of Ilorin did not eradicate Afonja's bloodline from leadership in the city. *Emir* Abdulsalami incorporated some members of Afonja's surviving family members into his governing council by appointing Afonja's oldest son Ladejo as *magaji are* (Afonja's heir) and his brother as *baba isale* (chief adviser). The *magaji are* title is still held by Afonja's descendants.

Like their kinsmen in Borno, it appears that the Fulani jihadists at Ilorin were acting on their own initiative without sanction from the jihad leaders at Sokoto. In 1828 or 1829, Abdulsalami wrote a letter to the *Emir* of Gwandu, Abdullahi, to introduce himself, pledge himself to Abdullahi, and ask the Sokoto Caliphate to formally recognise him as the *Emir* of Ilorin. Gwandu's reply to Abdulsalami indicates that the Sokoto Caliphate's leaders did not know who he was, nor did they pre-authorise his actions in Ilorin. The letter in response from Gwandu stated:

we have understood your letter and have pondered your excellent message in which you inform us that you are under our supervision and judgment, and *in which you tell us of your origin* [italics added] ... You also tell us that you will never defy our command,

---

28　Reichmuth, 1993, p. 168.

and that you pray God to prevent you from deviation in this regard. This is the substance of your message. Know therefore with certainty, my brother, that we accept unreservedly all you have spoken of in your letter ...[29]

This reply from Gwandu confirmed Ilorin's incorporation into the Sokoto Caliphate as its southern-most emirate. Although Gwandu accepted Abdulsalami as the *emir* of the new emirate of Ilorin, it was retroactive consent to a jihad they had not authorised in advance. The person who replied from Gwandu also gave some bad news which confirmed the writer's identity: 'This is also to inform you that the Shaikh our father (May God Almighty be merciful to him) has died.'[30] The deceased 'Shaikh our father' that the letter referred to was Usman Dan Fodio's younger brother Abdullahi; the prior *Emir* of Gwandu. This means that the person that replied to Abdulsalami was the second *Emir* of Gwandu: Abdullahi's successor and son Muhammed. Since the reply from Gwandu referred to Abdullahi's death, it probably means that Abdulsalami's letter to Gwandu was sent to Abdullahi, but that Abdullahi had died by the time it reached Gwandu.

While the Fulani consolidated power in Ilorin, Oyo was in freefall. The *alaafin* seemed to be a king in name only and had lost control of Oyo's provinces. By the time Europeans first visited and set eyes on Oyo, it was a shadow of its former self. When the British explorers Richard and John Lander visited Oyo in 1830, they reported that the kingdom had lost its lustre and that its people seemed hospitable and sedate (in contrast to their prior warlike reputation). They described Oyo's people as 'a simple, honest, inoffensive, but weak, timid, and cowardly race'.[31] By this time, the jihad and Hausa slave rebellion had forced Oyo's people to come down from their horses. Oyo had lost its famed cavalry, had only a small force of glorified ponies at its disposal, and Ilorin had become the new equestrian military power in the region. Dahomey had also success-

---

29 Sa'ad, 2015, p. 108.
30 Ibid., p. 291.
31 Lander, 1832, p.176.

fully revoked its vassal status to Oyo after its King Gezo led and won a successful war of independence in 1818.

'negligent and imbecile monarch'

The Lander brothers were so appalled by the people and their *alaafin*'s indifference to Ilorin's independence and the threat of invading Fulani horsemen on their doorstep that they described the *alaafin* they met as a 'negligent and imbecile monarch'.[32] The *alaafin* requested assistance from Clapperton and Richard Lander to help him expel the Fulani invaders from his kingdom. The identity of this *alaafin* who was the first to meet a white person is uncertain. Although the Lander brothers claimed that the *alaafin* they met was named 'Mansolah', Oyo had no *alaafin* named Mansolah. Johnson claimed that the Scottish explorer Hugh Clapperton visited Oyo in January 1826 and met *Alaafin* Majotu.[33] Whether or not Mansolah and Majotu are the same person, the Lander brothers accused *Alaafin* 'Mansolah' and Oyo's people of an 'unpardonable indifference to the public interest, and neglect of all the rules of prudence and common sense' for not being more alarmed about, and for not taking sterner measures to resist, the Fulani threat that lay less than 50 miles away at Ilorin. The Landers predicted that Oyo's indifference would inevitably lead to the Fulani conquering them.

Despite the Landers' criticism of Oyo's passive response to the Fulani threat, Oyo made a massive attempt to reclaim Ilorin from the Fulani. In an effort to shake off the humiliating reversal of Oyo being a vassal to its former province of Ilorin, one of 'Mansolah's' successors, *Alaafin* Oluewu formed a military alliance with the kingdom of Borgu to Oyo's north-west. The ensuing conflict (which took place sometime between 1830 and 1835) became a battle of military coalitions. Having acknowledged Ilorin as part of the Caliphate, Gwandu sent military reinforcements to help Ilorin (including Muhammadu Buhari and Muhammadu Abdul-

---

32 Ibid., p. 177.
33 Johnson, 1921, p. 210.

lahi – respectively, the sons of Usman Dan Fodio and his brother Abdullahi). The joint Oyo–Borgu attempt to drive the Fulani out of Ilorin ended in defeat and the deaths of two kings: Oluewu of Oyo and Eleduwe of Borgu, both of whom were killed in battle while trying to retake Ilorin from *Emir* Shitta (who had succeeded his brother Abdulsalami).[34] Oluewu's death marked the end of a dynasty, as he turned out to be the last *alaafin* resident at Oyo.

Six years after the Lander brothers departed Oyo, their prediction was fulfilled. In 1836 *Emir* Shitta's armies also invaded, sacked, and destroyed Oyo's capital. The Oyo who had menaced their neighbours with raids by armed mounted horsemen were now receiving a taste of their own medicine. The Muslim armies also invaded and destroyed at least 130 towns in northern Oyo.[35] Refugees fled south to escape the invaders and founded new cities at Ibadan and Abeokuta. Less than a century after reaching the zenith of its power and being the most powerful state in its region, the Oyo Empire spectacularly imploded. After Oyo's capital fell, the city evacuated, and Oluewu's successor *Alaafin* Atiba fled south and founded a new capital at Ago-Oja about 80–90 miles further south.

THE BATTLE OF OSOGBO

Not only had Oyo lost Ilorin and its capital to the Fulani, but it had no guarantee of safety in its new location. The continued Fulani push southwards threatened not only the wandering Oyo, but also the host communities where they fled. The jihad's southward trajectory created a morbid fear among the Oduduwan kingdoms that the Fulani would not stop until they were able to 'dip the Koran in the sea'[36] (a euphemism for extending the jihad all the way to the southern Atlantic coastline). Ecology, which had restrained Oyo's imperial expansion, ironically became its saviour, and cur-

---

34 All subsequent *emirs* of Ilorin have been Alimi's descendants. Additionally, the mother of the former *Emir* of Kano Aminu Ado Bayero is a descendant of Alimi.

35 Page, 1908, p. 82.

36 Johnson, 1921, p. 288.

tailed the Fulani in the same way it curtailed Oyo. In 1840 at the town of Osogbo (pronounced 'Oshogbo'), which is now located in Osun State in south-west Nigeria, the Fulani cavalrymen fought a pivotal battle against a joint alliance of warriors from Ibadan, Osogbo, and Oyo. Although the date of the battle is unconfirmed, it likely occurred in 1838. An informant wrote in 1841 that the battle took place 'about three years ago'.[37] For about three weeks the two sides were in stalemate as Ibadan, Osogbo, and Oyo were afraid to confront the Fulani horsemen in open fields, and the Fulani were unable to get their horses through the forest belt. The southward advance of the jihad that Usman Dan Fodio started around 35 years earlier was halted not by a superior military power, but instead by two ecological forces that even the conquering Fulani armies could not overcome. The dense forests of the south proved impenetrable for their horses, and the tsetse fly lurking in those forests menaced their horses with sickness. Hence, the joint Ibadan, Osogbo, and Oyo military alliance won a famous battle at Osogbo, stopped the jihad there, and prevented it from penetrating further south into the other Oduduwan kingdoms. Osogbo's victory had massive repercussions for the religious character of the Oduduwan region and of the future Nigerian state which arose in the following century. By insulating the southern territories from the jihadists, Osogbo's victory reserved a southern territory that was open for Christian evangelisation.

Alaafin Atiba revived the Oyo kingdom in the new location he fled to (which he also renamed Oyo) and reinstated the royal court, offices, and titles which were used in the old capital at Oye-Ile ('Original Oyo'). The Oyo dynasty continued at 'New Oyo', but its territory became emasculated and it never regained its former glory. Although Oyo had in the past operated from exile before returning to reclaim its territory, it never returned to its destroyed capital city at Oyo-Ile which remained deserted and is now grassland. Moving to New Oyo represented a geographic about turn.

---

37 Journals of Ajayi Crowther, in Schon and Crowther, 1842, p. 318.

Oyo had migrated north following its founder Oranmiyan's move from Ife, and was forced into moving its base south again.

THE HANDS OF TIME

Trying to unravel the source of Oyo's implosion is made more difficult by the utterly confused and opaque chronology of the events that preceded it. Those who recorded the events immediately preceding and following Oyo's collapse rarely dated them, or when they did, disagreed on issues of fact and timing. The oral histories collected were dated not on the Roman calendar, but based on other notable contemporaneous events. For example, even though Johnson wrote the most comprehensive history of these times, he did not date events that occurred before 1830. As a result, it is not possible to date with absolute certainty key events such as Abiodun's death, Afonja's coup against Awole, or the date that Alimi died.

Abiodun's death is an apt event from which to start the dating investigation as it preceded Afonja's rebellion. Based on the various accounts, Abiodun died at some point in time in the 21-year period between 1789 and 1810. Crowther claims that Awole succeeded Abiodun around the year 1800, reigned for seven years, and died in 1807.[38] If Crowther is correct, it would mean that Abiodun died in 1800 and that Afonja's coup against Awole occurred in 1807. However, this timeline is potentially contradicted by a letter that a French trader at Whydah wrote in June 1789 to the French minister of the navy. In this letter, the trader reported the death of someone he called the '*Roy des Alliots*' (King of Alliots): 'I have the honour of informing you that the King of Alliots died around the same time as the King of Dahomey; maybe last April.'[39] An academic argued in a PhD thesis written in 1963 that 'the "Roy des Alliots" referred to here could be no other than the redoubtable Abiodun'.[40] If this claim is correct, then it would mean that Abiodun died around April 1789, and that Afonja's coup against Awole would have to

---

38   Crowther, 1852, p. v.
39   Akinjogbin, 1963, p. 257.
40   Ibid., p. 257.

be backdated to 1796. However, placing Abiodun's death at 1789 and Afonja's coup at 1796 creates serious incoherence to the timing of later events. Accepting these dates would mean that after overthrowing Awole, Afonja waited over 20 years before inviting Alimi into Ilorin and igniting the Hausa slave rebellion (events confirmed to have occurred in 1817). The 1789 and 1796 dates are also made less likely by one of the informants (David Kukomi) that Johnson consulted for his book regarding the Oyo Empire. Johnson claimed that:

> Kukomi was a young man in the days of King Abiodun and it was his fortune (or misfortune) to take part in the wars and other national movements of the period as a common soldier, and was thus able to give a clear and reliable account of the sayings, persons, and events of those stirring times.[41]

If Abiodun died in 1789, and we assume that Kukomi was around 20 years old in 1789, then Kukomi would have had to be an elderly man of a very improbable age over 120 years old by the time Johnson consulted him.[42] The unlikelihood of such advanced age, and the irrationality of Afonja waiting in limbo for 20 years after his coup against Awole before the slave rebellion, suggest a more likely possibility that Abiodun did not die in 1789, but rather died in the early 1800s.

The distance in time between Afonja's coup and the Hausa slave revolt is another one of the historical unknowns. Prior accounts make it seem as if Afonja incited the Hausas into rebellion immediately after overthrowing Awole. This is given credence by the Lander brothers who, when they visited Oyo in 1830, claimed that the slave rebellion 'took place as far back as forty years'[43] (which would place it around 1790). However, the Hausa slave rebellion is one of the few events of the era to have been reliably dated (to 1817). Accepting the Landers' testimony on this issue requires us to

41 Johnson, 1921, p. vii.
42 Kukomi died in 1895, and at the given age of 98 (Law, 1984, p. 196).
43 Lander, 1832, p. 176.

accept the very unlikely probability that the slave rebellion started in the late 1700s and continued raging for some 40 years until they arrived at Oyo in 1830. Thus we are left with a series of spectacular events that definitely occurred, but no certainty as to exactly when each of them occurred in the approximate 41-year period between 1789 and 1830.

Afonja's traitor status has persisted because his enemies wrote most of what is known about him. Traitor or not, the consequences of his rebellion endured long after his death. The uprising he led created a domino chain of events that advanced not just Islam in Oduduwa-land, but also ironically advanced the cause of Christianity there too. It advanced Islam by extending the Sokoto Caliphate into northern Oduduwa-land. It also accidentally created a Christianisation movement. Apart from throwing the region into ferment, the exodus of refugees who fled southwards to escape the jihad caused long-standing societal changes. Some of these refugees and other captives (such as young Ajayi mentioned above) that the jihadists sold into slavery later regained their freedom, converted to Christianity, and returned to their ancestral lands to evangelise and Christianise the region. The descendants of these refugees and freed slaves became not just Christian evangelists, but also the primary actors in writing the history of the Oduduwan kingdoms and creating their modern identity as one people. As will be shown later in this book, one person in particular played a critical role in these processes.

Oyo Timeline

* 1754   Gaha becomes *bashorun*
* 1770–74   Abiodun becomes *alaafin*
* 1774   Death of Gaha
* 1789–1800 Death of *Alaafin* Abiodun
* 1796–1807 Afonja starts rebellion/*Alaafin* Awole commits suicide
* 1817   Afonja invites Alimi into Ilorin
* 1823   *Jamaa* mutiny and kill Afonja
* 1823   Fulani armies invade and capture Ilorin

* 1823/24   Death of Alimi
* 1836   Fulani armies invade and capture Oyo
* 1838–40   Battle of Osogbo between Ibadan and Ilorin army

7
The Kings from Heaven

The so-called 'Benin Bronzes' have recently attracted great publicity in the mainstream media. Benin was first catapulted into international news after British soldiers invaded and destroyed its capital Benin City in February 1897, and then after discovering a spectacular array of bronze sculptures, ivory terracotta, and other artworks (popularly known as the 'Benin Bronzes') there, looted over 2000 of them and dispersed them around the world. Although non-Africans have known about Benin's looted artwork for over 125 years, the outside world's preoccupation with the aesthetic aspects of the artwork and the moral restitutional arguments regarding whether or not they should be repatriated to Benin means that far less is known about the culture, history, and technical ingenuity of the people that produced the artworks.

Benin was not just a place where art treasures were found. It was a highly developed society with a powerful government that projected its power beyond its territory, inter-continental diplomatic relations with European countries, a powerful military, and a gifted guild of artists that created artworks which British art specialists later admitted were 'well able to hold their own for freedom of design and successful mastery of the most difficult technical details, with the best works of the European renaissance, with which period they are practically equal'.[1]

Although Benin's precise formation date is uncertain, its current monarchy was likely formed around the twelfth or thirteenth century. Benin's original territory was located in what is now southern Nigeria (mostly in modern-day Delta and Edo Sates – see Map 2), but it later extended its influence as far as 200 miles to the west of its capital city and made Lagos (Nigeria's first post-independence

---

1   Gaskell, 1902, p. 103.

capital city) its vassal. Benin was multi-ethnic and multi-lingual, and located in a green forest belt with the Atlantic Ocean and several creeks and rivers to its south. The Edo people (sometimes also called 'Bini') were its most numerous ethnic group and lived mostly in and around the capital of Benin City, while Benin's other ethnic groups such as the Afenmai, Esan, Igbo, Isoko, Itsekiri, and Urhobo lived in towns and villages that encircled Benin City.

THE *OGISOS* AND THE *OBAS*

Benin's history is marked by two distinct epochs; the first of which is little known but whose chronology is widely agreed, and the second of which is more well known but whose origin, chronology, and facts are hotly disputed. Prior to the twelfth century, Benin was ruled by mysterious deified rulers who had the title of *ogiso*[2] ('king from heaven' or 'king from the sky'). Some of the early *ogisos* were women. The *ogisos* were simultaneously heads of state and religion and, like the Japanese and Roman emperors and Spartan kings, were the leaders of a divine monarchy which in the eyes of their people, derived its authority from God. The first *ogiso* was called Igodo. Benin was originally named Igodomigodo ('the land of Igodo') after him.[3] The *ogiso* dynasty had 31 kings, the last of whom was named Owodo.

After a political crisis, Benin's people deposed and exiled Owodo after accusing him of cruelty and misrule. His only heir (his son Ekaladerhan) was unable to succeed him as he too had earlier been exiled to a town called Ughoton. Due to the leadership vacuum, Benin's people instead created a republican government led by a powerful man named Evian. However, political ferment again erupted after Evian named his son as his successor. Sometime in the twelfth or thirteenth century, Benin's people again rebelled, this time against what seemed to be Evian's attempt to resume monarchy via his lineage. What happened next has been subject to prolonged controversy and dispute for centuries. A new line of

2   A phrase compounded from the Edo words *ogie* (king) and *iso* (sky or heaven).
3   Osadolor, 2001, p. 52.

monarchs known as *obas* succeeded the *ogisos*, but the manner in which this transition occurred is shrouded in mystery.

MORE OFFSPRING OF ODUDUWA

While the popular Benin and Ife versions of the Oduduwa legend agree that Oduduwa's family tree gave birth to a new Benin monarchy, the manner in which it allegedly unfolded has many different variants. The Benin and Ife versions agree that due to the political vacuum caused by the downfall of the *ogisos* and the crisis with Evian, Benin's kingmakers travelled to the kingdom of Ife (approximately 150 miles to Benin's west) and appealed to Ife's ruler (the *ooni*) to send one of his sons to rule Benin. The then reigning *Ooni* of Ife (Oduduwa) granted Benin's request and sent Oranmiyan (who was either his son or grandson) to rule Benin after being assured that he would be welcome in Benin. After Oranmiyan arrived at Benin, he married and had a son named Eweka with a Benin woman. However, Oranmiyan abdicated and refused to stay after being unable to acclimatise to the culture or learn the language of his hosts. After Oranmiyan departed, his son Eweka re-established the Benin monarchy with himself as its king under a new title of *oba*, while Oranmiyan founded a new kingdom at Oyo and became its first king.

Although the Benin and Ife versions of this legend agree that Eweka was the first *Oba* of Benin, they have several irreconcilable inconsistencies. Firstly, they serve different purposes. Ife's version explains the origins of all life and the monarchies of the Oduduwan peoples. In contrast, Benin's version explains only the origin of its current *oba* ruling dynasty, and does not explain the origin of the *ogisos* or of Benin's people. Since the Benin version confirms that 31 *ogisos* ruled before Oranmiyan came to Benin, it punches a massive hole in the Oduduwa legend's claim that Oduduwa marked the beginning of Ife kingship and society. Oduduwa is unlikely to be an Adam-like father of the Oduduwan people, when less than 200 miles away, 31 different kings ruled in succession to each other before he was born. If Benin's monarchy existed before that of Ife, then it would be bizarre for Benin's leaders to approach a newly formed monarchy at Ife led by Oduduwa (who was allegedly Ife's first king) to provide a new monarch for Benin which by then had already had 31 different kings over several centuries. Even if we ignore the Oduduwa legend's obviously allegorical claim that all life on earth started at Ife, the *ogiso* lineage supports the argument made in Chapter 5 that a different monarchy ruled at Ife before Oduduwa arrived there.

Secondly, controversial variations of the Benin oral tradition arose in the twentieth century. Some of these variations claim that Benin's exiled prince Ekaladerhan (son of the last *Ogiso* Owodo) left exile at Ughoton, and after wandering for several years, sojourned to, and started a new life in, Ife. After a long search for him, a delegation from Benin found him at Ife many years later, where he was living under a new identity as Oranmiyan. The now elderly and infirm Ekaladerhan/Oranmiyan refused to return to Benin with them and instead sent his son Eweka to rule Benin.[4] If this alternate Benin version is accepted, it would mean that the first *Oba* of Benin was not the son of an Ife indigene, but was instead the son of an exiled Benin prince. This variation has some logic to it. Accepting the Ife version would mean that the Benin royalty are descended from a foreigner, and would require explanation as to why Benin's people (who had rejected rulers from their own community) went to so much trouble to get a new foreign king. If Oranmiyan was actually from Benin, then his people's quest to convince him to return home is logical. A knock-on effect of this is that if Eweka's father was actually the son of the last Igodo, then the *ogiso* and *oba* dynasties are not different after all. The two eras would be the same dynasty, albeit temporarily interrupted by a republican era. The start of the *oba* era could then be viewed as a resumption and reformation of Benin kingship (perhaps with influence from Ife).

In a further twist, another slightly different version of the Benin oral tradition claims that Ekaladerhan and Oduduwa were the same person.[5] These contradictory accounts can be explained as

---

4   Akinola, 1976, p. 24.
5   Osadolor, 2001, p. 59.

ethnic and politically motivated propaganda between Benin and Ife to claim ascendancy over each other. The 'Ekaladerhan is actually Oduduwa or Oranmiyan' story seems to be a twentieth-century Benin alteration to its ancient oral traditions. After British troops captured Benin in 1897, Consul-General Sir Ralph Moor and Acting Resident Captain Ernest Roupell prepared and sent an intelligence report to the Foreign Office in London regarding Benin's culture and history. The report was based on Moor's and Roupell's interviews with seven senior surviving personnel of the vanquished Benin government[6] (including the deposed *oba*'s official royal historian) in November 1897. This report was the first time that anyone recorded Benin's ancient history in writing. The Benin informants' account of the origin of the *oba* dynasty made no reference to Ekaladerhan or Oranmiyan but instead stated:

The people of this country [Benin] sent to Ufe [Ife] ... for a king. Eweka was sent to them – he came with a few men – he came to Benin city; he went softly, softly into all the country. If the people were weak, he fought with them and caught them; if strong, he talked cunningly with them, and he and his men sat down there and took their daughters to wife.[7]

Not only is this nineteenth-century Benin account closer to the Ife version, but intriguingly it suggests that Benin resisted Eweka's arrival, and that he and his allies from Ife had to fight wars of conquest to establish his rule. It also has great veracity as it was provided by officials of the Benin government (including Benin's official government historian) – provided of course that the British officials correctly translated and recorded their testimony.

There is an irrational element to the Benin and Ife origin folklore. Both the Benin and Ife versions make it seem as if the relationship between Benin and Ife started after the Benin delegation travelled

6   Chief Ariyo (who was described as the 'Court Historian' – presumably the *ihogbe*), Esseri, Ossa, Osuon ('Ju Ju Men'), Ihollo (master smith), Ihollo II (master wood carver), Ine (master ivory carver).
7   Read and Dalton, 1899, p. 5.

to Ife to find a new king. If we believe the Ife version, a pertinent question is why in its time of distress, Benin chose of all the
places in the world, to appeal not to a nearby neighbour, but only
to a faraway kingdom at Ife. If we accept the Benin version which
claims that Oranmiyan (or Oduduwa) was their exiled prince Ekaladerhan, then we must ask: of all the places a fugitive prince of
Benin could flee to, why did he choose to embark upon a dangerous
journey of over 100 miles on foot, without mechanised transport or
horses, and risk falling sick on the way, being robbed, kidnapped, or
murdered, all in the name of getting to Ife? The dogged determination of Benin's leaders to reach and seek assistance from nowhere
else but Ife suggests that Benin already had a pre-existing relationship with Ife that pre-dated Eweka and the *oba* dynasty, or that
Ife had an important political or spiritual meaning to Benin. The
political transition from the *ogiso* to *oba* dynasties was probably a
continuation of Benin's relationship with Ife, not the beginning of
it. We still do not know how and when this relationship started,
or how far back it goes. Benin's oral stories about the breakdown
of the *ogiso* lineage in Benin might even be Benin's version of the
overthrow of the pre-Oduduwa Ife monarchy that is discussed in
Chapter 5.

British explorers inadvertently found supporting evidence for
the link between Benin and Oduduwa-land. When Richard and
John Lander (brothers) visited Oyo in 1830, they reported that:
'It has been expressly and repeatedly told us, that the monarch
of this empire is brother to the King of Benin ... they assert that
Mansolah [the then reigning *alaafin*] and the King of Benin "were
of one father and one mother".'[8] The reference to the *Alaafin* of
Oyo and the *Oba* of Benin being siblings was a historical reference
to the two kingdoms being founded by Oduduwa's offspring. When
the Landers tried to get more information about this family link
between the Oyo and Benin monarchs, their Oyo informant tired
of their questions (some might say nosiness) and 'soon silenced our

---

8   Lander, 1830, pp. 167–8.

remarks by observing that we were too inquisitive, or, to use his own words, "that we talked too much".[9]

THE OBA ERA

After the transition from the *ogiso* to the *oba* era, Eweka renamed the kingdom 'Ubini' (the phrase that the names Benin and 'Bini' are derived from). The *oba*'s person was regarded as sacred and like his Oduduwan counterparts, one of his praise names is *ekeji orisa* ('deputy to the gods'). To maintain the *oba*'s supernatural mystique, most of his subjects were not allowed to see him. This seclusion allowed apocryphal legends about the *oba* to emerge. For example, many maintained the pretence that the *oba* did not eat as he did not require food to live. Such mystique was easy to maintain about a monarch that left his palace only a few times a year.

When the British army officer Lt-Colonel Henry Galway arrived for a meeting at *Oba* Ovonramwen's palace in 1892, Galway was received by people whom he sarcastically described as 'splendid specimens of manhood, whose tailor's bill was absolutely nil'.[10] These were members of the *oba*'s large retinue of attendants, some of whom were not permitted to wear clothes in his presence. The *oba* was very pampered and had staff for every conceivable purpose. He even had personal attendants who gently clasped and held his arms aloft at right angles when he walked. Some of his attendants were recognisable by their distinctive ceremonial haircuts that split their hair into three sections separated by partings.

'the largest single archaeological phenomenon on the planet'

Benin's oral history credits the *obas* for the major advancements in Benin's architecture, culture, and territory. Benin City was surrounded by several ditches and large walls. The ditch was dug in the late thirteenth century on the orders of the fourth *oba*, Oguola, and in the fifteenth century one of Benin's legendary rulers *Oba* Ewuare

---

9   Ibid., p. 168.
10   Galway, 1930, p. 233.

ordered the construction of Benin's famed walls and Benin City in a new symmetrical pattern. The walls credited to *Oba* Ewuare required the labour of 5000 men working throughout a dry season to construct.[11] Benin City was distinguished by great feats of engineering and technology, some of which were unprecedented in its era. It was surrounded by massive external and internal walls which both marked the city's boundaries and also segregated around 500 separate villages within it. The total length of these walls extended for over 16,000 kilometres. The 1974 edition of the *Guinness Book of Records* recorded Benin City's walls as the largest earthworks ever constructed in the world prior to the mechanical era. Another source claimed that the walls took an estimated 150 million hours to construct, and described them as 'perhaps the largest single archaeological phenomenon on the planet'.[12] Benin City was also one of the first places in the world to have street lighting. The 120-feet-wide roads to the *oba*'s palace were illuminated at night by palm oil-fuelled street lights that stood several feet high. Benin houses also had distinctive architectural customisations. For example, most houses had open moon roofs, which in a humid climate provided ventilation, sunlight, and importantly acted as a water supply by catching and draining rainwater into an internal water tank in the style of a Roman *impluvium*. A British visitor to Benin claimed that 'no one who went there in the old days came away without being impressed'.[13]

Commencing in the late fifteenth century and continuing into the late sixteenth century under the leadership of the warrior *Obas* Ewuare, Ozolua, Esigie, Orhogbua, and Ehengbuda, Benin embarked upon an era of imperial expansion through military conquest. During this era Benin expanded from a small size of only 15 kilometres in circumference, and overran neighbouring communities among the Oduduwan Owo kingdom to Benin's west, and some Igbo communities to its east. It became an empire with vassal states, and a 270-mile distance between its eastern and western

11   Posnansky, 1975, p. 118.
12   *Guardian*, 18 March 2016.
13   Roth, 1903, p. vi.

borders (as long as travelling from Brussels in Belgium, across Holland, and into northern France).

During the sixteenth century, *Oba* Esigie commissioned a guild of professionally trained bronze and ivory sculptors. The members of this guild were visual historians as well as sculptors. It was they who created the famous Benin Bronzes. The Bronzes served as Benin's Mount Rushmore of its great kings, victories, and other significant events and people. Thousands of the Bronzes adorned the *oba*'s palace. They were not purely aesthetic, but also had a functional purpose as physical narratives of Benin's culture and history. The variety of the people and themes depicted in the Bronzes was astonishing, and included kings, servants, enemies, deities, religious figures, soldiers, and even animals. The patience and skill required to make the Bronzes, and the precision of their finishing, marked Benin as a giant factory for great art.

'the skill of the Benin native in the casting of metal'

After destroying Benin and looting it in 1897, British military and colonial officers sent several hundred of the Bronzes to the British Museum in London. Their arrival in Europe and dissemination to the outside world caused a publicity sensation, and extremely uncomfortable European reassessments about the then prevailing theories of African intellectual and technological inferiority. When English reporters saw the Bronzes, *The Times* newspaper conceded that 'the novelty of the subject and the technical perfection of the work, are surprising evidences of the skill of the Benin native in the casting of metal'.[14] Museum curators were stunned by their decorative artistry and the technical expertise required to make them. Charles Read of the British Museum admitted to being amazed 'at the first sight of these remarkable works of art' and that 'we were at once astounded at such an unexpected find, and puzzled to account for so highly developed an art among a race so entirely barbarous as were the Bini'.[15] British Museum officials refused to believe that

---

14   *The Times*, Saturday 25 September 1897.
15   Ratté, 1972, p. 82.

the Binis, whom they viewed as primitive savages, were capable of creating art with such attention to detail, using the same 'Lost Wax' technique (which is further described in Chapter 9) as Europe's best sculptors. They instead speculated that an alien race from North Africa, China, or the Mediterranean had taught the Binis how to make the Bronzes.

Although the vast majority of the Bronzes depicted men, a few of them depicted a majestic-looking woman with a distinctive curved conical, elevated hairstyle covered in royal beads, wearing a coral embossed necklace, and sometimes surrounded by attendants and soldiers. This woman's sculpture was so striking that in 1902 a British art magazine described it as a 'really exquisite head of a negress in bronze, which, for accuracy of modelling, delicacy of finish, and fineness of patina, might well belong to the best period either of Classical or Renaissance art'.[16] The figurines of this woman were copied multiple times and became so iconic that a photo of an ivory carving of her face is a familiar image on the front cover of several books and was the logo of Nigeria's 1977 World Festival of African Arts and Culture. Who was this elegant and mysterious woman?

'the only woman who went to war'

Oba Esigie is one of Benin's most famous kings. He lived a drama-filled life even before he became the *oba*. After his father *Oba* Ozolua died in the early sixteenth century, a succession struggle ensued between Esigie and his brother Arhuaran. This was common in polygamous families where several children were born in close temporal proximity and there is no undisputed candidate among the potential heirs. The rivalry caused an intra-palace military clash, and Esigie's mother Idia interfered and sided with her son as violence erupted between him and his brother. Idia's intervention on her son's behalf ensured that he prevailed and succeeded her husband Ozolua. Although it was tradition for the *oba*'s mother

---

16   Gaskell, 1902, p. 100.

to be banished and secluded as soon as her son was coronated, Idia did not retire quietly to the background in satisfaction that her son was the new *oba*. Esigie rewarded his beloved mother by creating and elevating her into a new official title of *Iye Oba*[17] (mother of the king), and built a palace for her at the walled town of Uselu (about 3–4 miles outside Benin City) – complete with her own retinue of attendants. Uselu became known as *n'evbo iye oba* ('the land of queen mothers') and the official fiefdom of all subsequent queen mothers. Like her son, she also enjoyed the privilege of being escorted by servants who attended to her every need and who held her arms aloft as she walked. Idia and Esigie were so close that they even circumvented the royal edict which forbade the *oba* and his mother from seeing each other, by using messengers to communicate with each other. Invested with her new and unprecedented *ex officio* position of *iye oba*, Idia became her son's political and spiritual adviser and a famed warrior. Idia's influence was so significant that she conscripted her own army regiment which helped her son win a war against the Igala people of Idah in the sixteenth century. For this encroachment into the military domain traditionally reserved for men, Idia became known as 'the only woman who went to war'.

Idia's sculptures were not the only outliers among the Benin Bronzes. Some of them depicted people wearing crosses that bore a remarkable resemblance to the symbol of an ancient Knights Templar order. How and why did West Africans start wearing the insignia of a European religious order?

Benin had a geographic and trade advantage with the outside world as it was close to the Atlantic Ocean and had navigable rivers leading to its interior. This topography made it almost inevitable that people with advanced ship technology would eventually find Benin. Clues that ancient Benin hosted people from very far away are shown in some of the Bronzes which depicted people with straight hair, handlebar moustaches, and aquiline physical features. Moreover, these strangers wore sixteenth-century European clothing and hats, and carried firearms. Who were these mysteri-

---

17   This is a compound phrase of the Edo words *iye* (mother) and *oba* (king).

ous un-named people with non-African features that made enough of an impression for the *oba*'s guild of sculptors to include them in their Bronzes?

HENRY THE NAVIGATOR

In the fifteenth century, Iberians were at the forefront of advancements in ship design and technology. As ships became bigger, faster, and could sail further, Portugal's Prince Henry acquired the nickname of 'Henry the Navigator' for encouraging a daring era of Portuguese exploration to parts of the world that were then unknown to Europe. Portuguese determination to find a sea route to India, conquer new-found lands, and its messianic mission to spread Christianity, sent a generation of daredevil Portuguese explorers to West Africa. Portuguese explorers first arrived in West Africa in 1472, but did not enter Benin's interior until 13 years later in 1485 during an expedition led by Joao de Aveiro. This was only 2–3 years after Portuguese explorers reached Congo in Central Africa for the first time. The Portuguese were impressed with Benin City and referred to it as 'Great Benin'. They realised that they were in the midst of a society with impressive architectural and engineering skills. A Portuguese explorer who visited Benin in 1691 wrote that:

> Great Benin, where the king resides, is larger than Lisbon; all the streets run straight and as far as the eye can see. The houses are large, especially that of the king, which is richly decorated and has fine columns. The city is wealthy and industrious. It is so well governed that theft is unknown and the people live in such security that they have no doors to their houses.[18]

THE SPECIAL RELATIONSHIP: BENIN AND PORTUGAL

Portugal's voyage to Benin started a lengthy commercial and diplomatic inter-continental relationship that continued for over two centuries. The seeds for Benin–Portugal cooperation were laid 15

18   *Guardian*, 18 March 2016.

years before the Portuguese arrived in Benin. In 1470 the Portuguese found a small uninhabited island in the Atlantic Ocean off the West African coast and called it São Tomé (St Thomas). They decided to establish plantations on the island. Since São Tomé had no indigenous population, the Portuguese decided to buy slaves to work on its plantations. As Benin was only 400 miles away from São Tomé, it was within sailing distance and a source of slaves. In addition to slaves, Portugal also imported elephant tusks, palm oil, redwood, and gum from Benin, and in return gave silk (and other European fabrics), coral beads (which the Edo regarded as precious jewellery akin to gold and diamonds today), brass manilas (which was a form of currency), rum, and salt to Benin. Portuguese traders were so at home in Benin and did such a brisk business there that they built a factory at Ughoton (about 20 miles south-west of Benin City) and several of them had Bini wives and lovers.

'the law of God forbids it'

Trade and diplomatic relations between Benin and Portugal were so cordial and frequent that in 1514 the *oba* sent two of his ambassadors (whom the Portuguese referred to as 'Dom Antonio' and 'Dom Jorge') to Portugal to request Christian missionaries and weapons (including cannons) from Portugal. Benin's people had already demonstrated their interest in European weaponry that year when some of them seized a cannon from a Portuguese ship on the Benin River. This incident may have made Portugal vigilant because in the same year the crew of a Portuguese boat called *Sao Miguel* that was sailing in the Forcados River near Benin had orders to maintain tight security and to prevent any natives from accessing the boat's weapons.

While Portugal was enthusiastic about deepening its relationship with Benin, its assistance to Benin had strings attached. In December 1514, Portugal's King Manuel I agreed to send priests and Christian books to Benin. However, he found Benin's request for weapons problematic. In an ancient precursor to the manner in which in the modern era, America and European countries make aid and military assistance conditional on recipient states adopting their values such as capitalism and multi-party democracy, King Manuel declined to send the weapons until Benin's people converted to Christianity. Portugal had high hopes that Benin could be Christianised because its people already believed in a supreme god they called Osanobua. King Manuel sent a letter to the *oba* stating:

> We earnestly exhort you to receive the teachings of the Christian faith with that readiness we expect from a very good friend. For when we see that you have embraced the teachings of Christianity like a good and faithful Christian, there will be nothing in our realms with which we shall not be glad to favour you, whether it be arms or cannon and all other weapons of war for use against your enemies; of such things we have a great store, as Dom Jorge your ambassador will inform you. These things we are not sending you now, as he requested, because the law of God forbids it so long as you are ...[19]

The *oba* replied to King Manuel's letter, sent another envoy to Portugal in autumn 1515 (whom the Portuguese referred to as 'Pero Barroso'), allowed Portuguese priests into Benin City, and gave them consent to build a church and to baptise and teach his son to read.[20] The *oba's* Portuguese guests enjoyed his hospitality so much that in October 1516 Duarte Pires (a Portuguese royal emissary residing in Benin) wrote to King Manuel to inform him that:

> I am a friend of the King of Benin ... no part of his court is hidden from us, rather all the doors are open[21] ... We eat with his son ... When the Missionaries arrived the King of Benin was very delighted, the Missionaries went with the King to the war and remained a whole year. At the end of the year, in the month of August, the King ordered his son and those of his greatest

---

19 Ryder, 1961, pp. 234–5. The end of this sentence is incomplete due to a tear in the original document.
20 Ibid., p. 235.
21 Ibid., p. 239.

noblemen to become Christians, and he ordered a church to be built in Benin, and they learnt how to read and did it very well.[22]

'he needed leisure for such a deep mystery as this'

However, the Portuguese were sceptical about the *oba*'s commitment to Christianity and claimed that 'He sought the priests rather to make himself powerful against his neighbours with our favour than from a desire for baptism.'[23] Portugal's demand for the *oba* to convert to Christianity as a condition of providing military aid was extremely problematic since the *oba* was a divine king and the living embodiment of Edo traditional religion. Expecting him to abandon the religion of his ancestors and community was as realistic as expecting the Pope to abandon Catholicism and encourage the Vatican to replace Christianity with Buddhism.

When the Portuguese missionaries arrived in Benin in 1516 they found the *oba* engaged with one of his wars and thus he deferred the issue of Christian conversion until after the war's conclusion 'because he needed leisure for such a deep mystery as this'.[24] Inference from Portuguese accounts suggest that this *oba* died in late 1516 or early 1517. A Portuguese letter written in 1517 stated that the *oba* was a minor and that 'he is not ruling, except through two of his captains because he is a youth and under their control'.[25] If the 1516 *oba* died and his young son succeeded him in 1517, its portent would not have gone unnoticed in a society intensely preoccupied with finding and interpreting omens. The fact that Benin's king died shortly after permitting priests into Benin and authorising them to build a church would not have encouraged his subjects to convert to Christianity. Benin continued its warm friendliness towards Portugal (for example, it was customary for Benin to welcome visitors by washing their feet at Ughoton using water

---

22 Bradbury, 1959, p. 277.
23 Ijoma, 1982, p. 144.
24 Ryder, 1961, p. 235.
25 Ibid., p. 236.

from an ancient brass bowl which commemorated *Oba* Esigie) but without the mass Christian conversion that Portugal requested.

During another visit in 1538–39, Portuguese missionaries found that the young *oba* they baptised as a child more than 20 years earlier was still on the throne. However, as an adult, the *oba* seemed to have little more than an experimental interest in Christianity. Nonetheless, he recognised some benefits attached to Christianity, such as literacy. He employed Christians to teach Benin children to read and write. However, Portugal's insistence that Benin's people and their king should convert to Christianity was a bridge too far to cross for Benin. Portuguese emissaries and missionaries complained that the *oba*'s staff repeatedly blocked them from meeting with him to petition him regarding Christianity, and refused to provide interpreters for them. They turned to self-help and tried to learn the Edo language by themselves, until a Benin official casually told them that any Benin native caught teaching them Edo would be executed. The missionaries spent a fruitless year and a half trying to reach the *oba*, during which they engaged in a battle of wits with his staff to schedule a meeting with him. When they sent letters to the *oba*, his staff refused to deliver them. Portuguese missionaries even tried to deliver an alarm clock to the *oba* as a gift; knowing that it would arouse his curiosity enough for him to demand a meeting with the people who sent the gift. However, the *oba*'s staff saw through the cunning and simply returned the gift. An amusing and popular story states that an *oba* agreed to convert to Christianity on one condition (which he thought Portuguese missionaries would find impossible to fulfil): if they brought a white woman for him to marry. The missionaries were so determined to thwart this *oba*'s attempts to evade their religion that they left and returned with a white woman for him to marry.

'idolatries and diabolical invocations night and day'

Although the *oba* tried to meet the Portuguese halfway by allowing them to baptise his and other Edo children, his attachment to his traditional religion displeased his Portuguese allies. The Portuguese missionaries became exasperated and wrote home to their king to complain that the *oba* engaged in 'idolatries and diabolical invocations night and day'.[26] The Portuguese rarely documented the exact nature of the 'idolatries' they repeatedly complained about, however, subsequent British accounts were far more descriptive and grisly.

THE 'CITY OF BLOOD'

The topic of human sacrifice has received plenty of airtime in European writing about Benin. British officers who entered the abandoned Benin City in 1897 after invading and destroying it reported seeing horrendous scenes of blood and sacrifice with mutilated corpses laying around the city. The medical officer Dr Roth wrote in his diary: 'Dead and mutilated bodies seemed to be everywhere – by God! may I never see such sights again!'[27] Such gory and vivid accounts led Britons to conclude that Benin was a land of mass human sacrifice, and to nickname Benin City the 'City of Blood'. Many of the corpses that British officers saw were undoubtedly casualties of the British machine gun, artillery, and rocket fire which destroyed Benin City in what seemed to the denizens to be an apocalyptic fireball. Yet even if some corpses were casualties of a British military assault, the British allegations were not without foundation. Although these accounts were written by British enemies of Benin, their vivid descriptions and cross corroboration of each other are very convincing.

'mostly criminals who deserve death'

The stigma attached to the term 'human sacrifice' and the reluctance of Benin's people to admit to, or discuss it, makes it extremely difficult to provide more context. What has been presented as 'human sacrifice' in the writing of European observers was, from Benin's perspective, the capital punishment of criminals under its

26 Ijoma, 1982, p. 144
27 Roth, 1898, p. 218.

penal justice system, and the practice of its indigenous religion. In late 1897, officials who worked for the deposed *Oba* Ovonramwen claimed that Eweka 'made human sacrifices, and taught his son to do so too', and that 'The people who were kept for sacrifice were bad men, or men with bad sickness.'[28] Such sacrifices were conducted in a highly prescriptive way; and only at a few predetermined times a year. Animals such as cattle and chickens were also sacrificed during the religious rituals. At such occasions, murderers and other criminals, slaves, and those accused of witchcraft were executed to serve a dual purpose: to execute justice on the condemned and to provide them as atonements to the gods in order to pre-empt curses and other misfortunes such as droughts and epidemics. In a rare departure from the usual accounts of human sacrifice, the British anthropologist Henry Ling Roth (whose brother worked as the medical officer for the British invasion force in 1897) admitted that those killed 'are mostly criminals who deserve death'.[29] The sacrifice and offering of animals and people to the gods is similar to Old Testament Bible practices in which ancient Hebrews sacrificed animals to the Abrahamic God.

By 1652, Portuguese missionaries had not given up on Benin. However, the persistence of Father Felipe de Hijar and another missionary in entering the *oba*'s compound without invitation to witness an indigenous religious ceremony was the last straw. By their own admission they interrupted the ceremony and 'began speaking to the king and chiefs of the evil they were doing'.[30] This desecration of an indigenous religious rite so angered the *oba*'s staff that they finally tired of their nagging Portuguese guests, declared them *persona non grata*, and expelled them.

THE PORTUGUESE KING IN WARRI

While Benin had to endure the presence of Christian missionaries longer than it wanted to, the neighbouring Warri kingdom on

28   Read and Dalton, 1899, pp. 6–7.
29   Roth, 1903, p. 72.
30   Ryder, 1961, p. 245.

Benin's south-eastern border could not get enough Christian missionaries or as frequently as it wanted. In the mid to late sixteenth century, Portugal sent monks to Warri, and they built a settlement there they called 'Santo Agostinho'. Their efforts to Christianise Warri's indigenous Itsekiri ethnic group gained traction when a priest called Francisco a Mater Dei chopped down a sacred tree that Warri's people had shunned as they feared it was cursed. When no ill fate befell Dei, he gained enough esteem for the *Olu* (King) of Warri to give him permission to baptise the *olu*'s son and give him the Christian name Sebastian (after King Sebastian of Portugal). Sebastian (of Warri) in turn sent his oldest son Domingos to Portugal in 1600. Domingos lived in Portugal for over ten years, and after studying at the Augustinian and Jesuit Colleges in Lisbon, married a Portuguese noblewoman (the niece of the Count of Feira), returned to Warri with her, and succeeded his father as *Olu* of Warri.

Warri's lineage of Portuguese-speaking Christian kings continued for over 100 years. One of the most famous of them was on the throne in the mid-1600s, and many accounts of the time described him as a 'mulatto' named Dom Domingos II. This *olu* was either the bi-racial son of Domingos I (who studied in Portugal) or may be identified as a king called Oyenakpara who, according to Itsekiri oral traditions, was the son of a Warri princess and a Portuguese man. Regardless of his parentage, Domingos II spoke and wrote fluent Portuguese, wore Portuguese clothing, and walked with a sword by his side in a scabbard in the style of a Portuguese nobleman. On 20 November 1652 he wrote a letter to the Pope in Portuguese from 'Oery [*sic* – Warri] city of Santo Agostinho' pleading with the Pope to send priests to Warri, referring to Portugal's King John as 'my cousin', and insinuating that the Pope had mistakenly sent priests to:

> the Kingdom of Benin, a people neighbouring mine, who rejected the favour offered them and expelled the fathers from their Kingdom; nor did they tell the fathers anything about me and my Kingdom. I truly believe, Holy Father, that Your Holiness

intended these priests to come to me ... my kingdom is on the same coast adjoining Benin and distinguished from it only by the fact that mine is called Oery. I am acting as a preacher myself, as far as I am able, urging my subjects to trust in the mercy of God that all will soon be set in order ... I beg you therefore by the blood of Our Lord Jesus Christ to come to my aid and send me a mission of Capuchin fathers who ... will do great good to me and my kingdom ... I will give them all the help in my power and reliable interpreters so that they may bring my neighbour, the King of Benin, and others to the faith ... I am writing to my cousin King John of Portugal asking him to help me by assisting the fathers with their passage and the necessary provisions.[31]

This letter's existence is virtually unknown; which is remarkable as it is probably the oldest surviving letter ever written by a Nigerian. Although the Pope responded favourably to the letter and a Catholic and literate minority population emerged in Warri, the inability to keep sending priests (and the high mortality rate of those that went to Benin and Warri) meant that Christianity was largely an incubated religion of the Itsekiri royalty and a few others, the religion's flame could not be kept burning, and Itsekiri Christians relapsed to their traditional religions.

Christianity's inability to take deep roots in the region had a knock-on effect on trade. Although non-military trade between Benin and Portugal continued, Portugal imposed an arms embargo on Benin. Benin somehow circumvented the arms embargo because Benin soldiers obtained and used firearms during at least one of Benin's sixteenth-century wars. There are even reports that Portuguese mercenaries marched alongside Benin soldiers in at least one war (possibly against the Igala), and helped force the Igala army to retreat after the shattering experience of being on the receiving end of cannon fire for the first time demoralised the Igala soldiers. While it is unlikely that the Portuguese government sanctioned this involvement in a Benin military campaign, the Portuguese traders

31   Ryder, 1960, pp. 11–12.

in Benin had a motive to support Benin's wars (even if surreptitiously without their government's approval) because Benin sold the prisoners of war that it captured to Portuguese slave traders and Christian missionaries.

Whatever his moral views on slavery, the *oba* recognised that it deteriorated his kingdom's economy by draining its working population and military recruits. In the sixteenth century the *oba* outlawed the sale of male slaves. The Benin–Portugal alliance lost momentum and never recovered. The two sides began to regard each other as difficult and expendable trading partners. The cross embargoes of slaves and weapons hurt Benin more than Portugal. Portugal found other trading partners (such as Congo) and sources for its cherished imports of peppers (India) and slaves – in neighbouring lands to Benin's south (Warri) and west (Ijebu), and in other areas that it described as '*Licomin*' and '*Terra Nova*' (Oduduwa-land). The Atlantic coastline to Benin's south became so notorious as a source of slave supply that it was called the 'Slave Coast'. Dutch and English explorers and merchants also arrived in Benin and jostled with the Portuguese to make conflicting bargains with Benin – each with their own languages and trading terms which further complicated economic relations with Benin.

'WHODUNNIT'

It is very difficult to identify the reigning *oba* when the Portuguese first visited Benin and which *oba* is responsible for the various actions and incidents described above. Both the indigenous Edo chroniclers and European visitors are to blame for this problem: the former for not paying sufficient attention to the reign lengths and ages of their monarchs, and the latter for not recording the names of the Benin kings they met. The challenge of matching the chronology of events to specific *oba* reigns is made even more formidable by multiple indigenous oral traditions which contradict each other, confusing syntax errors in written accounts, and that after being coronated, *obas* stopped using their personal names and adopted regal *noms de guerre*.

The names of three *obas* in particular frequently recur in Benin's oral traditions regarding its legendary exploits and relations with Portugal: Ewuare, Ozolua, and Esigie. Their names are synonymous with Benin's most famous advancements, conquests, and innovations (to an extent that their legends are amplified to include events that preceded or followed their reigns). For example, radiocarbon dating confirmed that some parts of Benin City were built in the eleventh century, two centuries before the *oba* dynasty which is widely credited as the architects of all that is good about Benin.[32] The key *obas* to identify are the reigning *oba* when Portugal first arrived in Benin, the *oba* who sent his ambassadors 'Dom Antonio' and 'Dom Jorge' to Portugal in 1514, and the reigning *oba* when Britain first arrived in Benin in 1553.

Fusing Benin's oral history alongside accounts that European visitors wrote in the fifteenth and sixteenth centuries gives very strong clues about the identity of the *obas* who established strong relations with Portugal. Different conflicting oral accounts claim that the Portuguese first came to Benin during the reign of one of Ewuare, Ozolua, or Esigie. The Moor-Roupell report referenced above suggested that the Portuguese first arrived during *Oba* Esigie's reign, but the report phrased it very confusingly by stating that after becoming frail and immobile in his later years, Esigie had a habit of telling his staff 'that he was a white man when he was born, and he wanted to see white man again before he died' [*sic*].[33] This confusing statement that Esigie 'was a white man' set off wild speculation that Esigie was bi-racial or part Portuguese. However, the 'was' in the 'he *was* a white man' seems to be a typographical error which should have stated that Esigie '*saw*' a white man when he was young. A horrid syntax error is the only way to make sense of the remainder of this passage which also stated that Esigie sent a delegation from Benin to visit Portugal as he wanted to meet white men again before he died. If the Portuguese had been visiting Benin since Esigie was a child, then it means that Joao de Aveiro's first

32   Posnansky, 1975, p. 119.
33   Read and Dalton, 1899, p. 5.

visit to Benin in 1485 occurred during the reign of Esigie's father Ozolua or grandfather Ewuare.

OZOLUA THE CONQUEROR

The next significant 'who was it?' question is the identity of the *oba* that sent his ambassadors 'Dom Antonio' and 'Dom Jorge' to Portugal in 1514 to request Christian missionaries and weapons. *Obas* Ozolua and Esigie were warrior kings who kept their armies very busy. Ozolua was reputed to have prevailed in 200 battles and was nicknamed *Ozolua n'Ibaromi* ('Ozolua the Conqueror'). Ozolua and Esigie presided over two of Benin's most famous wars; against the Esan people of Uromi and the Igala people of Idah, respectively. Since Ozolua and Esigie ruled in the sixteenth century and are famed for their military campaigns, they are very likely candidates to request military assistance from Portugal. When the Portuguese visited in 1516, they found the *oba* at war. Although the Portuguese did not state where this 1516 war took place or whom it was against, this *oba* may have died during or shortly after this war because by August 1517, the reigning *oba* was so young that two Benin officials were appointed as regents. This suggests that the reigning *oba* in 1516 probably died in late 1516 or early 1517, and was succeeded by his young son. Since Esigie reigned until he was elderly, he was very unlikely to have been leading his troops at the warfront in 1516 during the final year of his life. If the 1516 wartime *oba* was someone other than Esigie, his father Ozolua is the most likely candidate. If an *oba* died in the midst of a war in 1516 or 1517, then that would also dovetail with Benin's oral history which states that Ozolua died during the Uromi war against the Esan people.[34] If Ozolua was the *oba* that died in 1516 or 1517, then the successor boy king who was baptised as a youth would have been Ozolua's son and successor Esigie. If Esigie was still a boy when he first came to the throne, it would also explain his mother Idia's extraordinary protectiveness and support for her son who was still a minor.

---

34 This would also mean that Ozolua died about 10–12 years later than the dates usually given for his death.

On 12 August 1553 the first British expedition to Benin commanded by Captain Thomas Windham set sail from Portsmouth. The three-ship[35] convoy of the supposedly British expedition had an experienced Portuguese-Jewish co-captain named Antonio Anes Pinteado. The fact that Pinteado and Windham arrived in Benin before one of them killed the other was a minor miracle. Pinteado had led an eventful life. He was a former member of the Portuguese royal court but fled to England to evade imprisonment after losing favour. While in England he convinced English traders to embark on an expedition to West Africa in search of the economic opportunities there. His life was about to get even more eventful. During the journey Windham (who at times behaved more like a pirate than an emissary of the British government) flew into a rage, called Pinteado 'This rascally Jew', and threatened to 'cut off his ears and nail them to the mast'.[36] Fortunately, Windham did not carry out his threat. When the expedition's members arrived in Benin, they were astonished to discover that Benin's 'king … had been brought up to speak the Portuguese language from his youth'.[37]

Fortunately for the British crew, this *oba's* command of Portuguese was so fluent that he communicated with them by conversing with Pinteado in Portuguese. Acting on the *oba's* orders, Benin's people provided the British crew with 80 tonnes of peppers within 30 days, and the *oba* was so generous that he even offered them credit if the goods on their ships were not enough to pay for the peppers. In 1997 the then reigning *Oba* of Benin Solomon Akenzua mentioned '*Oba* Orhogbua, who spoke Portuguese, like his father, *Oba* Esigie'.[38] Since both Orhogbua and Esigie reigned in the sixteenth century and we know that two sixteenth-century *obas* allowed the Portuguese to teach their sons Portuguese and how to read and write between 1516 and 1538, the reigning *oba* by the time Britain arrived in 1553 was probably Esigie or his son and successor Orhogbua. Thus, a reasonable summary of the reigning *obas* during

---

35 Three ships named the *Primrose*, the *Lion*, and the *Moon*.
36 Kerr, 1812, p. 225.
37 Read and Dalton, 1899, p. 3.
38 Akpolokpolo, 1997, p. 30.

each inaugural point of contact with European nations can be sum-
marised as follows:

* First *oba* to meet the Portuguese: Ewuare or Ozolua
* First *oba* to send ambassadors to Portugal: Ozolua or Esigie
* First *oba* to meet the British: Esigie or Orhogbua.

THE 'OGANE'

The exchange of ambassadors between Benin and Portugal
unearthed intriguing information regarding the ancient origins
of Benin's monarchy, which both contradicts and reinforces its
oral history. Medieval European governments usually asked their
explorers to bring back economic, military, and political intelligence reports about the people and states they found. When the
first Portuguese expedition to Benin returned to Portugal in 1487,
the expedition's leader Joao Afonso de Aveiro brought back with
him a Benin indigene[39] who was an emissary of the *Oba* of Benin.
Both de Aveiro and this emissary provided Portugal's King Joao
(John) II with insightful intelligence reports regarding Benin and
its neighbours which included:

what they had been told by the inhabitants of those regions, was
that to the east of the King of Beny [*sic* – Benin] at twenty moons'
journey – which according to their account, and the slow pace
at which they travel, would be about two hundred and fifty of
our leagues – there lived the most powerful monarch of those
parts whom they called Ogane. Among the pagan princes of
the territories of Beny he was held in as great veneration as are
the Supreme Pontiffs with us. In accordance with a very ancient
custom, the Kings of Beny, on ascending the throne, sent ambassadors to him with rich gifts to inform him that by the decease
of their predecessor they had succeeded to the Kingdom of Beny,
and to request him to confirm them in the same. As a sign of

---

39 Some accounts claim that this emissary was an Olokun priest from Ughoton
(Egharevbal, 1968, p. 27).

confirmation this Prince Ogane sent them a staff and a head-piece, fashioned like a Spanish helmet, made all of shining brass, in place of a sceptre and crown. He also sent a cross, of the same brass, and shaped like those worn by the Commendadores, to be worn round the neck like something religious and holy. Without these emblems the people would consider that they did not reign lawfully, nor could they call themselves true kings.[40]

In 1507 the Portuguese explorer Duarte Pacheco Pereira (who visited Benin four times between the late fifteenth and early six-teenth centuries) wrote about a 'great lord who is called Hooguanee. He is considered among the Negroes like the Pope among our-selves.'[41] The 'Ogane' and 'Hooguanee' in these two accounts very likely refer to the same esteemed person whom Benin held in Pope-like reverence. The identity of this enigmatic 'Prince Ogane' who had confirming authority over the *Oba* of Benin, and who lived 'twenty moons' to the east of Benin has been a long-running and controversial mystery for over 500 years.

'free and exempt from all servitudes, and privileged in his native country'

Eyewitnesses and physical evidence corroborated the vivid testi-mony that Benin and Portuguese informants provided about the Ogane. When ambassadors from Benin arrived in Portugal in 1540, the Portuguese historian Joao de Barros noticed that one of them was wearing one of the crosses described in de Aveiro's account regarding the Ogane. De Barros claimed that when he asked the Benin ambassador how he obtained the cross, the ambassador replied that when an *Oba* of Benin dies, it is customary for ambas-sadors from Benin to travel to the Ogane to report the death to him. The Ogane then ensured that as 'a kind of reward for the labours of such a journey the ambassador receives a small cross ... which is thrown round his neck to signify that he is free and exempt from

40 Ryder, 1965, p. 26.
41 Bradbury, 1959, p. 276.

all servitudes, and privileged in his native country'.[42] Some of the Benin Bronzes depict people wearing Maltese-style crosses across their chests, helmets, and carrying staffs – exactly as both de Aveiro and the *Oba* of Benin's emissaries reported to King Joao II and de Barros.

Since the traditions of links between Benin and Ife have been transmitted orally for centuries, they are frequently dismissed as folk tales without supporting evidence. Yet these Portuguese accounts about the 'Ogane' both contradict and support these oral traditions. The instinct to reflexively conclude that the Ogane is the *Ooni* of Ife is made very difficult by at least three contradictory pieces of information in the Portuguese accounts that sound nothing like the *ooni*. Firstly, de Aveiro's account claimed that the Ogane lived 'twenty moons' journey' or 250 leagues to the east of Benin. This is a massive geographical discrepancy as 250 leagues (over 750 miles) east of Benin is in modern-day Cameroon, whereas Ife is over 100 miles to Benin's *west*. If the Portuguese geography is taken literally, the Ogane could not have resided in Ife. Secondly, the *Ooni* of Ife did not usually give crosses and metal helmets as rewards, nor have crosses been excavated in Ife. Thirdly, the people in the Benin Bronzes wearing the crosses, helmets, and staffs that the Ogane supposedly gave to them had distinctive facial markings that are alien to Benin indigenes, and which resemble those of the Igala and Nupe ethnic groups.

'it is common with all negroes, to exalt their native country above all others'

When the Scottish explorer Hugh Clapperton visited the Nupe area in the late 1820s, a local official informed him that Benin's people often visited Nupe to trade, and more startling: 'that the Nyife [*sic* – Nupe] people and those of Benin were the same people; that Benin paid tribute to Nyffe'.[43] Clapperton dismissed this testimony because according to him, it 'is common with all negroes,

---

42   Tunis, 1979, p. 166.
43   Clapperton, 1829, p. 122.

to exalt their native country above all others, in their accounts to strangers'.[44] Although problematic, these discrepancies do not conclusively prove that the Ogane, 'Hooguanee', and the *Ooni* of Ife are not one and the same person.

THE LEGEND OF PRESTER JOHN

The Portuguese had a long-standing fascination with a mythical Christian ruler they called 'Prester John' whom they believed ruled a mighty empire in central Africa. Portugal's Holy Grail-style quest to find Prester John led two Britons to dryly describe it as 'their favourite geographical dream'.[45] The Portuguese were greatly excited when they heard about the Ogane who handed out crosses to his vassals because it coincided with, and reinforced, their belief in Prester John's existence.

Portuguese belief that the Ogane was Prester John heavily influenced their geographical calculations and presumptions about where he lived. The reference to the Ogane residing east of Benin was as much based on their pre-existing assumptions as it was on translations of what their Benin informant told them. A Benin informant was very unlikely to have told the Portuguese that the Ogane lived 250 leagues 'east' of Benin. This was almost certainly a Portuguese insertion. European concepts such as 'east' and 'west' would have been utterly meaningless to a fifteenth- or sixteenth-century Edo, in a society which determined geographical directions using lunar metrics. In addition, Ife has long been poetically known as 'the land from where the sun rises'. If a Benin informant described it this way it would have further amplified Portuguese conviction that the Ogane lived east of Benin. Since the Portuguese *wanted* the Ogane and Prester John to be the same person, and believed that he was the Emperor of Ethiopia, the only way of coalescing the Ogane, Prester John, and the Ethiopian emperor was to situate him east of Benin. Despite being brilliant engineers, explorers, and sailors, the Iberians were not always great cartographers. The Portuguese

---

44   Ibid., p. 122.
45   Read and Dalton, 1898, p. 364.

drew scandalously inaccurate maps of ancient Africa, and Spaniards who landed in the Americas thought they were in India, and did not realise their mistake until several decades later. The haphazard sixteenth-century European knowledge of African geography and Portuguese confirmation bias explain why the Portuguese accounts claimed that the Ogane resided east of Benin. If the word 'east' is removed from the Portuguese account, the Ogane's identity suddenly becomes far less mysterious.

OGHENE

The Portuguese never found Prester John, nor were they aware of intricacies in Edo pronunciation. Until today, Binis still refer to the *Ooni* of Ife as the *Oghene*.[46] 'Ogane' is probably a Portuguese mis-transliteration of Oghene. When an *Oba* of Benin died, it was customary to remove and transport some of his body parts to Ife for burial there, and the *ooni* in turn sent messengers to Benin with congratulatory gifts for the new *oba*. In the first half of the twentieth century a British colonial officer named Henry Lewis Ward-Price met the then reigning *Oba* of Benin Eweka II who:

> showed me a brass crucifix which was attached to a cord around his neck ... when he pressed the crucifix to his forehead, and prayed for the Oni [*sic*] of Ife, the Alafin [*sic*] of Oyo and the Oba of Benin (that is himself); after which he prayed for all the [Oduduwan] kings. This had for long been the custom, he said, whether the Oba was a Christian or not.[47]

Even if we dismiss these accounts as latter-day attempts to give legitimacy to a fictitious ancient folk tale, it is difficult to explain why Benin's monarchs would falsely link themselves with, and give legitimacy to, a faraway kingdom at Ife, thereby giving foreigners the credit for establishing their lineage.

---

46 *Oghene n'Uhe* ('Oghene of Uhe' or *Ooni* of Ife). Oghene is also the Isoko and Urhobo word for God.

47 Eisenhofer and Egharevba, 1995, p. 150.

The similarities in royal administration and taxonomy between Benin, Ife, and Oyo are difficult to explain away as coincidence or mimicry and give further credibility to the oral traditions regarding ancestral links between them. For example, *oba* means 'king' in the languages spoken in the Oduduwan areas, and the crown and ceremonial attire of the *Oba* of Benin are remarkably similar to that of his Oduduwan counterparts. While meeting with *Oba* Ovonramwen in 1892, Lt-Colonel Galway noticed that 'on his head was a coral erection of quaint design' and that 'The King's face was partly hidden by a sort of visor'.[48] The 'coral erection of quaint design' and 'visor' that Galway saw was a sacred crown embroidered with coral beads – which as discussed in Chapter 5, was a special privilege given only to kings descended directly from Oduduwa. A council of seven officials known as the *Uzama* advised the *Oba* of Benin in a way similar to how the seven-member *Oyo Mesi* advise the *Alaafin* of Oyo. The *Uzama*'s titles and responsibilities also correspond to those of the *Oyo Mesi*. Other officials in the *Oba* of Benin's court also held titles that were functionally and phonetically identical or similar to those in the Oduduwn areas.[49]

The cross corroboration by informants from Benin, Ife, and Oyo, British and Portuguese explorers, British colonial officials, and by the Benin Bronzes, provides a mountain of supporting evidence regarding Benin royal links with Ife that is difficult (if not impossible) to dismiss.

Nonetheless, there are some unresolved mysteries about the relationship between Benin and Ife. The origin of veneration for Ife as the source of political and spiritual authority for Benin and Oduduwa-land remains obscure. Unlike Oyo, ancient Ife did not have a military or government that was significantly more powerful than that of its neighbours. Hence, we still do not know how or why Ife attracts so much respect from its neighbours. Another mystery

---

48 Galway, 1930, p. 235.
49 For example, the senior member of the Uzama that crowns the *Oba* of Benin is called Oliha, whereas the corresponding official that crowns the *Olowo* (King) of Owo is called Olisa. The Benin crown prince and heir apparent to the throne is called Edaiken, whereas his Owo counterpart is called Idaniken.

concerns the people depicted in the Benin Bronzes wearing the Maltese-style crosses and other paraphernalia that the Ogane supposedly gave to them. Deciphering how West Africans in Benin obtained crosses which resemble honorific insignia of the Knights Templar is a challenging puzzle to resolve. After the Knights Templar were dissolved in 1312, Portugal's King Denis I created the Order of Christ in 1319 as a refuge for its surviving knights. Knights from the Order of Christ became the arrowheads of Portuguese exploration and their cross insignia was prominently emblazoned on the masts of Portuguese ships that sailed to West Africa. Several Portuguese citizens that visited Benin were also members of the Order of Christ, and King Domingos of Warri was also awarded the Order of Christ after he studied in Portugal during the early 1600s. The reverence that Portuguese missionaries paid to the Order's cross symbol would not have escaped the attention of Benin's people. It is very likely that the crosses did not come from the Ogane, but instead entered the consciousness of Benin's people due to their frequent appearance and association with, Portuguese visitors to Benin, their power, and their religion. However, the identity of the people shown wearing the crosses is more puzzling. The indigenous cross wearers (who were supposedly Benin's messengers to the 'Ogane') have 'cat's whiskers' scars on their cheeks. This is a stark contrast to most other Bronzes which depict Benin's people with keloid scars on their foreheads rather than on their cheeks. The facial incisions of the people wearing the Ogane's gifts resemble those of non-Edo people such as the Igala or Nupe.

Benin's sculpting guild did not only make sculptures of their kinfolk, but also made sculptures of their neighbours and even enemies. For example, during the reign of Esigie's son *Oba* Orhogbua, Benin won a war against people whom nineteenth-century members of the *oba*'s court referred to as 'Igbon' and whom they said were from 'a country near the Niger'.[50] After capturing the 'Igbon' king and several of his soldiers, Orhogbua ordered his sculptors to make sculptures of them, some of which showed the defeated prisoners

---

50 Read and Dalton, 1899, p. 6.

of war being guarded at knife point by Benin soldiers. While there is no contemporary Nigerian ethnic group called 'Igbon', one of Benin's most legendary wars was against enemies from a land near the River Niger and whose people were renowned for facial scars that are virtually identical to those of the supposed Ogane messengers who wore crosses. During the Idah war in the sixteenth century between Benin and the neighbouring Igala people, the Igala nearly overran Benin, but Benin's forces repelled the Igala in one of Benin's most famous military victories. A 'comeback' victory in a war like this which severely threatened Benin's survival is so significant that it would justify the *oba* commemorating the victory with sculptures. It is almost certainly the 'Igbon' war referred to above. If so, it yet again introduces new twists to Benin's history. It would mean that the Benin–Igala war did not occur during the reign of *Oba* Esigie as almost unanimously assumed, but instead occurred later during the reign of his son and successor, Orhogbua.

While it was not unusual for Benin's sculptors to make bronze sculptures of their enemies, a bewildering unexplained question is why Benin's leaders allowed vanquished foes and prisoners of war to wear sacred emblems provided by the Ogane and/or which were inspired by an ancient order of European knights. Since the Benin and Ife royal courts are secretive and conceal information about their sacred rituals from outsiders, this last mystery is likely to remain incomprehensible forever.

WHAT MIGHT HAVE BEEN

The legacy of Benin's ancient relations with Portugal and other European countries still survives over 500 years later in the languages spoken in Nigeria and in countries such as Equatorial Guinea and São Tomé. Due to the frequent trading between Benin and Europeans, an expressive staccato language evolved in the southern coastal areas of West Africa where Europeans traded. This new language hatched out of Portuguese and became the language of commerce between Europeans and West Africans. It incorporated terms such as *sabi* (to know), which is derived from the Portuguese word *saber*, and *pikin* (from the Portuguese word for small – *pequenho*), which was used to refer to children. Today this language's descendant is one of the most widely spoken in Nigeria. The BBC has a version of its website in this language and words from it are found in the lyrics of popular modern music. In contemporary times it is called *pidgin*. The Portuguese creole language spoken in countries such as Equatorial Guinea and São Tomé also includes words from the Edo language (a linguistic legacy of the slaves that Benin sold to Portugal's plantation colonies in those areas).

Benin's relations with Portugal can be viewed as a series of missed opportunities and 'what if?' questions. Benin had an almost 400-year head start over many other Nigerian societies in access to European education, materials, technology, and weapons. It also had several other advantages to emerge as the pre-eminent economic and political power throughout what is now Nigeria. The first was favourable topography. Unlike Kanem-Borno, Oyo, and the Sokoto Caliphate, it was not landlocked. Benin had a coastline and access to the ocean which enabled it to trade and obtain goods from another continent, and its territories were crisscrossed by navigable rivers. Secondly, unlike most other Nigerian communities who met Europeans for the first time at the wrong end of a colonial machine gun, Benin met and traded with the Portuguese as equals – outside a colonial context of conqueror and colonised. At times, Portugal seemed like the more eager partner in the relationship, and it was Portugal that repeatedly sent ambassadors and traders, and promised even greater economic and military aid, only if Benin would adopt Christianity. Since Benin had leverage, its leaders could have made stronger demands for Portuguese engineers, navigators, ships, teachers, and weapons – instead of coral beads for their crowns and European fabrics. Benin's military encounter with Britain in 1897 may have unfolded differently in an alternate chain of events in which by the time Britain arrived, Benin already had a large stockade of Portuguese weapons and centuries of experience with handling military grade firearms.

There is, however, a darker alternate history that may have unfolded for Benin's neighbours. Had Benin capitalised on Portuguese technology and weapons to amplify its power, its neighbours would have been the most likely victims. In the ancient world it was rare for empires that were far more economically and militarily advanced to treat their disadvantaged neighbours kindly. Given the twitchy trigger fingers of warrior *obas* such as Ewuare, Ozolua, and Esigie, a likely alternate scenario is that a Benin Empire flush with Portuguese cannons and guns may have extended its boundaries even further in all directions. Their most likely victims would have been their familiar Igala enemies to their north, the Oduduwan areas to their west, and if they crossed the River Niger, the areas of Igboland on the east side of the River Niger.

The repercussions of *Obas* Ozolua's and Esigie's refusal to accept Portugal's conditions for enhanced trade transcended religion. The *obas* missed an opportunity to use Portuguese resources to give themselves an unassailable head start that would have placed Benin far ahead of its Nigerian contemporaries. Other Nigerians later discovered in the nineteenth and twentieth centuries (but Benin failed to realise 250–300 years earlier) that Christianity had a secular secret weapon attached to it: literacy. Wherever Christian missionaries went, they acted not only as proselytisers of their faith but also as proxy school teachers. The massive twentieth-century boom in mission school education in Nigeria occurred partly because Nigerians realised that their British colonisers seemed to store the secrets of their knowledge and technology inside a source that had hitherto been incomprehensible to them: books written in Latin script. Medieval Benin preserved its culture and resisted a Portuguese theological takeover, at a price that delayed its downfall but made it more destructive. What Benin did not accept from Portugal when it had a choice and leverage, it was forced to accept 380 years later by force after its capital city and king's and queen mother's palaces were reduced to smoke and ash, its king overthrown and exiled forever, its prized ancestral heirlooms looted and scattered across the world, and its people were on their knees and at the mercy of British conquerors.

8
A Remarkable and Mysterious People

A reader of the existing writing about the Igbo people would be tempted to believe that Igbo history began in 1967. The Nigerian civil war of 1967–70 (in which Igbos were the primary protagonists and victims) has preoccupied Igbos' psyche, and dominated others' perception of them, to such an extent that it is the overwhelming theme in writing about Igbos. Written works about Igbos rarely look back before the civil war to the pre-colonial period. Pre-colonial Igbo history is not as well known or studied as other Nigerian ethnic groups such as the Hausa, Fulani, Edo, and Kanuri because Igbos did not have large pre-colonial kingdoms or states, and because European explorers did not travel into their thickly forested homeland until the nineteenth century. Even when British colonial officers began to record Igbo history in the twentieth century, they did so almost grudgingly. Igbos spent more time than any other part of Nigeria in fighting against British colonial authorities. Hence, the British were more concerned with crushing the persistently infuriating rebellions of people they described as 'a population whose character I gather is not peaceable'[1] and 'constitutionally lazy and treacherous'[2] than they were about learning their history or trying to understand their culture. Igbos did not help themselves either. Their recording of their pre-colonial history was fragmented because their writing system was not as widely known as *Ajami*, nor was it committed to recording history, and they did not employ professional historians to preserve their history to the same extent as their western and northern neighbours. Hence, Igbos were a mystery to outsiders until the twentieth century. These are the

[1] Hyam, 1968, p. 541.
[2] Rudkin, 1907, p. 434.

challenges that one faces when trying to write about a people that are rarely understood, and frequently misunderstood by outsiders.

Despite the paucity of written records, archaeology and oral tradition plugs the gaps in the history of ancient Igboland.

WHO ARE THEY?

The River Niger bisects the southern part of Nigeria now generally accepted to be Igboland into western and eastern segments. The vast majority of Igboland is on the river's eastern side in the inland areas of south-east Nigeria, while the western segment (whose people are often referred to in modern times as 'Anioma', 'Ika-Igbo', or 'Ikwerre') is on the river's immediate western side, on the outlying areas of the Benin kingdom.

Identifying who Igbos are is a challenge. The origin of the word 'Igbo' is obscure. Oral tradition states that when Oduduwa arrived at Ile-Ife in south-west Nigeria, he and his group met and expelled people called 'Igbo'. However, these 'Igbo' people were another Oduduwan group, and not the same Igbos who now reside in south-east Nigeria. 'Igbo' is a fairly modern ethnic descriptor that became common only in the nineteenth–twentieth centuries to describe disparate groups of people who previously referred to themselves by cultural names such as Abam, Aro, Ezza, Ngwa, Nri, Ohuhu, or by using geographic descriptors to refer to their towns (such as *Enu-Ugwu* ('hill-top'), which has now been Anglicised to 'Enugu'). Although these groups had similar cultures, history, and languages, they did not regard themselves as one until the nineteenth and twentieth centuries. Even then, some of those who are described as Igbo were, and remain, hostile or reluctant to being described as such.

While the origin stories of Borgu, Hausaland, and the Oduduwan areas regarding Kisra, Bayajidda, and Oduduwa, respectively, try to create a common origin for disparate groups, those of the Igbo do the opposite. Igbo traditions of origin are usually limited to a clan, town, or village, and do not provide one macro story of origin for all Igbo sub-groups. They instead explain how each group is different from its neighbouring groups. For example, the Ngwa clan of the Igbo (who live in Abia State) have a colourful myth about their origin. According to this myth, the Ngwa patriarchs were a group of people who migrated away from a village called Umunoha near Owerri. While travelling, they stopped beside a river to rest and eat. As they were cooking yams beside the river, the river's water level began to rise. Three brothers[3] among the group hurriedly boiled and ate their yams, packed up their belongings, and crossed to the other side of the river, leaving behind the rest of the group who had decided to roast their yams. The three brothers were given the name '*Ngwa*' ('quick') on account of the quick manner of their crossing, while those who roasted their yams and remained on the other side of the river were called '*Ohuhu*' ('roasters'). Until today, the Ngwa still refer to their non-Ngwa neighbours as *Ohuhu*. Although such foundational myths serve little purpose other than to identify 'us' and 'others' among Igbo sub-groups, they are very common.

This lack of a unifying narrative created space for lots of speculative theories about Igbo origins to emerge. The English clergyman George Thomas Basden believed that some Igbo customs indicated Jewish influence and that their 'language also bears several interesting parallels with the Hebrew idiom'.[4] An Igbo wrote in the eighteenth century about 'the strong analogy which ... appears to prevail in the manners and customs of my countrymen and those of the Jews'[5] and described multiple similarities between Igbo and Jewish culture such as 'We practised circumcision like the Jews, and made offerings and feasts on that occasion in the same manner as they did[6] ... we had many purifications and washings; indeed; almost as many, and used on the same occasions, if my recollection does not fail me, as the Jews'.[7] Despite there being no archaeological evidence to support these claims of Igbo Jewish origin, Igbos have been nicknamed 'The Jews of Africa'.

---

3   Ukwu, Nwoha, and Avosi.
4   Basden, 1921, p. 31.
5   Equiano, 1789, p. 25.
6   Ibid., p. 20.
7   Ibid., p. 21.

'the Igbo knows no king'

Nigeria's indigenous 'Nollywood' film industry is replete with films that depict 'kings' in pre-colonial Igbo society. The vast majority of such kings are pure fantasy and never existed. A striking characteristic of several ethnic groups (such as the Igbo, Annang, Ibibio, and Ekoi) that inhabited the area which became south-east Nigeria was that their communities lacked paramount rulers. Leadership rarely extended beyond a family or a village of a few dozen or few hundred people. Igbos are the archetype for such decentralised social organisation and have a maxim of *Igbo amaghi eze* ('the Igbo knows no king').

'These Ibo are intensely democratic'

Pre-colonial Igbo society operated as an idiosyncratic democracy. The oldest male member of each family or clan that claimed descent from a common ancestor usually exercised authority over his lineage and was called upon to mediate disputes between different households in the same lineage. Upon his death, his authority transmitted to the next oldest male. The different lineage leaders belonged to a village council called *Ndi Ama Ala* ('The People of the Land'),[8] which presided over matters affecting the entire village. *Ndi Ama Ala* was like a people's parliament, and its proceedings were remarkably democratic. Any adult male had the right to attend and speak at the council's meetings. Hence power was decentralised, and each lineage group was represented and had the assurance that decisions affecting them could not be taken without their consent. As late as 1937, a British anthropologist working in south-east Nigeria noted that:

> These Ibo [*sic*] are intensely democratic, recognizing no central tribal authority and though coming apparently from the same stock and speaking the same language (although with strong dif-

---

8   This can also be translated as 'The People of the Community'.

ferences) are curiously individualistic. Their compatriots, living in another village-area only a few miles away but unrelated by kinship, are considered as 'foreigners' ... Daily methods of farming, methods of building, taboos, religious conceptions, vary bewilderingly so that the investigator finds, after months of work, that he has still nothing but bits and pieces that form no coherent whole.[9]

Pre-colonial Igbos were not the only decentralised society. Ancient Vikings in northern Europe also lived in decentralised 'stateless' societies, and had people's councils like Igbos did. Other examples of such decentralised ethnic groups in Nigeria include the Idoma and Tiv, who lived in the middle area of Nigeria, sandwiched between the northern Muslim areas and the south.

Igbos never recognised one person or political authority as their ruler. Each village or town was largely autonomous, and it was common for its indigenes to claim a family blood affiliation to each other through descent from a common ancestor. The importance of lineages is encapsulated by the fact that many Igbo town and village names have a prefix of *Umu* (children) and a suffix consisting of the name of the patriarch or lineage leader that the town or village traces their ancestry to. Hence, village names such as Umu-Ocha ('children of Ocha') and Umu-Oba ('children of Oba') are legion in Igboland. The Ngwa sub-group of the Igbo has a community called Mgboko Ama Iri (literally: 'The Ten Compounds of Mgboko'), a group of ten villages which claim descent from the same ancient ancestor. Despite having a population of several thousands, these ten villages still consider each other as family, and their indigenes are forbidden to marry each other (they would regard such marriages as incestuous).

Annang, Efik, Ejagham, Ibibio, and Igbo communities that did not have kings and political leaders nonetheless had other mechanisms for maintaining social control. In Igboland one of these was *Omenala* ('The ways of the land'), which was akin to a pre-colonial anti-immorality and anti-criminal code based on the morals,

---

9   Leith-Ross, 1937, p. 206.

taboos, rituals, and sanctions of the earth goddess Ala. Spiritual prohibitions and the fear of invoking supernatural sanctions were not the only methods of maintaining social order in decentralised societies.

Although many contemporary West African secret societies exist mainly to provide entertainment, in the pre-colonial era, secret societies were vital for preserving social order. Across pre-colonial West Africa secret societies had important functions such as preparing and initiating youths into adulthood, as a way to educate children, regulating societal morality, while others emerged only at times of public pageantry. The *Poro* and *Sande* societies of the Mande people of Liberia and Sierra Leone are vital to their societies' social cohesion. The most prominent sodality in pre-colonial south-east Nigeria and western Cameroon was the so-called 'Leopard' secret society known as *Ekpe* among the Efik, *Ekpo* by the Ibibio and Igbo, and *Mgbe* by the Ejagham.

The term 'secret society' is an oxymoron. The existence of societies such as *Ekpo* was not itself a secret and their existence was well known. However, their activities were shrouded in mystery and non-members knew almost nothing about what they did. Their members had excellent motivation to maintain their organisation's secrets as disclosing them was punishable by death. *Ekpo* was a multi-faceted cross between a masonic lodge, a covert intelligence agency, a political cabinet, and a druid cult.

Although contemporary *Ekpo* members are now regarded as no more intimidating than a scarecrow, in pre-colonial times they had a terrifying 'boogeyman' mystique. *Ekpo* means 'ghost' in the Ibibio language. This was apt as *Ekpo* members often claimed to be reincarnated dead ancestors, wore terrifying costumes and masks, portrayed themselves as supernatural beings, and performed judicial functions such as the execution of criminals. A British colonial district officer who lived in south-eastern Nigeria in the early 1900s admitted that:

It is difficult to discover more than the merest fragments of the secrets of Egbo [*sic*], as any known informant would meet with a speedy death … Certainly a considerable amount of hypnotism, clairvoyance and spiritualism is taught, and only too many proofs have been given, that some of the powers of Nature are known and utilised by initiates, in a way forgotten or unknown to their white rulers … For instance, some of the esoteric members seem to have the power of calling up shadow forms of absent persons.[10]

Ekpo members' reputation for wielding supernatural powers, and the fact that they often attacked and/or abducted criminal offenders in the darkness of night, added to their aura and terrifying mystique. *Ekpo* was so influential that slaves from south-east Nigeria who were transported to the Americas during the Trans-Atlantic slave trade exported it to Cuba, where it still survives and is known as *Abakua*. They also exported a secret form of writing called *Nsibidi* (which is further discussed in Chapter 11).

In decentralised communities that did not have royalty, sodalities also had another purpose. Admission to a society which conferred honorific titles on its members was a status symbol and evidence of achievement. Such societies bestowed prestige on their members such as that given to a knight or lord. Although title societies incentivised achievement and provided upward social mobility, having an honorific title in decentralised communities did not necessarily make the title-holder a political ruler. Admission was remarkably democratic and was rarely hereditary. There were few or no qualifications for admission other than demonstrating high achievement. Someone could be admitted into an elite title society so long as they demonstrated high achievements in their lifetime and raised enough funds to pay for admission.

'an order of knighthood to distinguish nobles from the commons'

Perhaps the most famous title society in Igboland is the *Ozo* society. Nigeria's first post independence President Nnamdi Azikiwe described the *Ozo* society as 'an order of knighthood to distinguish

---

10   Talbot, 1912, p. 40.

nobles from the commons ... an aristocratic circle'.[11] In Igboland, members of title societies wore insignia of their status such as ivory anklets, a red cap, eagle feathers, a horse plume, and hand-carried fan. Sometimes the insignia was permanent. *Ozo* members were ritually scarred with knife cuts that carved symmetrical scars into their foreheads.

Members of title societies had many privileges, were exempt from manual labour, had servants, had their meals prepared and served to them in a special way, and had special seating arrangements at public events. For example, if a titled man entered a room or went to sit down where others were seated, all those already seated had to stand up and vacate their seats for him. This may give historical context for the 'high tables' reserved for dignitaries and elders at contemporary Nigerian social events.

Admission to title societies was simultaneously a privilege and a burden. In decentralised societies such as the Efik, Ejagham, Ibibio, and Igbo, it also burdened the title-holder by entangling him or her in a web of behavioural, dietary, moral, ritual, and social rules and taboos. Violating such restrictions would result in their membership being revoked. A titled individual could not rest on their laurels after being initiated into a title society. The title-holder had to maintain arduous membership rites and their life became beset with restrictions which became more burdensome and expensive as (s)he became more senior in the organisation.

The *Igbo amaghi eze* maxim is simultaneously true and false. While the vast majority of pre-colonial Igboland did not have monarchs, some Igbo towns and villages on its western and northern periphery had kings. Onitsha (on the eastern side of the River Niger in Anambra State) is the most famous of such kingdoms, and has a king called the *Obi* of Onitsha. How and why a people who pride themselves on having an egalitarian society without blue bloods ended up having kings, and contradicting the maxim that 'the Igbo knows no king', is shrouded in mystery.

Onitsha's people claim that they are not aborigines, and that they are originally from Benin. There are multiple conflicting accounts

11   Azikiwe, 1930, p. 477.

of the Onitsha people's alleged migration from Benin, and of how other nearby Igbo monarchies emerged. Fortunately, Onitsha's most famous son Nnamdi 'Ben' Azikiwe provided the most detailed written account of how kingship first arose in Onitsha. In 1930 (33 years before he became Nigeria's first post-independence president), the then 26-year-old Azikiwe claimed that Onitsha did not get its present name until the seventeenth century, and that prior to then, its people lived in a place called 'Ado N'Idu, which was a subordinate district of the empire of Benin'.[12] Azikiwe also wrote that 'The Ado N'Idus were a sort of ally to Benin City … The relations between the two kingdoms was very close.'[13]

However, relations between the two allies ruptured when the *Oba* of Benin's mother trespassed onto a farm that belonged to the Ado N'Idus, and the farm owners physically assaulted her. When the queen mother returned home, she demanded that her son the *oba* should avenge the outrage against her. The *oba* ordered his brother Gbunwala to retaliate against the Idus. Gbunwala invaded and laid waste to Ado N'Idu. After several weeks of fighting, the surviving Idus and their leader, a mononymous man named Chima, held a meeting about how to respond to the military crackdown against them. Depending on which account one accepts, Chima was either a provincial chief of Benin, the son of a previous *Oba* of Benin, a servant or hostage of the *Oba* of Benin's court, or a wandering priest from Arochukwu. Chima and his supporters fled in different directions. Some of Chima's followers settled in satellite towns on the outskirts of the Benin kingdom, while the main group under Chima fled further east, crossed the River Niger (with help from Igala people who gave them canoes to cross), and settled in the present town of Onitsha on the river's eastern side. Chima (or one of his sons) became the first *Obi* (King) of Onitsha. Like the *Oba* of Benin, the *Obi* of Ontisha was a reclusive king who rarely left his palace except during annual commemorations.

Onitsha's alleged descent from Benin was so well known that Bishop Samuel Ajayi Crowther heard and wrote about it when he

---

12 Ibid., p. 474.
13 Ibid., pp. 474–5.

travelled to Igboland in 1857 to proselytise. Crowther noted in his journals that:

Onitsha is not recognized as an original Ibo [*sic*] tribe; the people come from the Ado country on the west side of the Niger, having crossed to the east on the borders of the Ibo country, and thus gradually became naturalized by frequent intercourse and inter-marriages; they still retain many customs and habits of their fatherland, handed down by tradition; their word of salutation is Do! the same as Ado and Benin and the Ondo.[14]

THE CHILDREN OF KING CHIMA

Apart from Onitsha, Chima and/or his sons and followers are reputed to have founded about ten kingdoms on the western side of the River Niger close to Benin.[15] The various monarchies that Chima's fleeing family members and supporters founded identify themselves as *Umu Eze Chima* ('The Children of King Chima'). The *Umu Eze Chima* story has credibility despite the unlikelihood of a serious military confrontation and mass population transfer being triggered by an innocuous trespass on a farm.

'the Coral King'

The customs and regalia of the *Obis* of Onitsha and Agbor, and other *Umu Eze Chima* kings are remarkably similar to that of the *Oba* of Benin. The town of Aboh to the west of the River Niger is one of the *Umu Eze Chima* kingdoms. British explorers and Christian missionaries who visited Aboh in the early to mid-nineteenth century repeatedly documented their meetings with the town's king who they referred to 'King Obi'[16] or 'King Obie' – without realising that *obi* was a title, not his personal name. Since they mistakenly

14 *Church Missionary Intelligencer*, 1876, p. 536.
15 Aboh, Obior, Onitsha-Ukwu, Onitsha-Ugbo, Onitsha Olona, Issele-Azagba, Issele-Mkpitime, Issele-Uku, Ezi, and Obamkpa.
16 Schon and Crowther, 1842, p. 282.

presumed that Igbos (like the Hausa and Oduduwan people whom they had already met) had a paramount king, they also described him as 'King of the Eboe Country'.[17] The person they met was perhaps the most famous *Obi* of Aboh. Although those who met this *obi* spelt his name as 'Osai' or 'Ossai', the etymology of his name demonstrates the cosmopolitan origin of Igbos on the west wide of the River Niger. His name would be spelled as 'Osayi' in contemporary syntax. Osayi is a name that people of Edo, Igala, and Igbo origin answer. When the Lander brothers met the affable, tall, and 'splendidly clothed'[18] *Obi* Osayi in 1830, they noted that his attire:

> somewhat resembles that which is worn, on state occasions, by the monarch of Yarriba [the *Alaafin* of Oyo]. Its appearance was altogether brilliant; and from the vast profusion of coral ornaments with which he was decorated, Obie [*sic*] might not inappropriately be styled, 'the Coral King'.[19]

'a particularly handsome man [who] stands above six feet high'

Two years later the Scottish businessman MacGregor Laird also met *Obi* Osayi, and described him as 'a particularly handsome man [*who*] stands above six feet high'.[20] Laird observed that Osayi's arms and neck were bedecked with coral chains, and that 'From his fondness for coral ornaments, I should imagine him to be of Benin extraction.'[21] It is striking that the first thing that the Lander brothers and Laird noticed on meeting *Obi* Osayi was the resemblance of his attire and jewellery to the kings of Oyo and Benin. While this can be explained away as a case of mimicry of, or influence from, Benin, other similarities between the *Umu Eze Chima* and Benin kings are difficult to dismiss. The titles of officials in the *Obi* of Onitsha's and other *Umu Eze Chima* kings' courts were iden-

---

17 Lander, 1844, p. 213.
18 Ibid., p. 214.
19 Ibid., p. 213.
20 Laird and Oldfield, 1837, p. 101.
21 Ibid., p. 101.

tical or remarkably similar to those of their Benin counterparts.[22] Only people intimately familiar with Benin's royal system and its officials could have transplanted such phonetic similarity in titles and regalia.

'ASIJE'

Other elements of the story also have veracity. Not only do the oral accounts of the *Umu Eze Chima* communities corroborate each other, but their details also coincide with, and corroborate, Benin's oral history. While the Onitsha stories are not certain about the name of the reigning *Oba* of Benin when Chima's clan fled, Azikiwe and a British army officer who visited Igboland claimed that the Benin queen mother whose trespass on a farm triggered the conflict was named 'Asije'.[23] Curiously, several sources have spelled the name of Benin's legendary sixteenth-century *Oba* Esigie as 'Asije'.[24] As the story was orally transmitted over several hundred years, the names of Benin's king and queen mother became conflated and inadvertently switched. This similarity with *Oba* Esigie's name, and several details in the Chima story which resemble Benin's history, make it very likely that the *Umu Eze Chima*'s migration from Benin to Onitsha occurred during the reign of Benin's legendary *Oba* Esigie.

For example, Azikiwe also claimed that the conflict that caused Chima to flee was caused by 'family disputes'.[25] Benin's oral traditions are unequivocal regarding the manner in which Esigie came to the throne. Before assuming power, Esigie fought a battle against his half-brother Arhuaran (who was a rival claimant to the throne), destroyed Arhuaran's town known as 'Udo', and forced Arhuaran's

---

22 For example, the *Obi* of Agbor has a council called the *Uzama* (which is the same title as the *Oba* of Benin's royal council). In Agbor, the title of the *Uzama*'s leader is *olihe* (*oliha* in Benin). The *Oba* of Onitsha's court also includes officials with the following titles that are similar or identical to those of the *Oba* of Benin's officials (Benin equivalent in brackets): e.g. *Araze (Arase)*, *Isama (Isama)*, *Iyasele (Iyashere)*, *Osuma (Osuma)*.

23 Azikiwe, 1930, p. 475 and Leonard, 1906, p. 35.
24 Such as Roth, 1903, pp. 54–5.
25 Azikiwe, 1930, p. 474.

allies to flee. Esigie's famous mother Idia also played a prominent role and helped her son to prevail over his brother. Idia's significant involvement in this fraternal conflict rationalises why Onitsha's version of the story includes Benin's queen mother as a major protagonist. Azikiwe's account also claimed that the *Umu Eze Chima* 'left Benin about the seventeenth century',[26] while the British army and colonial officer Major Arthur Glyn Leonard estimated that they left 'presumably between two to three hundred years ago'[27] (prior to him visiting Igboland in the late nineteenth century and collecting testimony about Onitsha's kingship). Esigie is reputed to have come to the throne in the sixteenth century, and since the exact dates of his reign are not known, the dates that Azikiwe and Leonard provided are within the bounds of a reasonable margin for error. These factual and temporal similarities between the Esigie–Arhuaran civil war in Benin's oral traditions, and Onitsha's lore about the conflagration that forced Chima and his allies to flee to Onitsha and other places, almost certainly refer to the same event. Chima was probably one of the refugees who escaped in the aftermath of Esigie's battle against his half-brother.

Given that Benin's kings were polygamous and often had several hundred wives and many children, Arhuaran was unlikely to be Esigie's only rival for the throne. Esigie likely exiled other family members who posed a threat to him. If these rivals were blue blood sons of Esigie's father *Oba* Ozolua (or other members of his family), then it solves the mystery of why they established copycat kingdoms in the places they fled to and how and why they knew and used royal systems and titles that were almost identical to those of Benin.

Integrating the *Umu Eze Chima* and Benin oral traditions does not leave the accounts without issues. Although the Chima story portrays him as the founder of Onitsha, the city was already populated when Chima's people arrived there. Hence, Chima and his fellow refugees from Benin could not have founded the city. Azikiwe's account admits that when Chima's group arrived at

---

26   Ibid., p. 474.
27   Leonard, 1906, p. 35.

Onitsha, 'they confronted a hostile tribe, the Ozes';[28] whom they enslaved and expelled. Chima and his followers were invaders who founded Onitsha's *monarchy*, not the city itself. Even if the invasion theory is correct, it does not explain why *Eze* Chima fled to Onitsha in particular.

Although the *Umu Eze Chima* portray themselves as Benin indigenes, who after settling in Onitsha and intermingling with the local population, lost their original language and adopted the language of their new home, Chima's obviously Igbo name suggests otherwise. The names and languages of the people living in *Umu Eze Chima* monarchies are closer to the Igbos residing on the east side of the River Niger than they are to Benin. Several migration patterns and aspects of Igbo culture suggest that the *Umu Eze Chima*'s journey to Onitsha was probably a repatriation home, rather than the emigration it has been presented as.

Much of pre-colonial Igbo life revolved around trade at markets. Igbos had their own calendar with days that were named after four market days (*Eke, Afor, Nkwo,* and *Orie*), with seven weeks in a month, and thirteen months in a year. The Igbo word for a week is *izu*, a month is *onwa*, and a year is *afo*. The names of Igbo days were more than nouns. They were so significant that parents often named their babies after the day on which the baby was born. For example, naming a child Nwankwo ('child of Nkwo') would indicate that the child was born on the market day of Nkwo (and likewise for other Igbo names such as Nwaeke, Nwafor, and Nwaorie).

'a great artisan tribe'

Like the Hausas to their north, Igbos did not limit their predilection for commerce to their homeland, and were famed itinerant traders. The Igbo area has been one of the most densely populated areas in the world. This may explain why Igbos are contemporary Nigeria's most prolific internal migrants. A 2018 World Bank research paper[29] revealed that almost a quarter of Igbos in Nigeria

28   Azikiwe, 1930, p. 476.
29   Okunogbe, 2018, p. 24.

live outside their homeland in south-east Nigeria and are dispersed around other parts of Nigeria (in contrast, only 4 per cent of Hausas and 4 per cent of those from the Oduduwa areas live outside their home regions). These wandering habits are not new to Igbos. In pre-colonial times, the high population density of their homeland created pressure for economically motivated Igbo migrations to other regions. Then, as now, several Igbo groups were renowned itinerant occupational specialists. For example, the famous Awka blacksmiths spent about 75 per cent of the year away from home as they travelled to work and sell their services in southern and central Nigeria and north-west Cameroon. Their clients included Benin, the Efik, Idoma, and Igala. As late as 1909, a British reverend in south-east Nigeria described Igbos as 'a great artisan tribe, and their smiths are to be met in every village in this part of the country'.[30] The Aros (who are further discussed below) also travelled throughout south-east Nigeria to trade, recruit, and provide supernatural services. Some of these Igbo economic migrants became indigenised by absorbing themselves into, and permanently living among, their host communities. Their westward outward migration to areas on the west side of the River Niger 'collided' with the Benin kingdom which was expanding eastwards in the opposite direction.

The *Umu Eze Chima*'s choice of Onitsha as their refuge point is unlikely to be a random choice. Onitsha probably had a big cultural or historical significance for them. Permanent migrations were common in pre-colonial Igboland and several communities have oral traditions of descent or migration from a faraway location. For example, among the Ngwa clan of the Igbo, the village of Obete has two quarters inhabited by people who migrated to the village from elsewhere hundreds of years ago. Although these migrations occurred so long ago that no one knows when or why they occurred, the descendants of the migrants still live in a separate section of the village and are exempt from certain rights and prohibitions that apply to the indigenes. One of these immigrant communities originally came from the village of Ohuru and live in a separate section

---

30   Macgregor, 1909, p. 209.

of Obete village called *Umu Atakpuo* ('Children of Atakpuo' – the patriarch of the original migrant group), while the other migrant group still periodically visits their ancestral kin in Abiriba.

The reasons for such migrations varied. Refuge was a popular reason. Chima fled from Benin with members of his *maternal* family. This seemingly innocuous detail is far more important than it seems. Given the penchant of ancient *obas* of Benin for multiple marriages and prolific procreation, it is almost inconceivable that one or some of them did not marry Igbo women. While Igbos could be sanctioned for crimes and other offences they caused while in the community of strangers or of their *umu nna* (paternal family), they enjoyed immunity and special privileges while residing in the towns or villages of their *umu nne* (maternal family). It was sacrilege to harm or spill the blood of an Igbo person while (s)he was present in their mother's hometown. In times of despair or to escape the wrath of vengeful foes, people often fled to their maternal homeland due to the immunity from harm and prosecution they enjoyed there.

The sixteenth- or seventeenth-century controversy which led to the *Umu Eze Chima* being expelled from Benin and fleeing to Onitsha was most likely a case of them returning to their ancestral homeland. It is likely that their ancestors migrated from Onitsha to areas under Benin jurisdiction, and that during a time of strife, their *Umu Eze Chima* descendants returned to their original homeland on the east side of the River Niger when under siege from Benin. When combined together, the high population density of Igboland, patterns of emigration, presence of Igbo migrants in Benin and other areas, and Chima's escape to Onitsha with members of his mother's family, strongly suggest that the *Umu Eze Chima* were returning to their ancestral homeland in Onitsha, rather than migrating there for the first time. Having returned home after a long sojourn away, they brought back with them traditions from Benin that they absorbed while living there.

While the *Umu Eze Chima* monarchies were imported, there was a different but very prominent example of what indigenous Igbo kingship was like.

'BIG IGBO'

The town of Igbo-Ukwu (literally: 'Big Igbo' or 'Great Igbo') is located about 25 miles south-east of Onitsha. Igbo-Ukwu's historical importance was accidentally discovered in 1938 while a man named Isaiah Anozie was digging a water cistern in his compound. As he dug, Anozie unearthed elaborately carved and decorated bronze ornaments and sculptures. When archaeologists heard of Anozie's discovery, they excavated the area – including the neighbouring compound of Richard Anozie, where they found even more bronze sculptures, some buried more than 20 feet beneath the ground. Their most startling discovery was an ancient wood-lined burial tomb about 11 feet beneath the ground. The person buried in it was elaborately dressed, buried in a seated position, and was surrounded by treasures. Apart from the bones of the buried person, inside the tomb they found even more bronze sculptures, jewellery, countless beads (which were a sign of ancient royalty), ivory tusks, and a headdress that looked like a crown. The bronze artefacts excavated at Igbo-Ukwu were stylistically different from the Benin and Ife bronzes, and were made via a complicated process known as 'Lost Wax' (which is further discussed in Chapter 9), a method mastered only by the world's most elite sculptors.

'an astonishing level of technical virtuosity'

About 800 artefacts and over 165,000 beads were discovered during the Igbo-Ukwu excavations.[31] A British historian described the artefacts as having 'an astonishing level of technical virtuosity, and a delight in intricate craftsmanship for its own sake'.[32] The importance of the Igbo-Ukwu artefacts transcends their aesthetic appeal and artistic quality. Like the Benin Bronzes, Igbo-Ukwu's art also acted as a visual record of its people's culture and history. There was also cultural continuity in the designs of the artefacts. For example, the facial scars on one of the sculptures resembled facial

31   Ukpabi, 1971, p. 337 and Isichei, 1976, p. 14.
32   Isichei, 1976, p. 12.

scars observed in twentieth-century titled men from Nri, and symmetrical designs on the sculptures similarly resembled carvings on contemporary wooden doors in Awka.[33] This cultural and stylistic continuity in Igbo-Ukwu's art leaves no doubt that the artisans who made them were indigenes of the area (and were probably the work of the legendary Awka blacksmiths).

Not only were their makers brilliant artisans, but the foreign origin of the beads and metal found at Igbo-Ukwu suggests that the locals obtained them from international and inter-continental trading partners. Some of the beads came from places as far away as India and Italy. An Arab chronicler wrote that in the eleventh century, copper was exported from Morocco southwards to the land of the Blacks.[34] While Trans-Saharan trade routes from Europe and North Africa reached the Hausa States, the presence of these imported beads and metals so far south in Igboland, suggests that Igboland itself was either connected to the Trans-Saharan trade routes or had intermediary trade links with other pre-colonial Nigerian societies that did.

The foreign origin of the objects in the tomb at Igbo-Ukwu, their richness, and the great effort required to import and make them, show that the person buried in the tomb was exceptionally important. Igbo-Ukwu is only 1 mile away from Oreri and 9 miles away from Nri. Both of these communities recognise an Igbo king of immense ritual and religious importance. The person buried with treasures in the tomb at Igbo-Ukwu was an ancient Igbo king.

The community of Nri, located about 25 miles east of the River Niger and 15 miles east of Onitsha, was regarded as 'a small town which is the headquarters of a priestly cult whose special functions are connected with the coronation of kings'.[35] If the *Umu Eze Chima* represent imitations of Benin's royalty, Nri is one of the rare instances of indigenous Igbo monarchy.

Nri had for its people, a special reverence akin to that which Ile-Ife had in the Oduduwan area. Although few Igbo communities have

---

33   Ibid., p. 13.
34   Thurstan Shaw, 1988, p. 481.
35   Basden, 1921, p. 27.

traditions of origin as ancient or detailed as those of other communities such as Benin and Ife, Nri is an exception. Nri's lore of origin has several parallels with the book of Genesis in the Bible, and Nri's people trace their lineage to a founding father named Eri and his wife Nnamaku whom God sent down to earth. However, since the land was covered by water, God sent an Awka blacksmith who used his bellows, charcoal, and fire to dry the land. God rewarded the blacksmith by granting him a special commission to the smithing profession. Eri and Nnamaku were Nri's equivalent of Adam and Eve, and their youngest son Nri was his community's Abraham. Nri's descendants refer to themselves as Umunri ('the children of Nri') and became the holders of the *Eze* Nri title.

THE KING OF NRI

Nri had a priest-like king who had the title of *Eze* Nri ('King of Nri'). Since carbon dating has dated the burial tomb at Igbo-Ukwu to the ninth century (the era when Vikings repeatedly raided England), the *Eze* Nri institution has existed for over 1000 years at the very least, and is older than the more famous southern Nigerian kingdoms of Benin, Ife, and Oyo. Although the word *eze* means 'king', *ezes* did not have the type of executive power that European kings and African kings such as those of Benin, Oyo, and the Hausa States had. The *Eze* Nri was a theocratic leader whose powers were ceremonial and religious, rather than political. If we seek modern parallels, his role was akin to that which the Dalai Lama has in contemporary times. If the *Eze* Nri was Nri's 'head of state', then he was so only in the ceremonial way that the Pope is the Vatican's leader.

'too sacred to take part in local government'

While it is known that the *Eze* Nri was both feared and revered, far less is known about what he actually did. The *Eze* Nri was a divine leader whose person was sacred. As late as 1956, a British colonial government report stated that the *Eze* Nri's 'powers were ritual rather than political and he played no part in the government of his village'.[36] It also stated that Nri's people 'do not wish him to play any part in their village or Local Councils. They say he is too big a person for such work'[37] and that he was 'considered too sacred to take part in local government'.[38]

The *Eze* Nri title was not hereditary (although the incumbent had to be a descendant of Nri). After an *Eze* Nri died, the position was left vacant for several years,[39] during which time a sacred guild of trained professional diviners known as *dibia* performed *Afa* (divination) and sought portents of who should succeed as the next *Eze* Nri. The *dibia* were presumed to have talents that enabled them to foresee and interpret the wishes of God and spirits. The successful candidate had to make three public and fulfilled prophecies, and any person with a living parent was ineligible.

In order to confirm the *Eze* Nri's passage from human to a deified role, his coronation ceremony involved him symbolically 'dying' as a human being, temporary[40] burial in a shallow grave, and then being 'reborn' as a divinity. While buried, his wives and family even mourned his 'death'. After being exhumed from his grave he was painted with white chalk as a symbol of his new immortality and purity. After his 'resurrection', the *Eze* Nri could never wear his former clothing again, and could wear only white- or blue-coloured clothing.

While several articles and books speak of an 'Nri Kingdom', Nri was not a *political* kingdom per se, but was a cultural group with shared beliefs and theological practices, including their belief in the *Eze* Nri's powers. Pre-colonial Igbo society was governed by a series of laws, restrictions, and taboos known as *Omenala*, which functioned as society's moral and legal code. Violation of *Omenala* was known as *aruru ala* or *nso ala* (abomination against the land, or violating the taboos of the earth goddess Ala) and was believed to

---

36 Jones, 1956, p. 21.
37 Ibid., p. 10.
38 Ibid., p. 54.
39 The position was left vacant for about 30 years between the 1920s and 1950s.
40 The length of the burial is uncertain. The contemporary *Eze* Nri claims that he was buried for three days before being coronated.

bring social and spiritual damnation on the violator. The *Eze* Nri's duties included nullifying curses on communities who violated *Omenala*, performing rituals to ensure yam and other agricultural fertility, and settling disputes. These were important roles in an ancient pre-scientific society of farmers where droughts and other adverse weather conditions could devastate agricultural production and people's livelihoods. In such an era, a spiritual protector such as the *Eze* Nri was considered vital to the community's preservation.

ATTAH IGALA

The *Eze* Nri had many parallels with the neighbouring *Attah* Igala (King of the Igala people) to Nri's north. Like the *Eze* Nri, the *Attah* Igala was also a divine leader who similarly underwent a symbolic death and rebirth during his coronation ceremony. Both the *Eze* Nri and *Attah* Igala were sacred and reclusive leaders who lived in seclusion and rarely left their premises. Despite both of them being responsible for performing ritual ceremonies that protected their respective people and preserved the prosperity of their societies, they were rarely seen by anyone other than their attendants. After an *Attah* Igala died, it was customary to bury him seated in a wood-lined chamber (exactly like the ninth-century *Eze* Nri found at Igbo-Ukwu).

While nothing about the Nri legend can be taken as historical fact, historical metaphors are often buried within these magico-ritual lores. Its inclusion of Eri's son Idah, who allegedly founded the Igala capital city of the same name, suggests ancient links between the Nri and Igala kingships, and the fact that the founder of the Igala capital was presented as a *younger* brother of Nri's founder may mean that the Igala capital was founded after Nri. One of Nri's oral traditions even claims that when the *Attah* Igala is coronated, 'an Ndri [*sic*] man has to be there to put the crown on his head'.[41] Nri's priests not only acted as special consecrating agents for the

41   Ogedengbe, 1971, p. 52.

Attah Igala, but were so venerated that they also did so during the coronation ceremonies of the *Oba* of Benin.

Despite the archaeological finds dating back to the ninth century, there is a huge 'hole' in Igbo history between ninth and nineteenth centuries. European-educated African and European missionaries and colonial officers who visited Igboland in the nineteenth and early twentieth centuries recorded much of what is now known about pre-colonial Igbo society. Most of these informants were aliens to the society they observed and recorded, and there is no direct confirmation of how different or similar their depictions of Igbo society in the nineteenth and twentieth centuries were, when compared to Igbo society centuries before. It is unlikely that the society remained static for hundreds of years until Europeans started observing and recording it. It is widely presumed that there were no written eyewitness accounts during this largely unknown millennium to fill in the gaps between the archaeological finds from the ninth century and the multiple foreign nineteenth-century accounts.

Fortunately, a book written in the eighteenth century corroborated subsequent accounts. Although the book was not about Africa, its first chapter inadvertently provided the first ever published indigenous account of what pre-colonial Igbo society was like.

THE MAN WITH MANY NAMES

Although the book was the first of the 'slave narratives' that raised awareness about the horrors of the 'Middle Passage' and Trans-Atlantic slavery (and inspired other books in the same genre), its importance transcended its author's intent.

The author was a slave kidnapped from Africa around 1756 and shipped to Virginia in America during the Trans-Atlantic slave trade era. While being transported on the slave ship, the slavers named him 'James', and one of his many slave owners again renamed him 'Jacob'. In Virginia, Lieutenant Michael Pascal (a British Royal Navy officer) bought him and renamed him 'Gustavus Vassa', after the sixteenth-century Swedish king Gustav Vasa. Although he objected to the name, he eventually submitted to it after his master Pascal gave him 'many a cuff'[42] for his resistance. It is the name that he was known by for the rest of his life. While working for Pascal, Vassa learned to read and write and became a Christian. He led a nomadic life and travelled widely as a servant and sailor, and was the first African to visit the North Pole. He also travelled to the Caribbean and Central America. In 1766, Vassa bought his freedom from a subsequent owner, Robert King (an American Quaker), and his life changed dramatically.

After regaining his freedom, Vassa settled in England, and in 1792 he married a white English woman from Cambridgeshire, Susannah Cullen. The couple lived in Cambridgeshire, and had two daughters, Anna Maria and Joanna (who died in 1797 aged only three years old). In 1789, Vassa published his autobiography.[43] Vassa's book was a bestseller and it turned him into a celebrity. Vassa and his wife Susannah went on a book tour that took them across the United Kingdom and to Ireland. The book was reprinted for nine subsequent editions and translated into Dutch, German, and Russian. It was so popular that highly placed members of society pre-ordered it (including the Prince of Wales, the Dukes of Marlborough and York, and several lords, ladies, and bishops). Vassa joined an organisation called the 'Sons of Africa', a group of twelve Black men who campaigned for slavery to be abolished, met and befriended prominent members of British society and in 1788, he even wrote to Queen Charlotte (wife of King George III) to enlist her support for the abolition of the slave trade. Although Vassa died in his early-50s in 1797, his book's importance outlived him by several centuries.

'red men living at a distance'

Unbeknown to Vassa, the first chapter of his book provided the first ever published eyewitness account of pre-colonial Igboland written

---

42   Equiano, 1789, p. 62.
43   *The Interesting Narrative of the Life of Olaudah Equiano: or Gustavus Vassa, the African.*

by an indigene. Although Vassa described himself only as 'The African', and mentioned 'our language' several times in his book, he never identified the ethnic group he came from or his native African language. Yet, several terms he used in his book gave away both.

Vassa wrote that he was born in 'a charming fruitful vale, named Essaka'[44] (which was a province of the Benin kingdom) in 1745 and kidnapped and sold into slavery around 1756 when he was about 11 years old. He spoke of a place called 'Eboe', and of 'stout, mahogany-coloured men from the south-west of us'[45] called 'Oye-Eboe, which term signifies red men living at a distance', who sold guns, gunpowder, hats, beads, and dried fish to his people. He also mentioned that 'our year [is] called Ah-affoe'[46] and that his 'father was one of those elders or chiefs … styled Embrenche; a term as I remember importing the highest distinction, and signifying in our language a mark of grandeur'.[47]

Many phrases that Vassa used are recognisable (albeit spelt differently) in modern Igbo. 'Eboe' refers to Igbo, 'Ah-affoe' (spelt *afo* in contemporary syntax) is the Igbo word for 'year', and 'Embrenche' was his spelling of the practice known as *Mgburichi*: ritually scarring the faces of men that have been initiated into the prestigious *Ozo* title society. 'Oye-Eboe' was Vassa's rendition of *onye Igbo* (literally: 'an Igbo person'). This linguistic resonance leaves little doubt that Vassa was from what is now the Igbo-speaking area of Nigeria.

Vassa's idiosyncratic spellings can be explained by the difficulty of a writer who was taken from his homeland as a child, and tried to transcribe words he learned in his native language as an infant, and which he had not used for decades, into a foreign language while writing decades later as an adult man in his 30s.

The first part of Vassa's book was a treasure trove about daily pre-colonial Igbo village life. It was packed with information about pre-colonial Igboland, such as family life, crime and punishment,

---

44 Equiano, 1789, p. 3.
45 Ibid., p. 22.
46 Ibid., p.22.
47 Ibid., p. 4.

leadership, and marriage customs. By confirming that some Igbo areas were vassals of the Benin kingdom at least 300–400 years ago, Vassa also inadvertently corroborated the *Umu Eze Chima* oral traditions, and other information about pre-colonial Igboland which did not become known by outsiders until centuries after his book was published. His reference to 'Oye-Eboe' people (while not describing himself as such) confirms that the term originally referred only to a sub-group and not all people currently regarded as Igbo.

'having a loud voice, and well spoken'

He also revealed for the first time his birth name: 'Olaudah Equiano'. This name is not consistent with the spelling of any contemporary Igbo name, and the idiosyncratic spellings of the eighteenth century make it difficult to decipher how his name would be spelled in contemporary times. He said that Olaudah 'in our language, signifies vicissitude, or fortunate also; one favoured, and having a loud voice, and well spoken'.[48] That is a tremendous amount of information to pack into one name. Since the Igbo word for 'voice' is *olu*, it is reasonable to assume that the 'Olau' part of his name would today be spelled *olu*. However, vicissitude, being fortunate, and well spoken cannot be stuffed into the syllable 'dah'. 'Udah' means 'noise' or 'sound' in Igbo. When combined with *olu* to form 'Olu-Udah'[49] it translates literally as 'noisy voice'. His second name 'Equiano' is also a riddle. Although Equiano did not state the meaning of his second name, he and other eighteenth-century writers used the letter 'E' to spell words which would begin with the letter 'i' in modern day writing. It can thus be assumed that the name Equiano would begin with the letter 'I' today. Since modern Igbo syllables such as 'kw' did not exist in eighteenth-century orthography, Equiano would probably be spelt in contemporary times as 'Ikwuano' (*ikwu* means 'to speak' in Igbo). His full name was probably 'Oludah Ikwuano'. Another point to amplify is that Igbos did not have surnames in the

---

48   Ibid., p. 20.
49   When written backwards as *Uda-Olu*, it would mean 'the sound of that voice'.

eighteenth century. Instead, in addition to their birth names, most Igbos also had other affectionate *noms de guerre* that grandparents and different members of their maternal and paternal families used to address them. Thus, Ikwuano was either one of such *noms de guerre* or his first and second names were actually one continuous name ('Oludahikwuano').

'when I first arrived in England ... I could speak no language but that of Africa'

However, his account has discrepancies. Firstly, his claimed birthplace of 'Essaka' does not correspond to the name of any known Igbo town or village. While he was still alive his critics alleged that he was born in the Caribbean island of Santa Cruz, 'stole' accounts from other African slaves he met, compiled them together, and published them as his own. To defend himself from such accusations which he described as 'insidious ... with a view to hurt my character, and to discredit and prevent the sale of my Narrative',[50] he asked British people who knew him in London to corroborate his claim that 'when I first arrived in England, [I] could speak no language but that of Africa'.[51] Centuries after his death, academics also unearthed documents which cast further doubt on Equiano's claim of being born in 'Essaka'. His 1759 baptismal record at St Margaret's Church in Westminster listed his place of birth as 'Carolina', and a Royal Navy roll from his expedition to the North Pole in 1773 similarly listed his place of birth as 'South Carolina'. Yet, Equiano's account of his childhood in Essaka is so compelling, vivid, laced with Igbo terminology, and so consistent with what is known about pre-colonial Igbo culture, that it is an utter mystery how he acquired such knowledge if he was born in Carolina as his detractors claimed.

The controversy regarding Equiano's origin and place of birth does not diminish the importance of his book. After Equiano's book, no direct eyewitness published another book about pre-colo-

---

50 Equiano, 1789, p. iii.
51 Ibid., p. iv.

nial Igboland until the Lander brothers visited Aboh over 40 years later in 1830 (around the time that Oyo was collapsing and *Alaafin* 'Mansolah' was on Oyo's throne).

THE SPEAR OF GOD

The town of Arochukwu (in modern-day Abia State of south-east Nigeria) was a fundamental commercial and religious confluence point in pre-colonial Nigeria. Arochukwu means 'Spear of God' in Igbo. Before the twentieth century, the town held a religious significance akin to that which Rome has for Catholics, Mecca for Muslims, and Jerusalem for Jews. Arochukwu was so important to the pre-colonial religion of multiple ethnic groups that pilgrims from far away places in the Annang, Efik, Ibibio, and Ijaw areas (in Cross River, Akwa Ibom, and Bayelsa States of current-day Nigeria) and even Cameroon made pilgrimages there. The town's indigenes were known as 'Aros' and were revered.

'a remarkable and mysterious people'

Many superlatives have been used to describe the Aros. A British missionary described them as 'a remarkable and mysterious people ... intelligent, subtle, and cunning'.[52] The Aros were held in awe throughout the area that became south-east Nigeria, and they had a reputation for wielding economic, military, and supernatural power that made them seem invulnerable.

'God lives there'

Although the Aros have been retrospectively presented as inveterate and villainous slave traders, their commercial interests encompassed much more than just slave trading. They were also renowned businessmen, money lenders, traders, arms dealers, and providers of mercenaries. Aros trained young boys from an early age to be

---

52   Livingstone, 1916, p. 191.

traders and had lucrative commercial interests from trading within Igboland, with other ethnic groups such as the Ibibio and Ijaw, and with Europeans. They were also skilled artisans. When the Scottish explorer William Balfour Baikie visited Igboland in the mid-nineteenth century, he heard about Arochukwu and reported that: 'The inhabitants are skillful artisans, and manufacture swords, spears, and metallic ornaments, specimens of all of which I have seen, and can therefore testify to there being very neatly finished.'[53] The Aros did not ascribe their commercial success purely to their acumen. Like the Nri to their north, the aura around, and special veneration for, the Aro, was due to their claims of controlling access to a special supernatural power. During his travels Baikie also noticed that Arochukwu 'is always mentioned with great respect, almost, at times, with a degree of veneration and the people say … God lives there'.[54]

In a society that did not accept the power of paramount rulers, supernatural oracles were an important avenue for settling seemingly intractable disputes and problems. These oracles performed multi-purpose roles as a supernatural judiciary that could confer blessings or condemn, investigative agency that could identify murderers, other criminals, and witches, and as a counsellor. There were several such oracles in pre-colonial south-east Nigeria such as Agbala at Awka (which was referenced in Chinua Achebe's classic *Things Fall Apart*), Igwekala[55] ('the king greater than the earth goddess' or 'the king greater than the land') at Umunoha, Kamalu[56] at Ozuzu, Odo at Nsukka, Idemili at Nnobi, and Ogbunorie at Ezumoha.[57] A British reverend who lived in Igboland during the early twentieth century described Awka as 'the home of a notable deity, reputed to be endowed with marvellous gifts of divination.

53 Baikie, 1856, pp. 310–11.
54 Ibid., pp. 310–11.
55 Also known as 'Igwekani' (in areas where the earth goddess was known as 'Ani' rather than 'Ala').
56 Also known as 'Kamanu'.
57 The present-day locations of these towns are: Awka (Anambra State), Umunoha (Imo State), Ozuzu (Rivers State), Nsukka (Enugu State), Nnobi (Anambra State), and Ezumoha (Imo State).

Strangers were conducted thither from all parts of the country in order that they might hold consultations with the deity.'[58] The deity he referred to was called Agbala and was reputed to be 'a discerner of the secrets of men, the judge of poisoners, the revealer of witch-craft, the omnipotent one, the forgiver of sins, and the dispenser of blessings of every kind, including the gift of children'.[59] Despite the prevalence of these oracles, the most famous of them was located in a secret shrine in a cave at Arochukwu. Its name was 'Ibini Ukpabi'.

Arochukwu's population was multi-ethnic and included Ibibio people. Ibini Ukpabi's origin is uncertain. Some claim that it was a pre-existing Ibibio deity which Aros appropriated and elevated for their own benefit, while others identify it as the same deity as Chukwu, the Igbo supreme god. Whichever version is true, Aros believed in Ibini Ukpabi's power, and also convinced people hundreds of miles away to share their beliefs about Ibini Ukpabi.

THE CHILDREN OF GOD

Ibini Ukpabi (which the British nicknamed 'Long Juju') gained international fame when the British colonial army placed Aro-chukwu in its crosshairs in the early twentieth century. The Aros claimed that Ibini Ukpabi favoured them and gave them special powers and protection which caused their commercial success. Ibini Ukpabi acted as an oracle and supernatural judge who adju-dicated on disputes and prescribed punishment for the offending party. Ibini Ukpabi's presence in Arochukwu made the Aros feared and respected, and since the Aros also presented themselves as Ibini Ukpabi's agents and interlocutors, and claimed that only they could communicate with him, they held a special status as a 'chosen people' akin to ancient Hebrews. Others referred to the Aros as *Umu Chukwu* ('children of god'). This special status and the Aros' presumed role as Ibini Ukpabi's exclusive intermediaries, enabled them to charge others for access to Ibini Ukpabi. Payment for access to Ibini Ukpabi became a lucrative money-making machine for the

---

58   Basden, 1921, p. 245.
59   Ibid., p. 246.

Aros. The Aros' invincible aura was not only about the supernatural gateway to Ibini Ukpabi that they promoted. Although the Aros were not themselves a warrior nation, they entered into wise alliances and contracts with martial clans such as the Abam, Edda, and Ohafia. The Abams were famed warriors who 'were in a state of perpetual readiness for war whenever it was made worth their while'.[60] The Abams' military reputation was so fearsome that they were known as 'the dreaded Abams',[61] 'the fighting Abams', and as 'a fruitful source of fear'.[62] By contracting the services of warriors from such communities, the Aros were simultaneously able to hire others to do their fighting, punish enemies and uncooperative former allies, and act as military contractors who loaned out mercenaries. These proxy military campaigns were also money-making enterprises for Aros as they turned the survivors of the losing side into 'war booty' whom they would sell into slavery.

Being associated with a feared deity, and being able to conscript the support of dreaded warriors made the Aros one of the few groups that could travel through foreign towns and villages without inquiry or fear of molestation.

'a brilliantly perpetuated confidence trick'

However, not everyone was convinced by the claims of Aro economic and religious invincibility. An emancipated Igbo slave in Sierra Leone wrote about the Aros 33 years before Britain invaded Arochukwu, and claimed that the Aros used manipulation to maintain their supernatural facade. According to this account, when a pilgrim travelled to Arochukwu to consult Ibini Ukpabi, Aro emissaries outside Ibini Ukpabi's shrine met and blindfolded the pilgrim before bringing him into Ibini Ukpabi's presence. The Aros would allegedly contrive a justifiable explanation for the disappearance of pilgrims they deemed expendable, by either killing a fowl or spilling red dye into a stream, which an Aro priest would

---

60 Ibid., p. 208.
61 Ibid., p. 205.
62 Ibid., p. 37.

proclaim to be the blood of a pilgrim that Ibini Ukpabi had executed.[63] Instead, the Aros had secretly sold the unfortunate pilgrim into slavery.

When Britain prepared to invade Arochukwu in the early 1900s, it released a constant stream of anti-Aro propaganda which condemned Ibini Ukpabi as a fraud, and 'as little more than a racket by which the gullible peoples of the interior gave themselves over to the Aro as slaves and human sacrifices in payment for worthless religious and judicial services'.[64] The propaganda campaign was extremely successful and stuck. Almost 70 years after a British invasion force destroyed Ibini Ukpabi with explosives, a British historian described Ibini Ukpani as 'a brilliantly perpetuated confidence trick, by which the Aro enhanced their elite role as traders and slavers'.[65] The Aros' relationship with Ibini Ukpabi retroactively changed their reputation from that of a chosen people who resided in a holy city, to that of being one of the earliest perpetrators of the now infamous Nigerian '419' fraud.

THE IGBO JIGSAW PUZZLE

It is ironic that Igbos (who in contemporary times are stereotyped as Nigeria's most clannish ethnic group) were politically and socially fragmented in pre-colonial times. Pan-Igbo identity did not exist in the pre-colonial era and they did not regard themselves as one people. 'Patriotism' was usually limited to an individual clan or lineage group. If one accepts the accuracy of Igbo oral traditions such as those of the *Umu Eze Chima*, then many Igbo groups are either migrants or the descendants of amalgamations between indigenous and outside groups. Northern Igbo groups (in modern-day Anambra State) claim descent from Benin or Igala areas, Igbos on the west side of the River Niger (in modern-day Delta State) also claim Benin descent, while many inland Igbo groups claim to have migrated from other hinterland areas.

---

63 Horton, 1868, p. 185.
64 Jackson, 1975, p. 27.
65 Isichei, 1969, p. 127.

Yet paradoxically, despite living in independent social units and taking pride in their independence, there was much cultural and religious unity among them. The itinerant businessmen and traders such as the Aros and Awka blacksmiths assisted cultural consolidation by exporting their language, customs, and religion to where they travelled. Inter-group oracles such as Agbala and Ibini Ukpabi also created inter-ethnic and intra-ethnic religious solidarity by attracting pilgrims from afar. The different Igbo sub-cultures also shared the four-day Igbo week and market calendar.

Some generalisations still emerge despite this mass of divergent cultures and information. Firstly, Igbo oral traditions corroborate and reinforce the history of their neighbours. The 'family disputes' that triggered the *Umu Eze Chima*'s exile from Benin confirm that a seismic conflict erupted in Benin in the sixteenth or seventeenth century. The *Umu Eze Chima* oral tradition is an alternate non-Benin account of the conflict or civil war that involved *Oba* Esigie and his mother, Idia. Rather than the clash between two brothers which the Benin accounts portray it as, it probably involved far more protagonists, family members, or rival claimants for Benin's throne. Moreover, the *Umu Eze Chima* story is only a microcosm of the pre-colonial relations between Benin and its Igbo neighbours. Contact between the two peoples was not limited to a fraternal conflict during *Oba* Esigie's reign. Like the Igbos, Benin's Edo people also have a calendar of four market days with names (*Eken, Orie, Okuo*, and *Aho*) that are remarkably similar to their Igbo counterpart days. The Nri legend claims that God revealed these four days to Nri's people. Curiously, Benin's royalty trusted Nri's consecrating priests enough to allow them to participate in the *Oba* of Benin's coronation. This similarity is almost certainly the outcome of close ancient trading and/or religious links between Edo and Igbo peoples.

Secondly, *political* kingship that vests entire government responsibility in a head of state-type ruler is alien to Igboland. However, spiritual kingship (of the *Eze* Nri type) is not. It is highly unlikely to be a coincidence that the Igbo monarchies mostly exist in areas on Igboland's northern and western outskirts that border other areas such as Benin and the Igala – which have long-standing kingship traditions. These Igbo monarchies are curiously similar to the non-Igbo monarchies closest to them. Even then, no pre-colonial Igbo kings ruled anything bigger than a small town or village, let alone the entirety of Igboland. Such kings were the exceptions, and the *Igbo amaghi eze* maxim holds true in Igboland's interior, and the further one moves away from its border areas that are in close proximity to large kingdoms such as Benin and the Igala.

Thirdly, when indigenous kingship existed, the king was a ceremonial spiritual leader who was the living embodiment of his community's survival, but not its actual ruler. The revolt that greeted the twentieth-century British colonial policy of indirect rule in south-eastern Nigeria is great evidence that *political* kingship was alien to Igbos. In areas where the British colonial government could not find a chief, it found someone who it presumed was powerful or had leadership qualities, and appointed him as a chief by giving him a certificate of appointment called a 'warrant'. The appointment of such 'warrant chiefs' inspired anti-colonial revolts against both the warrant chiefs and the British authorities that appointed them. The warrant chief system was described as a 'disaster for traditional leadership in Igboland'.[66] The fact that the British colonial government had to create warrant chiefs, and that Igbos so bitterly resisted the warrant chiefs, was to a large extent because kingship was an alien imposition unfamiliar to the Igbo indigenes. This explains why indirect rule worked in northern and south-west Nigeria, but was such an utter disaster in south-east Nigeria.

---

66 Ubah, 1987, p. 172.

9
The Masterpieces of World Sculpture

The content of the previous chapters may tempt the reader into thinking that Nigeria's pre-colonial story was only about conquest, wars, and other upheavals. However, there was a gentler and more holistic side to pre-colonial Nigeria which often found its outlet in artistic expression.

Nigeria's three most famous twenty-first-century artistic exports to the world are firstly, its 'Nollywood' film industry which is the third largest film industry in the world. Secondly, is its burgeoning Afrobeat music scene, which has been popularised by musicians such as Burna Boy, Davido, Flavour, and Wizkid – household names that roll off the tongue to a worldwide Gen-Z and Millennial audience. Thirdly, are physical arts such as paintings and sculptures which are presented as an emerging industry in contemporary Nigeria, but which are actually a renaissance and continuation of the area's ancient tradition of artistic excellence.

So many superlatives have been used to describe Nigeria's ancient artworks that an entire book could be written about the praise for them alone. As far back as 700 years ago, West Africans at Ife in what is now south-west Nigeria were creating artworks which the renowned British anthropologist Professor Frank Willett later claimed 'would stand comparison with anything which ancient Egypt, classical Greece and Rome, or Renaissance Europe had to offer'.[1] Some of Nigeria's ancient artworks are now so valuable in the contemporary world that a Museum curator said that one of them 'has no price ... it is priceless'.[2] Those that have a price have been sold for as much as $10 million a piece.

1   Willett, 1960, p. 239.
2   'Head of an Ife King from Nigeria – Masterpieces of the British Museum', www.youtube.com/watch?v=3mtvcl1EjgM (accessed 8 July 2022).

'there is absolutely nothing like them in any other part of the world'

Although the Benin Bronzes are the most well known ancient Nigerian artworks, they are not the only great artworks that emerged in ancient Nigeria. The Bronzes get more airtime than other ancient artworks because there are thousands of them, and because European art experts and museum curators who examined and wrote about them concluded that 'there is absolutely nothing like them in any other part of the world'.[3] European museum curators who struggled to reconcile how people they considered as primitive savages produced artworks whose execution was so impressive that a British Museum curator admitted that: 'The skill with which the casting has been done is remarkable.'[4] The Bronzes also had a mysterious aura for at least two reasons. Firstly, there was great disagreement about the identity of the people who made them and how they learned how to make them. Secondly, although Nigeria's ancient societies left a legacy of highly sophisticated art, no one knows for certain why they were originally made, and what function they were supposed to serve when originally made.

There was no shortage of exotic nineteenth-century and early twentieth-century European explanations for the non-African origin of ancient Nigerian artworks, and of how Benin acquired bronze-making skill. The earliest was included in the Moor-Roupell report referenced in Chapter 7. The report's authors claimed that they gathered their information from senior Benin royal officials, who allegedly told them: 'When the white men came, in the time when Esige [sic] was king, a man named Ahammangiwa came with them. He made brasswork and plaques for the king.'[5] Although the attentive head of the British Museum's Department of British and Medieval Antiquities and Ethnography Charles Hercules Read and his assistant Ormonde Maddock noted that the mys-

---

3   Roth, 1903, p. 234.
4   Read and Dalton, 1899, p. 43.
5   Ibid., p. 6.

terious Ahammangiwa 'need not have been himself a Lusitanian',[6] the claim that he came with white men led subsequent accounts to jump to the conclusion that he was Portuguese and that six-teenth-century Portuguese visitors to Benin taught Benin's people how to make bronze sculptures. This claim had merit because the technical mastery of the Bronzes peaked in the sixteenth century – which coincided with the height of Benin–Portugal rela-tions. British Museum curators speculated that a Portuguese ship armourer that visited Benin made some of the Bronzes. When it became apparent that the Bronzes' design was beyond the capability of even the most extravagantly talented ship armourer, they devel-oped another theory, which claimed that a Portuguese sculptor or another superior alien race visited Benin and taught the natives how to make bronze sculptures. Sculptures excavated in other parts of Nigeria elicited similar European reactions. When the German archaeologist Leo Frobenius excavated 500-year-old bronze sculp-tures at Ife in 1910, he had an elaborate explanation for why they were not of African origin (despite being found in Africa and made before Europeans arrived in Africa). Frobenius' theory was that he was not in Africa after all, but had discovered in Ife the mythical lost city of Atlantis.

Despite the incredulity of European commentators, there is plenty of evidence to show that bronze sculpting was a native African skill and was not acquired from the Portuguese. Firstly, if Ahammangiwa was Portuguese, it is remarkable that the Portu-guese records made absolutely no mention of them sending one of their citizens to teach Benin's people a transformative artistic skill. The Moor-Roupell report also claimed that Ahammangiwa 'had many wives'.[7] A polygamous sixteenth-century Roman Catholic Portuguese citizen who lived several years in Benin and dedicated his life to teaching Benin's people how to make sculptures is very implausible. Moreover, there is no evidence that the fifteenth- and sixteenth-century Portuguese possessed bronze casting skills to an extent where they could export and teach it to foreigners living in

6   Ibid., p. 7.
7   Ibid., p. 6.

another continent. The British anthropologist and museum curator Henry Ling Roth conceded that: 'we are still quite in the dark as to any existence of such high-class art in the Iberian Peninsula at the end of the fifteenth century; and we know there was not much of this art in the rest of Europe'.[8]

The name 'Ahammangiwa' is clearly not European. The last four letters of his name ('Giwa') is a common Edo name and is also common among the Oduduwan people to Benin's west. The theory of European bronze sculpting origination is further discredited because sixteenth-century Benin pupils of Portuguese bronze casting education could not have acquired such a highly remarkable level of sculpting aptitude immediately after the Portuguese taught them. Even if the Portuguese began teaching Benin's people how to cast bronze on the very first day they set foot in Benin in 1485, it is inconceivable that immediately afterwards, the Bini would learn how to make better sculptures than their own teachers. It would be expected that Benin graduates of the Portuguese school of bronze casting would have at first made bad and clumsy sculptures before getting progressively better at them after several years or generations. Yet excavations have not found such preparatory models showing the sculpting naivety of a student, and then the improvement of increasingly better and experienced sculptors. These inconsistencies so puzzled a British curator that he admitted: 'It is not conceivable that an introduced art could have developed at so rapid a rate.'[9]

'LOST WAX'

Nineteenth- and twentieth-century Europeans were reluctant to attribute the artworks they found to Africans, and tried to find a European link to them – no matter how outlandish or tenuous, because they were technically brilliant, visually striking, and the method for making them was complex and laborious. To admit that Africans made world-class artworks that equalled or surpassed the quality of what Europeans were capable of, and using the same

---

8   Roth, 1903, p. 232.
9   Ibid., p.29.

techniques as Europe's best sculptors, would raise disturbing impli-
cations. Firstly, it was incendiary to the then prevailing European
presumptions that Africans were primitive luddites. The Benin and
Ife bronze sculptures were made using a complicated process known
as the *cire perdue* or 'Lost Wax' method. Lost Wax is the colloquial
term for a sculpting method which involves shaping the outline of
the sculpture in wax, then covering it in clay and perforating holes
in it. After the clay hardens, the sculpture is heated to a red hot
temperature to melt the wax out of the hardened clay, and allow the
wax to ooze out of the holes perforated in it. Bronze is then subsequently poured into the space that the wax was melted out from. The
fact that Europe's best sculptors also used this elaborate Lost Wax
method flummoxed nineteenth- and twentieth-century European
chroniclers who found it impossible to accept that Africans were
capable of such technical artistry. One such European commenta-
tor confidently claimed that 'It is almost certain that prior to the
discovery of Benin by the Portuguese the art of casting bronze by
the *cire perdue* process was unknown to its inhabitants'[10] and that
'To anyone acquainted with the negro character ... the Negro is
imitative, versatile, and tractable to a high degree, but absolutely
devoid of individual initiative, application, or power of retention,
and decidedly, ambition is not one of his strong points.'[11]

Unbeknown to European chroniclers, the skill was indigenous
and pre-dated European arrival in Africa. For example, the people
of Igbo-Ukwu in what is now south-east Nigeria made elaborate
bronze bowls, cups, and pots over 500 years before Europeans first
visited Nigeria, and the Ashanti of Ghana made bronze jugs as far
back as the 1400s (almost 100 years before Europeans first arrived
there). As shown in Table 9.1, there were at least four centres of
artistic excellence in ancient Nigeria starting from the Iron Age and
continuing until the sixteenth century. In chronological order these
were: Nok, Igbo-Ukwu, Ife, and Benin.

Hundreds of years before the Colossus of Rhodes was built, and
before builders laid the first foundation stones in the Great Wall of

---

10   Gaskell, 1902, p. 102.
11   Ibid., p.103.

Table 9.1   Chronology of ancient Nigerian art

	Era	Location
Nok	800 BC–200 AD	Middle Nigeria
Igbo–Ukwu	ninth–tenth centuries	South-east Nigeria
Ife	thirteenth–fifteenth centuries	South-west Nigeria
Benin	fifteenth–sixteenth centuries	South-central Nigeria
Tsoede bronzes	sixteenth century	North-west Nigeria

China, the mysterious 'Nok' people in Nigeria's Middle Belt region made terracottas that were described as 'some of the most iconic objects from ancient Africa'.[12] The bronze sculpting industry of the ancient city of Ile-Ife in south-west Nigeria peaked between the thirteenth and fifteenth centuries, and preceded that of Benin (which gives chronological support to the oral tradition that Ife's artisans exported their bronze casting expertise to Benin). In 1939 a German anthropologist wrote that Ife's bronze sculptures 'are masterpieces and could not technically be improved upon'[13] and the British historian Michael Crowder claimed that they 'rank among the masterpieces of world sculpture'.[14] Apart from their quality, the Ife sculptures had other notable traits. Firstly, the brass used to make them was imported from thousands of miles away (across the Sahara Desert). This shows the extent of long-distance trading routes in pre-colonial West Africa. Secondly, the Ife bronzes have a mystical aura. During excavations at Ife in the early 1970s the *Ooni* of Ife Adesoji Aderemi had recurring nightmares in which he saw his ancestors walking past his bed in a procession.[15] These nightmares made the *ooni* aware that archaeologists were excavating at Ife's royal cemetery, and disturbing his deceased ancestors. He ordered the excavations to stop.

---

12   Atwood, 2011, p. 35.
13   Meyerowitz, 1939, p. 152.
14   Crowder, 1973, p. 55.
15   'Head of an Ife King from Nigeria'.

'the front ranks of all known bronze statuary throughout the world history of art'

While most of the sculptures described above emerged from powerful large and/or powerful states such as Benin and Ife, some were excavated in obscure and surprising locations. In addition to the Nok, Igbo-Ukwu, Ife, and Benin sculptures, there is another group of mysterious bronzes whose origin cannot be easily attributed to any particular society. Several bronze figurines made in the sixteenth century were found at the small towns of Jebba and Tada (near the River Niger) in an area populated by the Nupe ethnic group. A German anthropologist said of them: 'Some of these – and here I have been confirmed by leading artistic and scientific experts in England, Belgium and France – must be placed in to the front ranks of all known bronze statuary throughout the world history of art.'[16] How brilliant bronze sculptures arrived at two small towns, outside of the most well-known and powerful pre-colonial Nigerian societies is a head-scratching mystery to outsiders. However, the bronzes hold no such mystery to the locals. To them, their origin is certain and they believe that a legendary man brought them.

THE LEGEND OF TSOEDE

Like Benin, the Hausa States, the Onitsha kingdom, and the Oduduwan kingdoms, there is a legend that traces the lineage of the Nupe monarchy to one man. According to this legend which is known by both the Nupe and Igala ethnic groups, prior to the fifteenth century the Nupe were vassals to the Igala. When an Igala prince travelled to Nupeland, he fell in love with, and impregnated, a Nupe princess. Before the princess gave birth, the prince was summoned to return home. Before departing he gave the princess a ring to give to their baby when he was born. After he departed, she gave birth to a boy named Tsoede.[17] As part of the Nupe's tribute obligations to the Igala, the Nupe were obligated to send slaves

---

16 Meyerowitz, 1941, p. 90.
17 Hausas call him 'Edegi'.

to the *Attah* Igala (King of the Igala). During one of these annual tribute payments 30 years later, the Nupe sent Tsoede to the Igala. When he arrived the Igala king noticed that he was wearing a ring. It was the same ring that the king (while still a prince) gave to the Nupe princess he impregnated. The king recognised Tsoede as his son, officially made him a prince of the Igala, and anointed him as his successor. However, Tsoede's half-brothers became jealous and conspired against him. Fearing that Tsoede's life was in danger, his father advised him to flee back to Nupeland. To aid Tsoede's escape, his father gave him gifts including a bronze canoe, large chains, and a trumpet as insignia of authority and kingship with which to take leadership in Nupeland. As Tsoede fled, his half-brothers pursued him. His escape from them was ascribed to the magical powers of the bronze artefacts that his father gave to him. When Tsoede returned sometime in the sixteenth century, he united the Nupe (who were then separated into several different clans) into one kingdom, declared himself as their first *etsu* (king), and freed the Nupe from Igala rule.

As the son of an Igala prince and a Nupe princess, Tsoede's legend survives in both Igala and Nupe oral traditions and his legend gave birth to a Nupe cult regarding him and the mystical bronze artefacts he brought from Igalaland – which are still regarded as insignia of royalty. Tsoede's legend is not limited to the establishment of the Nupe monarchy. He is also given credit for advancements in craftmanship and technology. He apparently brought blacksmiths from Igalaland with him to Nupeland; who taught improved smithing techniques to the indigenous Nupe blacksmiths. Tsoede is also credited with introducing canoe-building expertise to Nupeland.

'clever blacksmiths'

The fact that these centres of artistic excellence at Nok, Igbo-Ukwu, Ife, Benin, and Nupe are so widely separated by geography and a time continuum of over 1000 years suggests that artistic talent and technology was widespread among Nigeria's pre-colonial people. There are clues as to how and why mysterious sculptures of unknown origin were scattered so widely around Nigeria. Some pre-colonial blacksmiths (especially among the Igbos of south-east Nigeria) were itinerant professionals who travelled to sell their metal welding expertise outside their homeland. In contrast to the Benin sculptor guild who were servants of the king, the famous blacksmiths from Awka in what is now south-east Nigeria worked and earned a living as expatriate private professionals and were known as 'clever blacksmiths (who travel throughout the length and breadth of the land plying their trade)'.[18] The Awka blacksmiths travelled far and wide into Benin, the Efik-, Idoma-, Igala-, Ijaw-, Urhobo-speaking areas in the south-east and Niger Delta parts of Nigeria, and even into Cameroon. They did not just make sculptures for aesthetic purposes but also made functional items such as jewellery (including anklets, bracelets, and chains), weapons such as guns and swords, and farming tools such as axes, hoes, and shovels. When the English missionary George Basden visited Awka in the early 1900s, he got a front row seat to watch Awka's legendary blacksmiths at work. In return for a favour from Basden, one of Awka's blacksmiths immediately reforged an old cutlass into a patterned bracelet for Basden while he waited and watched. When Basden visited another blacksmith's shop, he witnessed the blacksmith reforge old cutlasses into a nearly complete gun. Basden was impressed that the blacksmith's work was 'so well executed that one could scarcely distinguish the result from an English-made article'[19] (comparing the output of an African's work to that of a European was the zenith of praise back then). The fact that several bronze artefacts of unknown origin were excavated at locations where the Awka blacksmiths travelled to may mean that the wandering habits of private blacksmiths, such as those from Awka and others like them, exported their skills into, and left traces of their work at, widely dispersed locations around southern pre-colonial Nigeria.

The indigenous Benin historian Jacob Egharevba popularised the tradition that Benin (Nigeria's most famous bronze sculpting centre) acquired its bronze sculpting skill from the same place as

18 Basden, 1921, p. 245.
19 Ibid., p. 174.

its monarchy: Ife. According to Egharevba, Benin's bronze casting first arose in the late thirteenth-century during the reign of *Oba* Oguola. Egharevba's account claims that after becoming aware of Ife's great bronze sculptures, Oguola asked the *Ooni* of Ife to send one of his bronze casters to teach Benin's people how to make them. In response, the *ooni* sent a master bronze caster called Iguegha to Benin.[20] Egharevba's account contradicts the earlier account that Benin's royal officials gave to Consul-General Sir Ralph Moor and Acting Resident Captain Ernest Roupell in 1897. The earlier account that Benin's officials gave to Moor and Roupell claimed it first arose later during the reign of *Oba* Esigie. This is a massive discrepancy as Oguola and Esigie reigned more than 200 years apart and there were at least ten other *obas* between their reigns. Also, while Egharevba claimed that Benin's first bronze caster came from Ife and was called Iguegha, the 1897 account claimed he was named Ahammangiwa but did not reference his homeland. Despite these contradictions, it is possible that Ahammangiwa and Iguegha are the same person – albeit differently transliterated, and with the era in which they lived being distorted in different oral accounts. Benin oral history's claim that Benin needed Ife to introduce bronze sculpting to Benin is puzzling. Other areas of southern Nigeria such as Awka and Igbo-Ukwu (which were closer to Benin than Ife) made bronze artworks centuries before Ife did. Some of their itinerant blacksmiths travelled to Benin and were closer teachers than Ife. It is unlikely that Iguegha introduced a new skill to Benin, but more likely that he introduced a particular *style* of bronze sculpting or an upgrade in its practice.

THE 'WEST AFRICAN CELLINI'

Until today, Benin's bronze casting guild still hero worships Iguegha. Although it is unlikely that a complicated skill such as bronze casting was taught by one man alone, the fact that Benin's bronze casting expertise peaked in the sixteenth and seventeenth centu-

---

20   Egharevba, 1968, p. 11.

ries suggests that a brilliant craftsman or group of sculptors worked in Benin during that era. The continued reverence for Ahammangiwa/Iguegha highly supports this and that he was the best of his kind. In 1902 a British art expert referred to Ahammangiwa as 'this West African Cellini'[21] and acknowledged that 'his technical and artistic skill is of the highest order'.[22] For early twentieth-century Europeans to compare Ahammangiwa's work to one of the greatest artists of all time (the Italian Benvenuto Cellini) was a rare form of praise, and was not the only reference that compared the Benin Bronzes to Cellini's work. The German archaeologist Felix Von Luschan claimed that:

> These Benin works notably stand among the highest heights of European casting. Benvenuto Cellini could not have made a better cast himself, and no one has before or since, even to the present day. These bronzes stand even at the summit of what can be technically achieved.[23]

The purpose for which Benin's master sculptor used his considerable skill is also shrouded in mystery. The most common assumption is that the Benin sculptures were made to glorify past kings and their achievements. However, these are twentieth- and twenty-first-century assumptions without the context in which they were made 400–600 years earlier. There is also a magico-religious or ritual element to them. Some of the Benin Bronze heads were attached to elaborately carved elephant tusks and used in religious rituals. No one is sure why. The Ife sculptures also have mysterious elements. Some have holes drilled along the foreheads and around the mouths of the people depicted in them. No one is sure why. While British and Portuguese visitors to Benin saw some of the Benin Bronzes hanging on the walls of the *oba*'s palace, British officials also found other plaque carvings covered in dust on the floor of a Benin palace courtyard – which suggests that they were disused or more likely

---

21 Gaskell, 1902, p. 101.
22 Ibid., p. 102.
23 Gunsch, 2013, p. 28.

that they were held in so much awe and reverence that frequently handling them was forbidden. We also do not know, for example, if the Bronzes were arranged in a chronological, symmetrical, or other order that when 'read' together, told a story about Benin. When British officers looted the Bronzes in 1897, they did not systematically catalogue exactly where they found each Bronze. As a result, much of the original knowledge regarding them has been lost.

These multiple unknowns are unsurprising because mystery was central to the profession of sculpting in ancient Nigeria. Blacksmiths and sculptors were not just regarded as skilled professionals. They were also custodians of sacred and secret knowledge. Smithing was more than an occupation, and was also regarded as a supernatural sodality. Ancient Nigerians regarded metals as mysterious materials that could be manipulated only by smiths who knew the secrets of their mystical qualities. Vikings had similar beliefs and also regarded their blacksmiths' skill in forging metal as the outcome of secret magic. Ancient Nigerian smiths reinforced their supernatural aura by incorporating religion into their work. For example, smiths from the Abiriba, Item, and Nsukka areas of Igboland worshipped an iron deity and sacrificed dogs to him in a way very similar to how smiths from the Oduduwan areas also worshipped and sacrificed dogs to their god of iron Ogun.

In medieval Nigeria, smithing was a special club where few were chosen. Smiths operated as a trade union that tried to institute a monopoly by prohibiting non-members from practising their arts. Professional sculptors and smiths jealously guarded the secrets of their knowledge and agreed to train others only in hereditary fashion within families. Smiths were very selective about, and tightly screened, non-relatives before agreeing to teach them. Even then, new inductees had to undergo ritual magic initiations. Smiths' mysterious aura meant that the anvils and hammers they used were regarded as dangerous and sacred implements with special powers that could harm or kill if people who did not undergo the initiation rites of the smiths' sacred guild used them. Even the water in which hammers were soaked was presumed to have special medicinal properties.

However, the secretive manner in which these artisans worked, and their reluctance to admit outsiders into their profession, came at a cost. For example, Benin's bronze sculptors were a royal guild in the king's exclusive service and could not make sculptures for others without the king's consent. As a profession that rarely trained new recruits, smiths inhibited their own succession and blocked knowledge transfer. When they spoke about the legendary Ahammangiwa in 1897, Benin's sculptors claimed that 'the king gave him plenty of boys [apprentices] to teach', but that 'We can make brasswork now, but not as he made it, because he and all his boys are dead.'[24] The sculptor guild's self-imposed limitations on knowledge transfer and succession meant that a sculptor's skills were often buried with him, and may explain why their skill peaked in the Middle Ages and was never restored to its former heights.

The importance of the artworks described in this chapter transcends their artistic merit. They say a lot more about the type of people who made them. There is a tendency to portray pre-colonial Africans as either subsistence farmers and/or hunters. Yet the massive array of sculptures in brass, bronze, clay, ivory, and wood, which depict monarchs, officials, royal servants, and others, the close attention paid to the details and minutiae of their clothing, insignia, and physical features so as to make them identifiable hundreds of years later, and the depiction of deities, glories, and military victories, means that the people who made these artworks were highly sophisticated. They were people who were not only aware of their culture and history, but who also had the skill and technology to expose and transport twentieth- and twenty-first-century people back into their era using nothing but visual art. Executing such complicated artworks using difficult techniques could not have been performed without a laser-like concentration, and years of dedication and training. In other words, these artworks were the work of exceptionally intelligent people with outstanding skill. Nigeria's contemporary artisan tradition should be viewed as a continuation of their legacy.

---

24   Read and Dalton, 1899, p. 6.

10
The God Who Carries the World

Indigenous West African religions have a bad reputation. They are usually maligned with derogatory terms such as 'black magic', 'juju', and 'voodoo', and have been ostracised to the realm of the occult. Indigenous beliefs are subject to so much social scorn that one is unlikely to find any information about them outside specialist academic texts. Oddly, much of the contempt for West African religions comes from West Africans themselves (especially Christians and Muslims).

The overwhelming dominance of Christianity and Islam in Nigeria often gives the erroneous impression that the area had no serious indigenous religion before the two Abrahamic faiths arrived. In the nineteenth century, Europeans dismissed adherents of African religions as 'for the most part degraded savages, worshippers of devils, and participators in horrible fetiche [*sic*] rites' living in a 'mass of dark humanity'.[1] A great irony is that the people who held such views about African religions and regarded their beliefs as preposterous 'superstition' or 'idol worship' irrevocably accepted the veracity of Christian teachings about talking donkeys, and a man surviving for 72 hours inside the belly of a giant fish. As will be shown below, pre-colonial West African religious beliefs were no more outlandish than, and in many respects resembled, those of Christian Europe.

Not only did religion exist before Islam and Christianity arrived, but it (as is the case in contemporary Nigeria) dominated private and public life. Very rarely was any event or occurrence deemed to be the outcome of coincidence. Rather, various deities and spirits were usually given the credit or the blame for blessings and ills such as plentiful farm yields, droughts, marriage, births, infertility, sickness, and unsuccessful business deals. Daily life involved

---

1   Bindloss, 1898, p. 2.

worship and sacrifice to maintain good relations with benevolent spirits that could confer blessings, and to placate malevolent spirits that could bring misfortune. Belief in the power of deities to affect natural forces and an individual's life created a powerful compulsion to engage with them.

IN THE BEGINNING: PRE-ABRAHAMIC RELIGIONS

The difficulty of revealing the extent and types of pre-colonial religion is amplified by the enormous variety of pre-colonial religions which varied from one community to another. For ease of reading, this chapter will focus on the major pre-colonial religions in the areas that later became south-west, south-east, and northern Nigeria.

Although the religions in each area were different, there were common themes between them. While pre-colonial West Africans are frequently portrayed as polytheists, they actually practised monolatry. Their beliefs were similar to ancient Hebrews, since they elevated and worshipped a supreme god, but simultaneously acknowledged the existence of other subservient supernatural deities. Belief in a supreme god that created the universe and everything in it was widespread in pre-colonial West Africa. The supreme god was usually regarded as remote and people normally approached him indirectly through a host of different subsidiary deities and spirits. Each of these subsidiaries had a specific power or responsibility entrusted to it. People believed that in addition to being emissaries of the supreme god, these subsidiaries governed aspects of daily life such as the weather, health, and fertility. Some deities were believed to have the power to ward off disease and epidemics, while other deities were invoked as sureties and witnesses for contracts and oaths.

OWNER OF HEAVEN

The pre-colonial religion of the Oduduwan areas is the most well-known and studied pre-colonial Nigerian religion because it was exported to the Americas and is still practised in faraway places such as Brazil, the USA, Cuba, Haiti, and other parts of the Caribbean. People in the Oduduwan areas recognised a supreme god they called Olorun[2] ('owner of heaven') who created the universe and life within it. Olorun (also known as Olodumare) also deputised subsidiary deities and spirits known as *orisas* (pronounced 'orishas'). Worship of *orisas* was so widespread that a Christian missionary's wife concluded that: 'one God is acknowledged, but the real worship is to the orishas [*sic*]'.[3] *Orisa* worship was so integral and widespread in society that the four-day week consisted of four consecutive 'sabbaths' named *Ojo-Awo, Ojo-Ogun, Ojo-Jakuta,* and *Ojo-Ose,* which were dedicated to the worship of the deities named Obatala, Ogun, Sango, and Orunmila, respectively. In contrast to the Igbo week which revolved around market days, and the Judeo-Christian seven-day week which has five working days followed by a Sabbath and two rest days at the weekend, the Oduduwan week was essentially a series of consecutive sabbaths every day.

THE *ORISAS*

There are over 400 different *orisas*. The pantheon of *orisas* are so numerous and varied that they rival the gods of Greek, Norse, and Roman mythology. The *orisas* are not competing or rival gods to Olorun, but are instead regarded as his lieutenants whom he delegated to supervise natural forces or different aspects of creation or the world's biological and environmental powers. Some *orisas* are supernatural (for example, Obatala), others are metaphors for natural phenomena (for example, Ogun), and a third category are deified ancestors or ancient rulers (for example, Sango). Although most *orisas* are territorial and worshipped only in a small geographic area, a few were worshipped in all or most of Oduduwa-land. Due to the massive number of *orisas*, the discussion below will focus only on five of the most significant and most widely worshipped *orisas*: Sango, Ogun, Obatala, Orunmila, and Eshu.

---

2   Olorun was also known as Eleda (the creator) and Oluwa (Lord).
3   *Church Missionary Intelligencer*, 1858, p. 260.

Olorun gave to the androgynous *orisa* known as Obatala the power to create land and to determine to shape of living beings. Women who wanted to become pregnant prayed to Obatala (also known as Orisala) since Obatala has the power to form a baby in the womb. The trademark of Obatala devotees is their all white clothing and white beads. Their attachment to the colour white means that they do not eat red meat or use red palm oil while cooking. Obatala's role as a supernatural sculptor that determined the shape of human beings meant that Obatala was held responsible for the fate of those born with physical deformities (such as albinos, dwarves, and hunchbacks). Such people were regarded as '*eni orisa*' (property of the gods) and were usually dedicated as priests and priestesses to Obatala (whom it was believed, caused their deformities due to being a mercurial and unpredictable artist, or capriciously to punish parents for slackness in their devotion). As discussed in Chapter 5, Obatala's role became conflated with that of Oduduwa, the presumed human patriarch of the Oduduwan area. In some versions of the Oduduwa legend, it was Oduduwa (not Obatala) that created land on the earth. The ancient political revolution in or around Ife which gave rise to the Oduduwan dynasty and kingdoms makes it likely that Oduduwa's legend was amplified by myths which attributed to him supernatural powers hitherto presumed to be the Obatala's. As a result, the story of one of them is also the story of the other. The Obatala–Oduduwa fusion is not the only instance where the stories of a deity and political leader were fused together.

The Stone Thrower

Sango (pronounced 'Shango') is the *orisa* of thunder and lightning, and worship of him can be simultaneously regarded as ancestor worship and a personality cult. Sango worship emerged from Oyo's royalty, and there is evidence that like Obatala, Sango's character and legacy has been combined with that of a human being. Sango was a tempestuous, larger than life early *Alaafin* of Oyo. He and his wife were also skilled supernatural practitioners. After being deposed and driven into exile following a people's uprising, the distraught Sango committed suicide. However, his reputation survived him. If lightning struck the house of a Sango enemy, his supporters claimed it was Sango's posthumous revenge and that he had paid a supernatural return visit from the afterlife back to this world. The site where lightning struck was regarded as sacred ground where people paid homage to Sango, who became a deified ancestor and gave birth to a religious movement that was based on a form of ancestor worship similar to ancient Rome's worship of deceased emperors. Sango's attributes, imagery, and visual depiction as a hammer-wielding bringer of wrath and vengeance are remarkably similar to those of Thor, the hammer-wielding god of thunder and lightning in Norse mythology. Since Sango was the fourth *Alaafin* of Oyo and lived in Oyo's early days, it can be presumed that worship of him is over 500 years old. However, thunder and lightning-centred religion and worship pre-dated Sango. Sango's nickname is Jakuta ('stone thrower'). Jakuta is more than a nickname. It was also the name of a god of thunder and lightning that pre-dated Sango. It is likely that Sango's explosive personality made it easy to nickname him after a thunder and lightning deity, and for some of his aggrieved and grieving followers to mount a successful posthumous public relations campaign that turned into a personality cult that coalesced Sango's legend with the attributes of a weather deity.

Ogun is the *orisa* of iron, and is associated with the shaping and transformation of iron and other metals. Ogun was reputedly a son of Oduduwa who left Ife, settled in a forest hideout. and converted it into a factory for manufacturing iron tools. Unsurprisingly, Ogun was very popular among, and was regarded as the patron of, professionals whose employment relied on the use of metal tools (such as blacksmiths, hunters, and warriors). The ability of blacksmiths to manipulate and change metals into different shapes was regarded as a skill so mysterious that it was the outcome of supernatural ability. Ogun's association with metals that could be forged into weapons also attached a martial image to him, and he was popular in areas that resisted conquest by Oyo (such as Ekiti, Ilesha, and Ondo). Ogun was probably less popular among dogs, as dogs were believed to be

Ogun's preferred sacrifice. Dogs were often beheaded as sacrificial offerings to him. In contemporary times, Ogun is popular among professional vehicle operators such as bus, lorry, and taxi drivers.

Rather than being simultaneous pre-human creations by Olorun, some *orisas* were by-products of socio-political forces. In the same way that different Oduduwan groups had their own versions of the Oduduwa legend that gave themselves primacy, they also had cultural or historical legacies that explain the emergence or predominance of *orisas* in their locale (for example, Sango's popularity in the Oyo areas where he reigned, and the preference for Ogun in the eastern areas of Oduduwa-land that resisted Oyo). The fact that some *orisas* had human-like idiosyncrasies also supports the position that some of them were humans that later became deified after their supporters posthumously fused them into folk tales regarding *orisas*.

Eshu: 'sowing dissension is my great delight'

Eshu (also known as Legba in Dahomey) is the most emotionally divisive of the *orisas*. Eshu (pronounced 'Aeh-Shu') is a trickster akin to Loki of Norse mythology. He is the *orisa* of chaos and disorder and a specialist agent provocateur. In an old allegory that demonstrates Eshu's mischievous aptitude for engineering disagreement, Eshu donned a hat with different colours on its left and right sides and walked back and forth between two neighbouring farms owned by friends. Eshu's appearance made the two friends quarrel so vehemently about the colour of his hat and the direction he was walking in that they came to blows. When the two friends later tried to hold Eshu accountable for the trouble he caused, he confessed that 'sowing dissension is my great delight',[4] then started a fire as he fled. As the townspeople tried to escape the fire, he further flummoxed them by mixing up their possessions, while laughing at the disorder he created. Eshu's propensity for mischief and for instigating conflict and mayhem led to him being later mis-characterised in Christianity as the devil. Yet, the incorporation of Eshu

---

4   Cosentino, 1987, p. 262.

into personal names such as Esutoyin ('Eshu is worthy of praise') demonstrates that Eshu was not initially regarded as the embodiment of evil. Instead, Eshu was actually the gateway to a divinatory system known as *Ifa*.

IFA DIVINATION: RELIGION MEETS ANCIENT ALGORITHM

Although Oduduwans recognised hundreds of *orisas*, a divinatory process called *Ifa* acted as an integrative system that linked the constellation of *orisas* to each other. *Ifa* is a term loaded with multiple meanings. *Ifa* is not an *orisa* but is simultaneously a religious system, a massive cultural and intellectual algorithm, a counselling service, and fortune telling. *Ifa* is often conflated with the name of the *orisa* of divination and wisdom called Orunmila[5] (who is also referred to as Ifa), and the word also describes the system of divination that Orunmila founded. According to the creation story popular in the Oduduwan areas, when Olorun deputised Obatala to create land and physical beings, he appointed Orunmila as a superintendent to observe and advise Obatala as he created. Being a direct witness to creation gave Orunmila sacred knowledge and wisdom. Orunmila's ability to migrate between heaven and earth and Abrahamic ability to be an interlocutor between Olorun and the human world led him to be revered by his followers as *ibikeji Olodumare* (second only to God). *Ifa* provided a means of accessing Orunmila's awesome knowledge of the universe.

Orunmila and Eshu are the twin patrons of *Ifa* divination. Although Eshu is now typecast by Christians as 'the prince of darkness'[6] and 'the supreme power of evil',[7] in the pre-Christian era, Eshu was akin to an agent that collected a commission for providing access or introductions to other *orisas*. Due to an ancient bargain between Eshu and Orunmila, Eshu was entitled to a share of the offerings and sacrifices made to other *orisas*. Thus *Ifa* divina-

---

5 Known as Orunmuola among the Owo in the eastern area of Oduduwa-land.
6 Farrow, 1924, p. 120.
7 Lucas, 1942, p. 60.

tion was activated by prayers to Eshu, who was the gateway through which Orunmila could be accessed.

Ifa is a diagnostic tool of wisdom that allows people to identify the supernatural forces affecting their lives, and which directs them on the form of sacrifice or worship they should make to achieve their desired outcome. For example, people may consult *Ifa* prior to significant decisions or life-changing events such as child birth or marriage, or to reveal the source of ill fortune, barrenness, or sickness in a family. *Ifa* is and was used in several West African communities such as those from the Oduduwan, Dahomey, Igala, and Ewe (Ghana) areas. The Idoma, Igbo, and Benin people also have similar divination systems, respectively called *Eba*, *Afa* or *Aha*, and *Ogwega*.

FATHER OF MYSTERIES

Ifa relies on the astute analytical insight of a professionally trained diviner known as a *babalawo* (literally: 'father of mysteries'). Due to their remarkable powers of memorisation, perception, and ability to decipher and diagnose complex social and spiritual problems, *babalawo* (who are known as *bokono* in Dahomey) are highly respected. They provided their services to royalty and commoners alike and sometimes served on the court of monarchs and advised kingmakers regarding royal succession, or the king on major decisions. For example, in the early 1840s, the *Alake* of Egbaland Sodeke agreed to allow Christian missionaries into Abeokuta only after concurrence by an *Ifa babalawo*.

Being a *babalawo* is a lifelong vocation involving lengthy training and memorisation, and secondment to international *Ifa* training centres. The level of aptitude and training required to become a *babalawo* accorded them great respect. The *babalawo* is part clairvoyant, and part behavioural psychologist. While in session he has a restrained and tranquil comportment and is hyper-conscious of his client's verbal and non-verbal behaviour and responses. During this heightened state of concentration and enlightenment, his job is to identify the client's problem and prescribe a solution to it by interceding with Orunmila to reveal the remedial steps that the client should take.

Faith in the *babalawo's* near supernatural powers of intuition was such that rather than directly inform the *babalawo* about the nature of their problem (the way a patient or church-goer would do to his doctor or pastor), the client would instead whisper their problem in a low tone that the *babalawo* could not hear, or whisper it to the instruments of divination. The *babalawo* is then expected to decipher the problem and its solution himself using his instruments and intuitive powers. Yet this does not mean that clients accepted their *babalawo's* skills as fact without scrutiny. A client may, for example, test a *babalawo's* aptitude by asking him to give details about the route and journey the client took to meet the *babalawo*.

Although the procedure of *Ifa* divination varied from one region to another, the two most common methods involved interpreting signs made by either casting a chain attached to 16 curved half-shells from the fruit of the *opele* tree (*anwa* tree in the Igala version of *Ifa*) or by the *babalawo* placing 16 palm nuts known as *ikin* in one of his hands and then clapping his hands together to try to catch all of them with his other hand.[8] The pattern that the shells fall in (for example, face up, face down) has a coded hidden meaning which the *babalawo* has pre-memorised as part of his training. There are 16 basic meanings that can be rendered, but when the pattern of the nuts are read in pairs, there are at least 256 possible meanings (known as *Odu*) which the *babalawo* recites to the client in the form of an allegory or proverb. These meanings are not improvised and have to be memorised.[9] Given that each meaning has a particular *orisa*, ritual, sacrifice, or sanction attached to it, that they had to be memorised and recited verbatim, and that it was sacrilegious to add or omit anything from the recitation, the *babalawo's* powers of memorisation and recall were extraordinary.

The *babalawo's* concern is not only to learn the source of the client's problem, but also to determine which *orisa* was responsible for it, and to appease and make offerings to. After identifying the client's problem, the *babalawo* prescribes a solution which may

8   In an alternate version used by Igalas and known as *Ifa ebutu*, the *babalawo* draws lines in sand.

9   Other accounts claim that there are over 1000 *Odu* meanings.

involve making sacrifices to a particular *orisa*, or secular behavioural modifications by the client (such as changing diet or abstaining from certain behaviour). A remarkable aspect of *babalawos'* work is how often they are right. As recently as 2018, an American academic who spent eight years shadowing a *babalawo* noted that:

> Indeed, it is rare that the advice given to an individual from Ifa by way of [the *babalawo*] has proven wrong or untimely. Having sat at his feet in training regularly from 2008 to 2016, I have borne witness to scores of clients coming through the door of his shrine proclaiming, 'Baba you were so right! Everything you said happened!'[10]

RELIGION IN THE SOUTH-EAST

Belief in a supreme god assisted by several supernatural deputies was also replicated in the area that is now south-east Nigeria. In pre-colonial times, belief in the supreme god that created the universe was so widespread in Igboland that when European missionaries arrived there to proselytise to what they presumed was a heathen population, several of them grudgingly admitted in their diaries and notebooks that Igbos already 'believe in the existence of one Almighty, Omnipotent, Omnipresent Being whom they worship as such, and regard as the Omniscient God'[11] and that 'Amongst the Ibo [*sic*] people there is a distinct recognition of a Supreme Being – beneficent in character – who is above every other spirit, good or evil. He is believed to control all things in heaven and earth, and dispenses rewards and punishments according to merit.'[12]

'the god who carries the world'

Igbos referred to their supreme god by a series of superlative names which varied depending on the geographic area where the god's

---

10   Wood, 2018, pp. 91–2.
11   Horton, 1868, p. 183.
12   Basden, 1921, p. 215.

devotees lived. These names included *Obasi ndi n'elu* ('the god who is above') and *Ose bulu uwa* or *Olisa bulu uwa* ('the god who carries the world') in the so-called Ika-Igbo or Anioma areas to the west of the River Niger (modern-day Delta State). In the southern areas of Igboland (modern-day Abia and Imo States), people referred to the supreme god as *Chi na eke* ('the creator god' or 'the god that creates').

'The Ibos are … a religious people'

Many missionaries' first visit to Igboland was to towns adjacent to the River Niger or northern Igbo towns such as Awka and Onitsha (modern-day Anambra State) where people referred to the supreme god by a word that to early European missionaries sounded like, and which they transliterated as, 'Tshuku'. Reverend James Schon observed that: 'The Ibos [*sic*] are, in their way, a religious people. The word "Tshuku" – God – is continually heard. Tshuku is supposed to do every thing [*sic*] … "God made every thing: He made both White and Black," is continually on their lips.'[13] The phrase the missionaries heard was actually *Chi-ukwu* ('the big god' or 'the mighty god'). *Chi na eke* and *Chukwu* later became contracted and transliterated as Chineke and Chukwu, respectively, and these remain the most common names and spellings for God in Igboland in contemporary times. God's importance was demonstrated by a plethora of Igbo names such as Chibueze ('God is king'), Chibundu ('God is life'), Chukwunyere ('the one that God gave').

WAMAH'S PRAYER

The prayers of Chukwu's adherents were almost indistinguishable from the prayers made today by followers of the Abrahamic religions. For example, in the late 1850s Reverend Taylor observed an Igbo woman called 'Wamah' (probably Nwama) praying in the town of Aboh (in modern-day Delta State). Taylor transcribed her prayer as follows:

---

13   Schon and Crowther, 1842, pp. 50–1.

*Biko Chi, mere'm ihe-oma. Gi nwe ndu. Biko kpere Chukwu Abiama,
gwa ya obi'm dum ma – biko wepu ihe ojo di na obi'm tsufu Amusu,
mekwa akku bia'm*[14] (Please God, give me blessings. You have
power over life. I beseech thee to intercede with God the Spirit.
Tell him my heart is clean. Please remove all bad thoughts from
my heart; drive out all witchcraft; let riches come to me)

A striking aspect of Wamah's prayer is how similar it was to a
modern Christian prayer. Not only were the general contours of
Igbo traditional belief in, and prayer to, God similar to Christianity in general outline, but so was Igbo belief in spiritual reward
for those who did good and retributive justice for those who did
evil. The former would be deemed as bound for *ala eze* ('the land
of kings') and the latter were condemned to punishment in a place
called *oku muo* (literally: 'ghost fire').

'Truly God has not left Himself without witness!'

Schon was so astonished by what he learned about Igbo religion
and the parallels between *ala eze* and *oku muo* with the Christian
concepts of heaven and hell, that he asked others whether the Igbos
who said and believed such things had interacted with Christians.
Even when he was told that they had not, he refused to believe it
until he confirmed what he had been told by his own investigations.
Having satisfied himself that Igbo traditional religion had a counterpart for heaven and hell, Schon exclaimed to himself: 'Truly God
has not left Himself without witness!'[15] These correlations between
what pre-colonial Igbos already believed and Christian doctrine
perhaps made them receptive to Christianity when it arrived.

CHUKWU'S EMISSARIES

Alongside their belief in Chukwu, Igbos also interfaced with a
pantheon of subsidiary deities that they regarded as Chukwu's emis-

---

14 *Church Missionary Intelligencer*, 1858, p. 260.
15 Schon and Crowther, 1842, p. 51.

saries. Although Igbos recognised several of such lesser deities, Ala was particularly important. Ala was a female deity akin to Mother Earth or Mother Nature. Ala (also known as 'Ana' in some dialects) was the god of agricultural and human fertility. Ala's role was important in an agricultural society of farmers where childbirth and crop fertility were essential for survival and social cohesion. The theft of seeds or deliberate destruction of crops was a capital crime. In Igbo, the word *ala* also means 'earth' or 'the land'. Ala also served as the guardian of the society's traditions. Many crimes and immoral acts were referred to as *aruru-ala* or *nso-ala* (cruelty against the earth or sacrilege against the land). Other prominent deities in Igboland included Amadioha (the god of thunder) and the sun god Anyanwu (literally: 'the eye of the sun').

Igbos also believed that the subsidiary deities and spirits could inhabit places such as caves, forests, rivers, trees, and even objects. The location where a spirit resided would be deemed sacred or haunted, and either have a pilgrimage of worshippers or shunned – depending on whether the spirit was regarded as benevolent or malevolent. To outsiders who observed the devotees of such spirits making sacrifices to, or praying before, such locations and objects, they may have appeared to be idol worshippers. However, people did not worship the locations and objects as such, but rather, gave them special recognition as the abode of a spirit or a holy location (in the same way that Catholics hold crucifixes to be sacred and bow before statues of the Virgin Mary, Jews pray at the Wailing Wall, and Muslims pray at the *Kaaba* in Mecca). In their reflexive rush to dismiss and ridicule pre-colonial beliefs, adherents of the Abrahamic religions often omit such similarities between their religion and the ancient indigenous religions that preceded theirs. In the pre-colonial era, religious devotees recognised that an object or sculpture was not by itself sacred, and would discard or declare it worthless once the spirit that inhabited it was deemed to have departed from it. The haunted forest or sacred object inspires fear or has value only when the spirit is inside it.

Igbos' simultaneous belief in Chukwu and in other supernatural deities did not necessarily render them polytheists. When a Christian minister interviewed an elderly illiterate animist Igbo man named Ezenwandeyi, the interview produced 69 pages of transcripts during which Ezenwandeyi confirmed that the other deities that Igbos believe in were simply metaphors for Chukwu.[16]

'the father of all wickedness'

Among Igbo Christians, a deity called Ekwensu is dreaded as 'an evil spirit, akin to some extent to the Satan or Devil of Christian, Jewish, and Muslim peoples'.[17] However, like Eshu, Ekwensu has not always been synonymous with the devil. Due to the reluctance of people to be associated with, or speak about, a deity that is now regarded as the ultimate embodiment of evil, Ekwensu's pre-colonial persona is contested and opaque. In Ika-Igbo towns (such as Agbor and Asaba) to the western side of the River Niger, Ekwensu was commemorated during annual festivals. Christian missionaries disapproved of these festivals which they claimed were held 'for the express purpose of extolling the devil and all his works'.[18] While such festivals undoubtedly took place, there were other social reasons for them – unconnected to devil worship. In some communities, Ekwensu festivals had a military character with war dances and were held in order to commemorate past battles, significant persons, and other events of historical significance from antiquity. These annual Ekwensu festivals were also important as their frequency was used to calculate the ages of boys and determine their eligibility for admission into age group societies. This is not to say that Ekwensu did not have any association with evil in the pre-colonial era. Ekwensu was also the name of a head-hunting cult, and those who killed were said to have been possessed by Ekwensu's spirit. Ekwensu was also associated with tragic or untimely deaths. For example, people who committed suicide, died in accidents such as drowning or in fires, and women who died during childbirth were said to have suffered *onwu Ekwensu* (death by Ekwensu) and were

---

16 Isichei, 1969, p. 122.
17 Meek, 1937, p. 39.
18 Basden, 1921, p. 221.

denied traditional funeral rites. Thus, although the post-Christian portrayal of Ekwensu as the devil, 'the Evil One ... the father of all wickedness, anywhere and everywhere'[19] is not accurate, Ekwensu had a sinister persona in pre-colonial times. Unfortunately, due to the reluctance of a society that is now Christian to disclose or discuss information about a deity that is now feared as God's 'eternal enemy',[20] Ekwensu's identity and role in pre-colonial times remains obscure.

OSU – THE OUTCASTS

In contemporary Nigeria, Igbos are usually stereotyped as the country's most egalitarian ethnic group. Unlike many of their compatriots such as the Edo, Fulani, Hausa, and Kanuri, most areas of pre-colonial Igbo society did not have hereditary blue-blooded royalty. Yet, also unlike many other Nigerian ethnic groups, Igbo society had a class of outcasts. The existence of this outcast group is utterly contradictory to Igbo society's egalitarian traditions. Even in the twenty-first century, the so-called *Osu* people are spoken about in hushed tones and often shunned, and/or regarded with dread and horror. Yet there is little understanding about the *Osu's* origins and why they are treated in this way. Unlike outcast or 'untouchable' groups in other societies, the *Osu* were formerly revered in ancient times and were not regarded as cursed, nor were they condemned to servitude. However, the social impression of them changed over time.

While pre-colonial Igbo society did not have a strict caste system like India, it had protected classes of persons who worked as specially dedicated attendants at the shrines of deities. These attendants were known as *Osu*. The heritage of *Osus* is preserved in contemporary Igbo names such as *Nwaosu* ('child of *osu*') or *Osuala* ('*osu* of Ala' – the earth goddess). In contemporary times, *Osu* is regarded as a 'caste system'. Yet originally, *Osu* was not a caste as such, and the cleavage between them and the rest of society was religious and social rather

19   Ibid., p. 221.
20   Ibid., p. 215.

than caste based. In ancient times, *Osu* people enjoyed an elevated social position and were venerated. Since the *Osu* were dedicated servants to deities, it was sacrilege to harm or mistreat them. Other than living pious lives and dedicating themselves to serving deities, the *Osu* were not forbidden from procreating or from social elevation. On the contrary, some of them were successful, wealthy, and held positions of influence. As recently as the 1940s (during British colonial rule of Nigeria), *Osu* held powerful positions in non-Christian areas of Igboland, and the Ngwa sub-group of the Igbo did not stigmatise them. In contemporary Nigeria, many influential Igbos (including some who served in the government) are *Osu*. Yet no matter how wealthy and successful an *Osu* became, even impoverished peasants would refuse to marry them.

People could voluntarily or involuntarily become *Osu* in different ways. For example, one could become *Osu* if a *dibia* (a supernatural diviner) revealed them as one who was born or destined to dedicate their life in service of the gods. Since *Osu* enjoyed immunity, people in distress such as debtors, those accused of witchcraft, and other offenders could escape sanctions for criminal or moral offences by fleeing to a deity's shrine and becoming an *Osu*. This social amnesty came at a price. Since *Osu* lived segregated lives separate from the rest of society, a cleavage opened up between them and non-*Osu*. The latter avoided and feared the *Osu* as they did not want to unintentionally invoke the wrath of gods by interacting with those dedicated to serving them. The social custom whereby whomever married an *Osu* also automatically became *Osu* (along with the children born from the union) led non-*Osus* to forbid their children from marrying an *Osu*.

The *Osu* were also victims of changing religious and societal conditions. The slave trade and introduction of Christianity into Igboland combined to transform the impression of *Osu* from revered to trepidation. As most people were unwilling to voluntarily submit themselves to a life of servitude to deities and the social isolation attached to that role, people instead bought slaves to work as *Osu*. Some communities also tried to mollify deities by offering people considered dispensable as sacrificial atonements to the deities. Hence, social stigma became attached to a status regarded as living sacrifices to deities. The penetration of Christianity into Igboland in the twentieth century simultaneously helped and hurt *Osus*. Christianity's teaching of the equality of all men and women attracted those who sought upward social mobility or inclusion in mainstream society. As a result, many early Christian converts were slaves or social outcasts such as the *Osu*. Becoming a Christian and receiving mission school education allowed a former *Osu* to look upon animist religious practitioners as equals or to even look down on them as pagans. Conversely, since Christianity encouraged Igbos to shun their pre-colonial religions, Christian converts also shunned those associated with such religions. Christianity combined with the social fear of interaction and intermarriage with *Osus*, to turn a formerly venerated class of religious devotees into outcasts.

PRE-COLONIAL RELIGION IN THE NORTH

Revealing the traditional religion of the land that became northern Nigeria is challenging because since many of its indigenes are now Muslims, there is hostility to pre-Islamic religious practices, and the iconoclastic Islamic Caliphate that preceded the formation of Nigeria destroyed the symbols of those pre-Islamic religions. However, residues of the pre-Islamic religion still exist among the so-called *Maguzawa* (singular *bamaguje*). The *Maguzawa* are Hausas that refused to convert to Islam. Although the *Maguzawa* are a small minority and Muslims regard them as pagans, the *Maguzawa* can claim to be custodians of traditional Hausa culture and religion since their beliefs harken to a bygone pre-Islamic era.

Hausa traditional religion is known as *maguzanci*. One of its most significant worship practices is known as *Bori*. The nineteenth-century religious revolution in Hausaland pushed *Bori* to the margins of Hausa society but did not eliminate it. The term *Bori* refers both to a spirit possession belief system and is also colloquially used to refer to temporary insanity. For example, a person that behaves erratically may be asked *kana bori ne?* ('are you possessed?' or 'are you insane?'). Although the *Maguzawa* believe in god (whom they call Ubangiji), their beliefs are dominated by supernatural spirits called *iskoki*. While the *Maguzawa* acknowledged that Ubangiji is the supreme god that created the universe, they do not pray directly to, or make sacrifices to, him. Instead they interacted directly with *Bori* spirits known as *iskokin gona* (benevolent spirts) and *yan dawa* (wild or malevolent spirts). *Bori* practitioners believe that benevolent spirits bring wealth and good fortune, while the malevolent spirts cause misfortune, ill health, and death. *Bori* practitioners also believe that these spirits can inhabit trees, hills, rivers, and other locations. Thus, they often offered sacrifices at the locations where spirits were believed to reside, in order to placate them and pre-empt them from afflicting people with diseases and other negative experiences.

Bori has a spirit possession ritual where its practitioners wear the costumes of spirits who possess them, seize control of their bodies, and communicate through their bodies and mouths. The possessed usually become frenzied, contort their bodies with irregular, hysterical body motions, and foam at the mouth. The spirit is deemed to have left the possessed person when (s)he coughs or sneezes.

Although it is common to presume that there is a clear demarcation between *Bori* and contemporary religious and supernatural beliefs in some Hausa areas of northern Nigeria, there is a direct lineage between the medical expertise and practices of the *Bori* and the amulets and charms that are popular in contemporary Hausa society.

Embedded within Bori are clues about the powerful political and religious roles that women held in ancient Hausaland. Curiously, most *Bori* members are women. Prior to the early 1800s, the chief *Bori* priestess (the *inna*) in the Hausa State of Gobir was usually chosen from the king's lineage (normally his sister or daughter) and was also the leader of Gobir's women. The sister of Yunfa, the last Hausa pre-jihad King of Gobir, was the *inna*. However, the transformed religious climate after the nineteenth-century jihad led to the abolishment of such powerful *ex officio* roles for women, or to them being transferred to Muslim women.

THE RETURNERS

Reincarnation was another widespread and convergent belief. The belief in reincarnation was demonstrated by names such as Apara ('one who comes and goes'), Yetunde ('mother has come again'), and Babatunde ('father has come again') which are commonly given in the Oduduwan to babies born shortly after the death of a sibling. If several children in a family died in early childhood, a common belief was that the same child was being reincarnated and repeatedly reborn to, and dying with, the same parents. Such children were known as *abiku* ('born to die') in the Oduduwan areas, *ogbanje* among Igbos, and *aman akpa* ('born to die') among the Annang and Efik people of south-eastern Nigeria. The Edo and Ijaw people also had similar beliefs. It was believed that the child repeatedly inflicts grief on their family by dying and repeatedly being reborn. A child that exhibited precociously manipulative behaviour, fits, hallucinations, or frequent illness was likely to be suspected of being a returner and would be closely watched as they were often suspected of possessing supernatural powers, and could depart at any time.

Although each society had its own localised explanation for the cause of such cycles of repetitive birth, death, and rebirth, they were generally believed to be the work of evil spirits (known as *emere* in the Oduduwan areas). Families of the 'returner' children did not accept their fate without resistance. To break the cycle of death and rebirth they often deployed supernatural devices such as adorning their children with amulets, making incisions in their flesh, or mutilating the 'returner's' corpse after death by cutting off a finger, and then closely observing future children born in the family for birthmarks or physical deformities that correspond to the injuries inflicted on the returner's corpse. For example, in Ile-Ife a mother was so distraught at the death of her first ten children (who were presumed to be *abiku*) that she threw the corpse of her tenth child on the floor, fracturing its jaw as a result. Her eleventh baby was born with a disfigured lower jaw.[21]

---

21   Stevenson, 1985, p. 23.

In much of pre-colonial Nigeria, names went far beyond words used to identify a person, and also had massive religious and social significance. Names were believed to have the power to influence a child's destiny. Hence, parents carefully chose the names of their children and used them as a preventive measure to immunise them from harm and to prevent the reappearance of a 'returner'. Among Igbos, names such as Onwuzuruike ('let death rest') and Ozoemena ('let it not happen again') were common.

Although 'returners' were attributed to evil spirits, it is likely that the belief in them was linked to the high infant mortality rate before the twentieth century, and/or to genetic illnesses such as sickle cell anaemia. A modern study revealed that 70 per cent of *ogbanje* children that were examined for the study carried the sickle cell trait.[22] In ancient societies without a way of diagnosing childhood illnesses such as sickle cell anaemia, autism, epilepsy, and psychiatric illnesses, the distinctive physical features, frequent illness, and premature death of children with such ailments may have become conflated with evil spirits at a time when they seemed to be incomprehensible afflictions.

WHEN BELIEFS COLLIDE

The discussion above has consistently revealed two groups of religious similarities between the West African religions and the Abrahamic religions that supplanted them, and between the macro structure of the pre-colonial religions practised in different areas. The first similarity is the widespread indigenous belief in the afterlife and heaven and hell, even before the arrival of Christianity and Islam. In the Oduduwan areas, there was common belief in two heavens: *orun rere* (good heaven) and *orun apadi* ('heaven of broken potsherds' – bad heaven). Heaven and hell were also known in the Igbo areas as *ala eze* or *elu igwe* and *oku nmuo*, respectively. Secondly, an analogy can be drawn between spirit intermediaries in indigenous African religion such as the *orisa*, and the constel-

---

22   Okonkwo, 2004, p. 654.

lation of supernatural agents that assist the Abrahamic god (such as angels, prophets, Apostles, and others that are given permanent or temporary supernatural powers). African religious adherents seeking divine guidance and intervention from *orisas*, *babalawo*, and *dibia* is not much different to Christians who believe in or pray to God through intermediates such as the Virgin Mary, saints, or who believe that the prayers of their pastor are more effective than their own prayer. The supernatural paraphernalia such as amulets and charms that adherents of pre-colonial religions wore may be viewed as equivalent to the crucifixes and Virgin Mary statues that Catholics carry, or the stained glass images of revered saints that frequently adorn churches.

The prominent role of pastors as celebrities and alternative authority figures in modern Nigeria is not new. Priests and religious diviners also had prestige in pre-colonial society and faith in their powers was great enough for some of them to earn a living by selling supernatural advice, devices, and protection. Although *babalawo* and *dibia* are now often derogatively dismissed as 'witch doctors', in the pre-colonial era they were multi-talented professionals, and working as a provider of supernatural services was a recognised profession. They also had non-religious skills as medical practitioners and herbalists who could treat illnesses and perform medical procedures. Such abilities were highly valued in societies where virtually every accident, personal or social misfortune, and unexpected death was attributed to the work of evil spirits and witches. They were also invoked as neutral judge-style third-party mediators to settle disputes between litigants. For example, in a contract or dispute, it was common for the parties or protagonists to swear by a deity and vow in the presence of a *babalawo* or *dibia* to forfeit their life if they broke the contract or oath (in the same way that witnesses in contemporary court cases swear on the Bible or Koran, or swear to tell the whole truth and nothing but the truth).

Supernatural vocations were not limited to animist religions and also existed within Islam. For example, prior to their involvement in the revolutions for which they later became famous, Muslim *mallams* such as Mohammed al-Kanemi of Borno and Alimi (in

Ilorin) earned a living by selling supernatural amulets and charms. As recently as 1841, Reverend Schon of the Christian Missionary Society (CMS) observed at Idah (in the modern-day Igala area of Kogi State) that 'The Mallams ... ministerial labours consist chiefly in selling charms.'[23] These concepts of blessings or miracles for sale still continue in contemporary Nigeria where pastors constantly demand and/or encourage their congregation to give offerings and tithes in the expectation of material rewards and wealth. This can be viewed as an indirect descendant of ancient practices of payments in exchange for supernatural assistance and protection.

Not only did several aspects of pre-colonial West African religion resemble Christianity and Islam, but the pre-colonial religions of different ethnic groups and regions also resembled each other and converged, even among ethnic groups that had little or no contact with each other. For example, the Igbo god of thunder and lightning Amadioha had remarkably similar counterparts called Sango in the Oduduwan area, Kenjo among the Jukun, Sokogba among the Nupe, and Xevioso by the Fon people of Dahomey. All four of these deities were reputed to have power over thunder and lightning. Their worshippers also believed that the thunder and lightning deities delivered retributive justice against the wicked, and being struck by lightning was a bad omen. Another example is Gajimare, a part serpent Hausa deity that had power over rainbows. Gajimare had a remarkably similar counterpart deity in Oduduwa-land called Osumare, an androgynous serpent who was the spirit of the rainbow. Gajimare and Osumare also had a rainbow-serpent counterpart in Dahomey called Damballa.[24] Another common belief was in trickster deities called Nakada, Ekwensu, Eshu, Anansi, and Damballa among Hausas, Igbos, Oduduwans, the Akan of Ghana, and Fon of Dahomey, respectively.

We learned most of what we now know about pre-colonial West African religions in the nineteenth century when African and European Christian missionaries started writing about their observations of those religions. Since such writing was produced

---

23 Schon and Crowther, 1842, p. 100.
24 Damballa is also worshipped in Haitian cosmology.

by people whose stated intention was to outlaw, overthrow, and replace the pre-existing African religions, they unsurprisingly concluded that the area was 'a country where fetishism is universal'.[25] Little is known about how the religions were practised before these narratives were written, and how different the nineteenth-century and early twentieth-century practices were from how they were practised before. In a little over 100 years, the pre-colonial deities that were universally worshipped were overthrown and pushed to the brink of extinction. Christianity and Islam's replacement of once dominant indigenous religions is one of the most rapid and remarkable religious transformations in human history. The Abrahamic faiths supplanted the *manner* of religious worship, but not the reasons for it. People converted to Christianity and Islam in order to address the same concerns and needs that pre-colonial religions addressed: assistance with family, health, and personal problems, and protection from evil forces. The most popular books in modern-day Nigeria are the Bible, Koran, and other religious instructional books. The religious symptoms have changed, but the causes remain the same.

---

25 Basden, 1921, p. 288.

Unknown Characters

Accounts of Nigerian education usually begin when British colonial officers and missionaries arrived in the nineteenth century. This is because of the incorrect assumption that education and writing were unknown to Africans until Europeans imported it and taught it to them. However, multiple forms of education and writing existed in pre-colonial West Africa hundreds (perhaps thousands) of years before Europeans arrived. These indigenous forms of education and writing were often 'invisible' to outsiders because sacred or secret orders utilised them in a subterranean form that was not immediately recognisable by Europeans. Hence, for a long time there has been a mistaken impression that Africans were 'A credulous and illiterate people'.[1]

The British colonial assumption that south-east Nigeria was a primitive place without a writing system was shattered by a coincidental conversation in the early twentieth century. British missionaries saw symmetrical signs on calabashes, ceramics, and musical instruments in the area but did not attach any importance to what they presumed were purely decorative designs. They also observed some natives communicating in sign language but did not realise that the sign language also had a written form. While teaching in the Efik area of south-east Nigeria in April 1905, Reverend James Kerr Macgregor was taken aback when one of his native pupils 'deeply resented the statement that the civilisation of the people in Nigeria was primitive because they had no writing'. The student let a secret out of the bag when he 'declared that they had a writing called *nsibidi*'. The encounter ignited Macgregor's curiosity and he decided to find out more about the native writing that the pupil mentioned. However, Macgregor initially met a wall

---

1 Burns, 1929, p. 213.

of silence and 'People smiled when I asked for information and declared that they knew nothing about it.'[2] However, the little information he was able to obtain led him to admit that 'The use of *nsibidi* is that of ordinary writing.'[3]

The British colonial officer Percy Amaury Talbot similarly encountered avoidance when he asked a local 'who had the reputation of knowing more Nsibidi ... than any man now alive ... to give me a little help in the study of this script'. The local 'refused point blank, though a good remuneration had been offered for his services' and 'refused to give any further information, and soon after went away'.[4]

Locals resisted Macgregor's and Talbot's attempts to learn *Nsibidi* because it was a covert form of communication used by secret society members. *Nsibidi* recently came to prominence when images of it briefly appeared in the blockbuster film *Black Panther*. *Nsibidi* is a pictographic form of writing that uses drawings and shapes to represent events, ideas, people, and stories. In addition to being a form of writing, *Nsibidi* was also a sign language, and a mystical communication method. Indigenes often feared *Nsibidi* as they believed that it had supernatural powers.

'delusion came to a screeching halt'

Nsibidi was so deeply associated with secret society members that when a twenty-first-century scholar tried to conduct fieldwork on it in Calabar, his 'delusion came to a screeching halt just days after spending time in that region ... I quickly realized the real study of Nsibidi, in any form, was nearly impossible without at least some cursory understanding of Ekpe and Mgbe [secret] society.'[5]

The *Ekumeku* secret society which fought an anti-colonial war against British colonial authorities in the late eighteenth and early nineteenth centuries provided a good example of how secret socie-

---

2 Macgregor, 1909, p. 210.
3 Ibid., p. 212.
4 Talbot, 1912, p. 39.
5 Hales, 2015, p. 115.

ties used secret communication. *Ekumeku* members swore lifelong oaths of allegiance and secrecy to each other, and communicated via non-verbal means such as silent gesticulations that could be recognised only by other members. Examples included covert finger gestures intelligible only to members, or shaking bullet containers in a manner that signalled the time of their meetings. *Ekumeku* also employed a trumpeter who blew his horn to convey coded messages about battle plans and the location of British troops. Professional guilds such as blacksmiths were also knowledgeable in *Nsibidi* and Reverend Macgregor noted that 'wherever a smith goes he carries with him the knowledge of *nsibidi*'.[6]

Knowledge of *Nsibidi* was geographically widespread and traversed the Efik-, Ekoi-, Ibibio-, and Igbo-speaking areas of south-east Nigeria and also north-west Cameroon. In the early 1900s, a British district commissioner in south-east Nigeria recorded 363 different *Nsibidi* signs in the Ikom district alone[7] (in modern-day Cross River State). Given the desire of people literate in *Nsibidi* to keep their knowledge secret, it is safe to assume that the number of *Nsibidi* signs far exceeded those he found. *Nsibidi* also had different levels and purposes. While some levels were reserved only for secret society members (for example, covert communications), other levels were outside facing (for example, public notices, warnings to stay away from a particular area, and dates and times of important events) and were known by people who were not secret society members. Some illicit lovers even used *Nsibidi* to leave secret messages for each other and hide adultery.[8] Reverend Macgregor's inquiries led him to discover a very detailed record of a court case transcribed in *Nsibidi*, and a woman who operated an *Nsibidi* teaching school.[9]

Nsibidi's advantages were its flexibility and multi-lingual usage. It was often printed on clothes, house walls, inscribed in body tattoos, cut or painted onto palm stems, and *Nsibidi* has even been found

6 Macgregor, 1909, p. 209.
7 Dayrell, 1911.
8 Ibid.
9 Macgregor, 1909, p. 212.

on gravestones in Virginia in America (presumably carved by Igbos who were taken to the Americas during the Trans-Atlantic slave trade era, or by their descendants). *Nsibidi* did not have strict rules of syntax like Latin script. For example, although some *Nsibidi* signs were common and mutually intelligible between different secret societies, some societies added their own custom signs that could not be understood by non-members. Multiple signs could also be grouped together to form a sentence, and changing the order in which the signs were placed did not alter their meaning. *Nsibidi* was also intelligible between different languages. Hence, an Efik person could read *Nsibidi* written by an Igbo person and vice versa.

WRITING IN MUSLIM PRE-COLONIAL AFRICA

After Muslim slaves of Hausa, Nupe, and Oduduwan descent rebelled in Brazil in 1835, chief of police Francisco Goncalves Martins wrote about the rebels as follows: 'almost all of them know how to read and write in unknown characters, similar to the Arabic, which are used by the Ussas, who today appear united with the Nagos'.[10] The 'Ussas' he referred to were Hausas, the 'Nagos' were Oduduwans, and the 'unknown characters' they wrote in was a form of West African writing that the slaves took from West Africa to Brazil.

Muslim education and writing in Africa mirrored that of Christian Europe. The history of writing in both continents was intertwined with religion. Whereas European education was based on Latin and Christianity, Africa's was based on Arabic and Islam. After the Romans conquered much of Europe and the Middle East in the first millennium, Christian Romans translated the New Testament of the Bible into Latin. This intertwined Latin and ancient Christianity as European Christians who lived in areas that Romans conquered had to learn to read Latin in order to read the Bible. After 1000 AD, the Latin script became more widespread as many Europeans adopted it to write their native languages.

---

10   Reis, 1982, p. 146.

After Islam spread from the Arabian Peninsula to Africa in the seventh century, it reached West Africa in the eleventh century. Since the Koran was written in Arabic, African Muslim converts also had to learn Arabic in order to read their holy book, just as European Christians had to learn to read Latin. Islam's propagation promoted literacy and writing, and many of pre-colonial West Africa's large empires such as Songhai, Timbuktu, and the Sokoto Caliphate employed calligraphers skilled in Arabic to write their official correspondence. West African Muslims eventually adopted the Arabic script to write their native languages in the idiosyncratic style that Brazilian police chief Martins described as 'unknown characters'. This Africanised form of writing was known as *Ajami*.

THE 'LATIN OF AFRICA'

Ajami is a derivative of the Arabic word *ajam*, which can be translated as 'mute' or someone unable to speak Arabic properly. Historically, it was also a racial slur and a synonym for something foreign. *Ajami* script spread and like Latin many Africans used it to write their native languages such as Fulfulde, Hausa, Nupe, Swahili, and Wolof, across a wide belt of Africa ranging from West Africa's coast with the Atlantic Ocean (modern-day Gambia, Senegal, and Guinea), northern and south-west Nigeria, to East Africa. South-west Nigeria's version of *Ajami* was known as '*Anjami*' or '*Anjemi*'. About 80 African languages have been written in Arabic script[11] and it became so synonymous with pre-colonial West African literature that a scholar referred to it as the 'Latin of Africa'.[12] *Ajami*'s emergence is the major reason why the sixteenth–nineteenth centuries are the best known era of pre-colonial West African history.

The earliest known *Ajami* writing in Nigeria was in Kanem in the seventeenth century, where an official wrote comments on the Koran in Kanuri.

In addition to *Ajami* and *Nsibidi*, the Vai people of Liberia and King Njoya of Cameroon also developed written scripts. Writing was

11 Mumin, 2014, p. 44.
12 Hunwick, 2004, p. 133.

taught in West Africa's ancient universities such as Sankore University (founded in the twelfth century) in Timbuktu, Mali, which is one of the world's oldest universities and pre-colonial West Africa's answer to Harvard. Timbuktu had about 180 Koranic schools and 15,000 students in its fifteenth–sixteenth-century heyday.[13] Sankore was not an island and had links with other universities around the world in Granada (Spain), Egypt, Saudi Arabia, Tunisia, Kano, and Zaria. The scholars and students from these pre-colonial universities toured West and North Africa to study and/or teach, and often travelled from the Senegambia and Timbuktu regions to visit large scholastic communities on the outskirts of big cities such as Kano, Katsina, and Yandoto (which the nineteenth-century jihadists destroyed). These scholars wrote frequently during their tours. In the fifteenth century, the famous Berber scholar Abd al-Karim al-Maghili (who was born in Algeria) visited Kano, Katsina, and several other West African states. While in Kano, he wrote for Kano's King Mohammed Rumfa a book entitled *The Crown of Religion Concerning the Obligations of Princes*, and a shorter treatise entitled *Brief Sentences*. The former was a constitutional template for the operation of an Islamic state, while the latter was a treatise on law and order. The legendary sixteenth-century Timbuktu historian Ahmed Baba also wrote about 70 works.

THE INTELLECTUAL JIHAD

Coverage of Usman Dan Fodio's jihad usually focuses on its military and religious aspects, and omits the fact that it was also an intellectual revolution led by radical scholars. The Sokoto Caliphate's leaders were extremely erudite scholars, teachers, and writers, some of whom spoke, read, and wrote in four different languages. Dan Fodio and his lieutenants were very well versed in Arabic and Islamic history and jurisprudence. They had a preconceived template of the ideal type of society they wanted to emerge after their jihad, and disseminated and implemented it with their written advocacy and political and religious reforms.

---

13 BBC, 2001.

The Dan Fodio family were so devoted to study and writing that scholarship was almost the family's addiction. Between the four of them, Dan Fodio, his brother Abdullahi, son Mohammed Bello, and daughter Nana Asma'u wrote about 300 books, articles, and poems on a wide range of subjects such as science, poetry, medicine, Islamic jurisprudence, history, and mysticism. Given that much of their writing has been lost, this is probably an undercount. Some of Mohammed Bello's writing (and his copy of *Euclid's Elements*) was destroyed in a fire at his house. Their polyglot skills meant that they wrote not only in their native Fulfulde language, but also in classical Arabic and Hausa. Their prolific writing is why the nineteenth century is the best known century in the history of pre-colonial northern Nigeria. Bello's book *Infaku'l Maisuri* ('The Wages of the Fortunate') is a part autobiography of Bello, part biography of his father, and part history book. It is the canonical work about his family and the Sokoto Caliphate. Bello's brother-in-law and best friend Gidado Dan Laima also wrote a biography of his father-in-law Dan Fodio called *Meadow of Paradise*.

Despite being ecologically confined by the Sahara Desert to its north and the Atlantic Ocean to its south, West Africa was not intellectually isolated from the outside world. The Caliphate's leaders were extremely well versed with global events and literature from outside Africa. For example, when the Scottish explorer Hugh Clapperton met Mohammed Bello in 1824, Clapperton was stunned to discover that Bello owned a copy of *Euclid's Elements*. Clapperton wrote in his diaries that during their first meeting, Bello bombarded him with questions about Britain's conquest of India, ancient Christian denominations, and asked for newspapers, which he asked Clapperton to read to him in English. Bello's choice of conversation topics became so esoteric that Clapperton admitted that 'To extricate myself from the embarrassment occasioned'[14] (by Bello's questions) he hurriedly changed the subject. Bello and his family's knowledge is made more impressive when one considers that none of them ever visited the Middle East (which is considered

---

14   Denham, Clapperton, and Oudney, 1826, p. 332.

the epicentre of Islamic knowledge) and that they lived their entire lives in West Africa.

Pre-colonial African societies that did not have literacy had other forms of education and intellectual transmission that did not involve a Europe-like model of education based on classroom reading and writing. For example, people in the Oduduwan areas used a symbolic communication method called *Aroko* to send messages to each other by tying cowrie shells together in different patterns. Each pattern had a different meaning. *Aroko* fell short of writing as it did not represent letters or even sounds, but instead conveyed ideas or coded messages. For example, a businessman could accept a business partner's business proposal by sending two cowrie shells facing each other. Or if a man courting a woman sent her six cowrie shells tied together, she could elicit that he was attracted to her because *efa* (six) also means to be attracted to/drawn towards something.

'the keeper of the old times'

In many areas of pre-colonial West Africa, the illiterate instead used oral tools such as folk tales, poetry, proverbs, and riddles to transmit knowledge. The use of such 'invisible' forms of knowledge transfer led many to mistakenly conclude that pre-colonial Africa had no traditions of artistic expression or scholarship. Such societies that relied on oral tradition employed special guilds of trained professional oral genealogists and historians to act as human knowledge repositories. These professionals have different names in different parts of West Africa. Among the Wolof of Senegal they are known as *griots*, as *ihogbe* in Benin, *ahanjito* in Dahomey, *maroka* in Hausaland, *gesere* in Songhai, *baba elegun* in Ketu, and as *arokin* in Oyo. Their role encompassed more than just history, and they served multiple roles as genealogists, musicians, praise singers, and storytellers. These professionals were responsible for memorising and transmitting their culture, knowledge, and history from one generation to the next. In Oyo the leader of the *arokin* was known as the *ologbo* ('the keeper of the old times'). His equivalent in Benin was the *esekhurhe*. The *arokin*, *baba elegun*, and *esekhurhe* were employed as official palace historians in their respective kingdoms and were responsible for memorising the chronology and genealogy of their kings, notable events during the reign of each king, and their society's history, then communicating them to the public. During royal coronation ceremonies, they had to recite the names and reigns of all previous kings. This was a serious responsibility as their rendition could elevate or destroy a king's legacy. Thus, deliberate misrepresentation or material inaccuracies in rendition carried severe consequences, and could lead to the *ologbo*, *baba elegun*, or *esekhurhe* being sentenced to death.

Their primary method of transmitting the histories they memorised was to compose and recite praise poems, rhapsodies, or songs that contained important historical information about their society or a particular family. In Oyo, these praise songs were known as *oriki*. Historical events were also preserved by re-enactment. For example, when a new *alaketu* (king) was crowned in Ketu, he was required to re-enact the experience of the first *alaketu* during his migration from Ife to Ketu, and when he died, all of his people extinguished their fires across the kingdom, then lit torches at a cave where their ancestors borrowed fire from their Fon neighbours when they first arrived in Ketu. While the employment of historical guilds within the king's employees preserved history, it also enabled royal control and editing of the historical narrative. However, the *arokin* sometimes found cheeky ways to surreptitiously criticise rulers with negative traits, such as by giving *Alaafin* Awole the nickname *Arogangan* ('the heavy-handed one').

Reverend Samuel Johnson's massive book *The History of the Yorubas* is a testament to the memorisation skills of Oyo's *arokin*. Johnson obtained much of the information he used to write his 671-page book from *arokin* employed by the *Alaafin* of Oyo. That *arokin* memories should produce such a large volume shows the vast amount of information that they memorised and could orally recite. Johnson's book also inadvertently demonstrated the limits of oral knowledge, and the different results it produced when compared to modern methods of knowledge transmission. While *arokin* were expected to accurately memorise and recite the list of their kings, they did not always do so in chronological order, and instead usually performed this task thematically. While reciting, they might group together kings who shared similar characteristics or who came from the same family. Johnson tried to create a chronological list of Oyo's kings using information that the *arokin* had memorised thematically. Hence, discrepancies arose when European-educated clergymen such as Johnson tried to record the *arokin*'s historical knowledge in writing. In 1852, Bishop Crowther wrote a brief chronology of the eight immediately preceding *alaafin* (including the then reigning *Alaafin* Atiba).[15] Seventy-eight years later Johnson's book (based on testimony he collected from *arokin* in the late 1800s) was published. Crowther claimed that *Alaafin* Ajagbo was Abiodun's predecessor, whereas in Johnson's list, there are 13 *alaafin* between Ajagbo and Abiodun. In 1914, the grandson of an *alaafin* published a brief account which chronicled many of the same *alaafin* and events as Johnson, but listed them in a different order.[16]

'the most remarkable proverbs in the world'

The use of memory and recitation was not limited to elites such as monarchs. It was also used as an educational tool to teach children. For example, Igbos used a popular rhyming riddle to teach rules of grammar and vocabulary to children. To demonstrate that the word *akwa* had several meanings depending on context and intonation, parents taught their children to memorise a rhyme which included five different meanings of the word *akwa* (which could mean cloth, cry, egg, bed, and to make something). The rhyme was *nwanyi na akwa akwa, ina akwa akwa na okuko yiri akwa na-elu akwa ikwara akwa ndi na-elu akwa* ('is this woman tailor crying because a hen laid an egg on the clothes she made, which are on the bed?'). Proverbs were also used to compress historical events and impart moral lessons. The Oduduwan areas were so replete with profound proverbs that the American missionary T.J. Bowen

15   Crowther, 1852, pp. iv–v.
16   Falola, Doortmont, and Adeyemi, 1989. For example, by stating that Majotu succeeded Amodo, whereas Johnson listed them in the opposite order.

(who visited there) said theirs were 'among the most remarkable proverbs in the world'.[17] Their proverbs provided so much guidance on a multitude of topics in daily life and relationships that Bowen described them as 'the poetry and the moral science of the nation'.[18] This was not an exaggeration. The proverbs were so well known and so often repeated that they became mentally submerged in everyday discourse and helped to shape people's etiquette and morality. For example, the grisly fate of Oyo's infamous eighteenth-century Bashorun Gaha led to phrases such as 'reflect upon Gaha's death and mend your ways' (a warning that retributive justice awaits the cruel and unjust).

The continual use of such commemoration and recitation led some to develop high levels of verbal and visual memory. British colonial officer Major Leonard visited south-east Nigeria and spoke of 'these illiterate people, with their tenacious memories'.[19] A nineteenth-century writer was stunned that emancipated illiterate slaves from the Oduduwan areas that he met:

> calculate figures in their memory to an extent which would surprise the most practised mathematician, without using any mechanical means for their aid. Thus an unlettered liberated African, whom I knew and repeatedly questioned, could calculate within an incredibly short space of time any amount of pennies, half-pennies, or farthings, reducing them to pounds, Shillings, and Pence. Some keep for years the debit and credit side of their account in their memory with great accuracy.[20]

Parents taught their children to count from an early age by getting them to count cowries (which were a popular pre-colonial currency). Such continual arithmetic practice led an English-trained missionary to remark that in south-west Nigeria 'A person cannot be more insulted for his stupidity in arithmetic, than by telling him ...

17   Bowen, 1857, p. 284.
18   Bowen, 1858, p. 56.
19   Leonard, 1906, p. 277.
20   Horton, 1868, p. 23.

you do not know nine times nine.'[21] After visiting Benin multiple times in the nineteenth century, the British trader Cyril Punch was astonished by the remarkable consistency between the protocols of Benin's officials he met and the eyewitness accounts about Benin he read from other Europeans who visited centuries earlier (including the Dutch merchant David van Nyendael over 150 years earlier). Punch noted that:

> there was little or no change in the ceremonies as recorded in the past, when compared with the ceremonies he himself took part in ... There are lapses of generations between the recorded visits [of Europeans], yet at the end of so many centuries the courtiers seemed to know all the details which were *en règle* when a European arrived. Practically, Nyendael's reception was the same as my own. It is remarkable that the traditions which regulate the ceremonies should have been handed down so carefully.[22]

'the shrewdest and most intellectual of their race'

Oral learning was not less rigorous than written tuition. While admission to guilds such as the *arokin* and *griots* was usually hereditary within specific families and outsiders could not be admitted, other professions such as blacksmiths, *babalawo*, and *dibia* involved formal apprenticeship and training before initiation into their professional guilds. Blacksmiths in the Igbo areas subjected their apprentices to a long, intellectually and physically demanding training regime, and a difficult examination before admitting them into the profession. For example, in elite Igbo blacksmithing areas such as Abiriba, Awka, and Nkwere, before being allowed to graduate, an apprentice would be invited to a proficiency ceremony that was like a final exam. The apprentice's trainer, the trainer's colleagues, and other blacksmiths from neighbouring communities also attended the ceremony. To prove his worthiness, the apprentice

---

21   Crowther, 1852, p. 39.
22   Ling Roth, 1903, p. 119.

had to instantly manufacture any item that any of the blacksmiths in attendance asked him to produce.[23]

Babalawos (professional diviners) in the Oduduwan areas had to train at specialist training schools for long periods of time sometimes exceeding five years before they could be admitted into the profession. The corpus of *Ifa* knowledge that formed the syllabus of *babalawos'* knowledge consisted of at least 256 different preset allegories, myths, and proverbs known as *Odu*, from which the *babalawo* rendered advice to their clients during *Ifa* divination. Each *Odu* had to be memorised and recited verbatim. The focus and powers of recall required for the *babalawos'* occupation led a British academic to comment over 100 years ago that they 'are the shrewdest and most intellectual of their race, profound thinkers, and of great subtlety and knowledge'.[24]

As colonial influence increased in the twentieth century, oral and written forms of indigenous knowledge became almost extinct. Despite its wide pre-colonial usage, by the twenty-first century *Ajami* had fallen into such disuse and become so esoteric that it was almost unknown in southern Nigeria. Twenty-first-century Nigerian discourse often features public rows between Christian southern Nigerians and their northern Muslim counterparts regarding the appearance of *Ajami* inscriptions on Nigeria's currency, the Naira. Many southern Nigerians objected to the use of 'Arabic text' on Naira notes, its 'foreign' origin, and its association with Islam (and ironically ignored the foreign origin of English text which also appears on the notes). Unbeknown to them, *Ajami* was indigenous and pre-dated (in Africa) the English text printed on the same bank notes by over 500 years.

Ajami and *Nsidibi* fell into disuse for several reasons, some of which were unique to one or the other, and others which were common to both of them. *Nsibidi* had three 'strikes' against it. Firstly, its secret status meant that it would lose its special quality if it became widely known and mandatorily taught to everyone like Latin script. Hence, those who understood *Nsibidi* were deter-

---

23   Njoku, 1991, p. 199.
24   Farrow, 1924, p. 203.

mined to conceal its existence and to ensure that as few people as possible would be admitted into the privileged class of persons who understood it. Secondly, *Nsibidi* was often written on surfaces such as ceramics, clothing, floors, pottery, and walls, which had a finite lifespan. Thirdly, after the *Ekumeku* secret society waged an insurgency against British colonial authorities and soldiers in the late eighteenth and early nineteenth centuries, the British colonial government enacted the Unlawful Societies Ordinance in October 1910, which banned *Ekumeku* and other secret societies and made membership of them a crime. Colonial authorities also launched a massive military crackdown against *Ekumeku*, and Christian missionaries refused to baptise anyone who was a member of a secret society. These legal, military, and religious assaults against secret societies inhibited them and their work, and drove them underground. As outsiders and British colonial officers discovered and started deciphering *Nsibidi*, its dual status as a written text and a sign language meant that its exponents could 'bury' its written form and instead prioritise its sign language form which was less easy to decipher.

The first challenge common to both *Ajami* and *Nsibidi* is that both of them were tools of sacred or secret orders that confined their usage within specialist circles. *Ajami*'s descent from the Arabic script which was closely associated with religion ironically helped it to fall into obsolescence. While religion was critical to the development and spread of education and writing, counter-intuitively, it also inhibited them. Between the fifteenth and early twentieth centuries, the most literate were also usually the most religious. Many of these holy people tended to use and view their literary skills as instruments for propagating their religion – nothing more. Hence, the trajectory of education and writing tended to reflect their choices and preferences. Arabic's special status as the language of the Koran meant that many of the literate scholars who could read and write it deemed secular matters not fit to be written in the same sacred text that the Koran was written in.

After the Scottish explorer Hugh Clapperton met Mohammed Bello and other Sokoto Caliphate officials in the 1820s, Clapperton was so excited by the encounters that he devoted several chapters of his two books (which spanned over 1200 pages) to describe his interactions with them. While in Sokoto, Clapperton lived in the house of Bello's *Waziri* Gidado Dan Laima, whom Clapperton described as 'an elderly man ... excessively polite[25] ... an excellent man, and has unbounded influence with the sultan, to whose sister he is married'.[26] Although Clapperton knew that Gidado was married to Bello's sister Nana, and mentioned that female members of Gidado's household repeatedly visited him, he did not state whether Nana was among them.

Yet excellent writers like Bello, Nana, and Gidado did not return the favour by writing about meeting Clapperton. Although Bello was curious about meeting a *Nasara* (Christian) like Clapperton for the first time and the technological 'toys' that Clapperton brought, he did not once mention meeting Clapperton in his large library of writing. Neither did Gidado, and nor did Bello's sister and Gidado's wife Nana. Clapperton's omission from their writing is made more curious when one considers how much they wrote, and that Clapperton was probably the only *bature* (European) and only Christian that they ever met in their lives. Thus, we are left only with Clapperton's impressions and recollections of them, but nothing about their impressions of Clapperton.

'[He] asked me a great many questions'

In Nana's case this may be because 'a reclusive Sufi woman' (as a Hausa informant described her to me) like her did not meet Clapperton, or if she did meet him, did not want to publicise the meeting. However, there is another more credible reason why such prolific writers did not deem their encounters with Clapperton worthy of their writing. Many learned scholars of their era regarded literacy as an instrument of religion, not of historical dissemination. Clapperton did not help himself by failing his religious 'audition' with Bello. Clapperton recalled that during his first meeting with Bello,

---

25   Denham, Clapperton, and Oudney, 1826, p. 81.
26   Ibid., p. 85.

Bello 'asked me a great many questions about Europe, and our religious distinctions. He was acquainted with the names of some of the more ancient sects, and asked whether we were Nestorians or Socinians ... He continued to ask several other theological questions.'[27] Bello's choice of conversation topics became so specialised that Clapperton admitted: 'I was obliged to confess myself not sufficiently versed in religious subtleties to resolve these knotty points.'[28] Clapperton's lack of knowledge about his own religion was unlikely to have impressed a deeply religious man like Bello whose title was after all 'King of the Muslims'.

After the jihad, the prioritisation of religious texts consequently deprioritised non-religious and *Ajami* writing. As late as the mid-1980s Mallam Bala dan Idi (a learned Muslim scholar who was the keeper of the official copy of the *Kano Chronicle*) did not bother to read or teach the contents of the special book in his possession. Although the *Kano Chronicle* is one of the most important written accounts about pre-jihad Hausaland, Idi admitted that 'it has plenty of dust' and that 'We aren't reading it'[29] because he regarded it as a secular historical document that did not merit the attention he devotes to his religious work. Mallam Saidu Limanin Sabuwar Kofa (a member of a Tijaniyya Sufi brotherhood) further explained Muslim scholars' disdain for history by stating:

> the knowledge of history is not important among us. Important knowledge among us is knowledge of the faith, exclusively. As for history, we know it, but we don't like to acquire it. We consider it to be nothing. It is only news fit for telling with your mouth. It has no reward ... we don't like to admit that we have it ... there is no use of history. It is just news. It has no use ... if you have history, you will just be considered a liar![30]

---

27 Ibid., p. 82.
28 Ibid., p. 82.
29 Starratt, 1993, p. 128.
30 Ibid., p. 121.

The second challenge common to both *Ajami* and *Nsibidi* is that unlike Latin script, they did not have widely agreed upon rules of syntax and usage. Hence, both were used with much improvisation, and there was no central coordinating organisation to either mass disseminate or standardise their use. The third and greatest challenge to both *Ajami* and *Nsibidi* came when European Christian missionaries and colonial officers arrived in the nineteenth century, started translating the Bible into African languages, opening schools, and sought to adopt or develop a script that could be understood by their multi-lingual congregations. After considering Arabic script (which was already known by some natives), unsurprisingly, the Church Missionary Society instead decided to use the script already known by its missionaries, and taught it to West African Christian converts (rather than the Christian missionaries having to learn native scripts). Reverend Samuel Johnson admitted that:

> the Roman character was naturally adopted, not only because it is the one best acquainted with, but also because it would obviate the difficulties that must necessarily arise if missionaries were first to learn strange characters before they could undertake scholastic and evangelistic work.[31]

Another factor that Johnson did not mention was that Christian missionaries were very unlikely to translate the Bible into a script that was closely related to a rival religion. Latin script's systematised format, with strict rules of syntax, meant that it competed with, and pushed, improvised texts such as *Nsibidi* and *Ajami* to the margins of literacy. Not only did British colonial authorities and missionaries import the Latin script as a vehicle for Christian evangelisation, but they also used it as the official text of secular education. After the ability to read, write, and speak English became a prerequisite for Nigerian school children, English literacy supplanted the pre-colonial forms of literacy. European educational

31   Johnson, 1921, p. xxxiii.

achievement became a prized status symbol that offered upward economic and professional mobility, both of which became associated with English-speaking school-educated people. As a result, contemporary Nigeria tends to conflate the ability to speak English with being educated, and forgets that English is just a language; not a barometer of intelligence.

The Black Bishop

For over 120 years, the monumental contribution of one of the most remarkable pre-colonial Africans has not been given due recognition. Unlike many others featured in this book, he was not a monarch or a legendary warrior. Since so many stories about pre-colonial West Africa are about its elite, this chapter is about one of the few 'local boy made good' stories. Although the leading personality in this chapter did not conquer or establish any empires, he perhaps more than any other pre-colonial West African helped to shape the emergence of the second most populous ethnic group in Nigeria, the religion of Nigeria's people, and their post-colonial educational and literary systems.

THE NATION WITH NO NAME

Two great ironies of Nigeria's second most populous ethnic group are that it was created in exile several hundred miles outside Nigeria, and that it did not exist 200 years ago. Despite their shared belief in common descent from Ife, and similar cultural and linguistic ties, prior to the late 1800s, the people who lived in the Oduduwan kingdoms did not consider themselves to be one ethnic or national group, nor was there one commonly accepted name by which all of them were known. In their homelands they identified themselves by their local identities such as Egba, Ekiti, Ijebu, and Ondo. The chaos that followed Afonja's coup, the Muslim jihad against Oyo, and Oyo's collapse, caused the enslavement of thousands of Oduduwans in the 1800s. Many of those enslaved were sold to Trans-Atlantic slave traders and dispersed around the Americas.

By the nineteenth century, Oduduwans were dispersed around the globe as far away as the Caribbean and North, Central, and

South America. They were referred to as '*Nagô*' and '*Lukumi*' in Brazil and Cuba, respectively, and Portuguese records in the sixteenth and seventeenth centuries referred to some of them as being from '*Terra Nova*' ('New Land'). Each of these names had a specific cultural and/or historical context. '*Nagô*' was a derivative of the name that Dahomey's people used to refer to Oduduwans: '*Anago*'. The Edo people of the Benin kingdom also used the term '*Olukumi*' to describe people who migrated to the Benin kingdom from eastern Oduduwan areas such as Akure and Owo. Among some Oduduwan groups, '*Oluku mi*' meant 'my friend'. Today, there are still communities known as *Olukumi* in the Anioma/Ika-Igbo areas close to Benin. *Terra Nova* probably referred to Trans-Atlantic slaves who originated from the western areas of Oduduwa-land (lands that provided a new source of slaves outside Benin). Yet all of these terms were colloquial, created and used by foreigners, and none of them was an official national name for the *Omo Oduduwa* (descendants of Oduduwa).

MOUNTAIN LION

After Britain made it illegal for its citizens to engage in the slave trade from 1808, it stationed a naval squadron off the West African coastline to intercept slave ships heading for the Americas. Since the slaves that the British Royal Navy rescued from slave ships were from several disparate places, it was not possible to repatriate them to their homelands. Back in 1787, the British government had bought a 20 square mile area of land from locals near the coast of Sierra Leone ('Mountain Lion' in Italian) and converted it into a freed slave colony. In 1787 it shipped the first batch of 400 freed slaves there along with white English prostitutes. This freed slave colony was later renamed 'Freetown', and it remains the capital of Sierra Leone until this day.

Freetown inadvertently became a production line for the export of a new religion to the land that later became Nigeria, thereby helping to create the only country in the world with its population equally split between Christians and Muslims. Developments in Freetown also turbo-charged English language education and literacy, and created a new ethnic identity which was exported from Sierra Leone in an easterly direction down the West African coast-line to the area that eventually became south-west Nigeria.

Sierra Leone had a large population of freed slaves of Oduduwan descent. In Sierra Leone, yet another term emerged as a descrip-tor for the Oduduwans in the diaspora. European missionaries in Sierra Leone nicknamed them 'Aku' or 'Ackoos' due to their habit of greeting themselves using the phrase '*Aku*' or '*E ku*'.[1] Reverend James Schon wrote of 'the Aku Nation in Sierra Leone'[2] and James Africanus Horton justified the use of Aku because it was 'the name which is given to the whole nation at Sierra Leone and which is generally adopted in every part of the Coast'.[3]

Even then, the use of 'Aku' as an ethnonym for all Oduduwans was a misidentification. Many of those at Sierra Leone were from Oyo, and it was the Oyo group that were prone to using '*Aku*' or '*E ku*' as a salutation. Hence, the term '*Aku*' conflated the Oyo with the other Oduduwan peoples. Since Oyo's population was not mono-ethnic, it is possible that speakers of multiple languages such as Bariba, Ebira, Hausa, and Nupe were sublimated into the '*Aku*' identity. However, *Aku* was a nickname localised to Sierra Leone and was an unknown term in Oyo itself (except as a greeting). Before the late 1800s, the vast majority of Oduduwan people had never heard of the terms *Aku*, *Lukumi*, *Nago*, and *Terra Nova* (except those who resided far away from home in the Americas and Sierra Leone where these terms were used).

THE 'WHITE MAN'S GRAVE'

In 1841 the Christian Missionary Society (CMS) launched a Niger Mission to spread Christianity among the many ethnic groups

---

1   The closest English translation of this term is 'may you live forever' or 'im-mortality', to which the appropriate and usual response was 'Oh!' (signifying as-sent). Bowen, 1857, p. 303.
2   Schon and Crowther, 1842, p. 367.
3   Horton, 1868, p. 159.

that lived adjacent to the River Niger. However, the Mission was a disaster; 130 of the 150 Europeans on the Mission became sick, and another 49 died. The CMS discovered why West Africa had the nickname of 'the white man's grave'. The CMS aborted the Mission due to the shocking mortality and sickness rate. However, the CMS refused to abandon its overall goal of spreading Christianity throughout West Africa. The Mission's failure unintentionally had a massive impact on the study of West African languages and led to the creation of a new ethnic nation.

Africa was of particular interest to European missionaries because in their view it was a 'huge mass of heathen darkness'[4] and unlike large parts of Asia and North Africa, it did not have one dominant indigenous religion to resist Christianity. However, 'the appalling death rate which hitherto had decimated the ranks of European missionaries sent to the west coast of Africa'[5] convinced the CMS that it could not accomplish its goal of Christianising West Africa without the aid of indigenous West Africans. Using Africans to convert their fellow Africans was a matter of preserving European lives 'for her [Africa] own sons would not be stricken down by fever as the white men were'.[6]

Missionaries valued being multi-lingual as it allowed them to spread Christianity to different people around the world. However, the Niger Mission's survivors realised that they faced an awesome linguistic challenge in West Africa. Nothing short of supernatural linguistic skills could help them when they were trying to convert people in a geographic region that had over 500 indigenous languages. The bewildering number of languages and dialects spoken by the people the missionaries wanted to convert amplified the need for African proselytisers who spoke the indigenous languages. In a letter to the lay secretary of the CMS, one of the Niger Mission's survivors, Reverend Schon said: 'It appears to me obvious, that not much good can be expected to result from Missionary labours

---

4   Hinderer, 1873, p. 360.
5   Page, 1908, p. 35.
6   Ibid., p. 35.

unless the various nations are addressed in their own languages, and portions of the Sacred Volume are put into their hands.'[7]

Using indigenous missionaries required the CMS to find West Africans who were not only Christian but who were also polyglots that could read and write English well enough to translate the Bible and preach scripture in native West African languages, and who had the motivation to devote their entire lives to propagating a foreigner's religion. Fortunately for the CMS agents, such an individual landed on their doorstep just when they most needed him. He was one of the survivors from the Niger Mission.

NIGERIA'S MOST FAMOUS SLAVE

A great irony of the nineteenth-century jihad that Muslims waged against Oyo was that it probably advanced the cause of Christianity more than it did that of Islam. As the rebellion swept across Oyo's northern territory, Afonja's *Jama'a* warriors raided the town of Osogun in 1821 and captured and enslaved a young boy who, unbeknown to them, would become their most famous victim. The boy's name was Ajayi. *Alaafin* Abiodun was Ajayi's maternal great-great grandfather. His paternal grandfather was also from a royal family and migrated from Ketu to Oyo. After capturing Ajayi, the *Jama'a* separated him from his mother Afala, two sisters, a cousin, and a newborn baby sibling that was only two months old. During the raid, Ajayi's father had rushed into the family home to warn his family to flee, before going outside to join the defence of the town. Ajayi never saw his father again. The process of selling slaves was so fluid that as Ajayi was sold from one person to another, he had three different owners in only one day. On one occasion he was sold in exchange for tobacco and rum. After approximately eight months of slavery during which he passed through at least six different owners, he was sold to Portuguese slave traders in Lagos, and placed on a Trans-Atlantic slave ship called *Esparanza Felix* on 6

7　Schon and Crowther, 1842, p. 358.

April 1822 for a one-way journey to Brazil. He was so distraught that he considered suicide many times.

However, the next day (7 April 1822), British navy ships HMS *Myrmidon* (commanded by Captain H.J. Leeke) and HMS *Iphigenia* (commanded by Captain Sir Robert Mends) intercepted the *Esparanza Felix* at sea, arrested its crew, rescued Ajayi and 186 other slaves on board, and dropped him at Bathurst in Sierra Leone on 17 June 1822 (about 7 miles away from the capital Freetown). The CMS placed Ajayi under the care of English guardians: Mr and Mrs Davey, who started teaching him how to read and write in English. He was such a good student that he was able to read the New Testament of the Bible after only six months in Sierra Leone. Ajayi was baptised on 11 December 1825 and received a new name. He was named after the vicar of Christ Church, Newgate Street, London, who was a CMS committee member: Samuel Crowther.

The CMS' interest in the newly renamed Crowther had more than humanitarian aims. It was part of a mission to further its Christianisation mission and save European lives. The large number of freed African slaves at Freetown made it an ideal laboratory to conduct the CMS' experiment of Christianising Africa using 'her own sons'. It placed at stake matters of religion, and also the future trajectory of native education, languages, and ethnic identity. Since some CMS members were sceptical about the intellect of Africans, to them the fate of Crowther and other freed African slaves like him was also a social experiment to test the intelligence of Africans. Could they read, write, and evangelise?

In 1827, the CMS sent a young German Lutheran missionary, Reverend Charles Haensel to open a school called the Fourah Bay Institution in Freetown. The school was located in an old disused two-floor slave house. Its first student was Samuel Ajayi Crowther. The house's veranda acted as a lecture theatre, and Haensel turned the house into a boarding school where the students lived downstairs, and Haensel and his wife lived upstairs.

'I wish ... to see him in that state of lowliness of mind which Africans so easily lose'

Fourah Bay was not a liberal environment. Haensel ran a puritanical regime with severe discipline. He expelled a bright and well-behaved pupil for the offence of refusing to sever contact with his unmarried sister who was living with a European man that was the father of her baby. Haensel suspended another student for writing love letters to a girl.[8] When Crowther arrived at Fourah Bay, he brought with him a mattress which he had been given when he visited England in 1826 with his guardians Mr and Mrs Davey. Haensel confiscated the mattress and refused to let Crowther sleep on it as, according to Haensel: 'this was too great a luxury ... I wish for the good of his own soul to see him in that state of lowliness of mind which Africans so easily lose by visits to England.'[9]

'a very clever lad'

As Fourah Bay's first student, the success of the institution, and European impressions of African intellectual ability, depended on Crowther and his classmates. He was an anomaly at the school. While most of his classmates were children aged between 9 and 15, Crowther was in his late teens and almost an adult. Despite the spartan environment at Fourah Bay and its European syllabus, Crowther became its star pupil. He excelled, learned Greek and Latin, and acquired a curiosity and aptitude for languages. Haensel reported that Crowther was 'a very clever lad' and that 'it is mere pleasure to instruct him'.[10] Crowther matured into a brilliant student and scholar who was the first on many lists. As well as being Fourah Bay's first pupil, he later became its first African teacher, and its first African principal. Crowther's ascent was meteoric. In 1821, he was a kidnapped slave heading to doom in the Americas. Less than a year later, he had been rescued, four years later he had become a

---

8   Paracka Jr, 2001, pp. 49–50.
9   Ibid., p. 37.
10 Ibid., p. 46.

Christian, six years later he was an enrolled student at what would become one of Africa's most famous colleges, and seven years later he was a teacher at that same college.

While learning to read and write with Mr and Mrs Davey, Crowther met and befriended another of their pupils. She was a girl from Oyo named Asano[11] whose story was remarkably similar to his. After being captured in Oyo and sold as a slave, she too was rescued by a British navy ship (HMS *Bann* under the command of Captain Charles Phillips) and taken to Sierra Leone only four months after Crowther arrived there. After becoming a Christian, she had changed her name to Susan Thompson. She later became a school teacher at Bathurst. Crowther and Asano married in 1829 and had six children (three boys and three girls).[12] All of their daughters married clergymen, and their second son Dandeson also became a clergyman.[13] Crowther and Asano[14] were also blessed to live long enough to become became great grandparents.

THE ATHENS OF WEST AFRICA

To address the linguistic challenge of spreading the Gospel in multiple languages, the CMS implemented a reverse Tower of Babel concept by trying to coalesce different African languages and dialects into new 'standard' languages into which they would translate the Bible. Reverend Schon's view was that along with the CMS' missionary work: 'the opportunity is presented of acquiring and fixing in Sierra Leone, for Missionary purposes, the principal languages of Western Africa'.[15] Due to the large number of polyglot freed slaves, linguistic scholars, and dedication to scholarship at Freetown, the city became such an educational and intellectual melting pot that it was nicknamed the 'Athens of West Africa'.

---

11 It is possible that Asano was formerly a Muslim named Hassana.

12 In order of birth: Samuel Jr (born in 1830), Susanna (born in 1834), Abigail (born in 1836), Josiah (born in 1838), Dandeson (born in 1844), and Julianna.

13 Dandeson was named after the former CMS secretary Dandeson Coates.

14 Asano died in Lagos in 1881. Her husband died ten years later in 1891.

15 Schon and Crowther, 1842, p. xiii.

Fortunately for the European missionaries, they found Crowther among the freed slaves at Sierra Leone, and that he shared both their interest in linguistics, and their ambition to spread Christianity across West Africa. Crowther became one of the leading linguists of the nineteenth century. The CMS had special plans for Crowther, and they recruited him to translate the Bible into a language that could be read and understood by all Oduduwans. The translation project rested on two unproven missionary assumptions: that the languages spoken by the Oduduwan people were simply different dialects of the same language, and that this language had an authentic 'parent' dialect from which all others derived. The project required Crowther to simultaneously be an anthropologist, clergyman, linguist, missionary, and translator. During the aborted Niger Mission he displayed a remarkable linguistic aptitude and curiosity, and studied the cultures and languages he and the other Mission agents encountered (such as the Edo, Fulani, Hausa, Igbo, Igala, and Nupe).

The Bible translation project was the seminal work of Crowther's life. It was of critical importance for at least three reasons. Firstly, the translation was not merely a mechanical exercise of repeating words in another language. It was also about creating a *new language format*. The translation transcended the Bible and would also determine the new form in which an entire language would be spoken, written, and read. At the start of the translation work, the missionaries considered using *Ajami* for the written script of the translation as literate West African Muslims were already familiar with it. However, this would require the English-educated, English-speaking translators such as Crowther to learn a script unfamiliar to them before embarking upon the awesome task of translating the world's most widely read book. *Ajami* also posed a theological challenge. It would cause some awkwardness for Christian clergymen to use the script of Muslim holy books and scholars to translate the Christian holy book. Ultimately, the missionaries decided that the Latin script of their European-educated translators would be the script of choice. Secondly, although the missionaries presumed that the Oduduwan people spoke different dialects of the same 'parent' language and thus were one nation, the level of mutual intelligibility between their languages back then is uncertain. What the missionaries presumed were dialects were regarded by their native speakers to be entirely different and autonomous languages altogether. Thus, while the missionaries thought they were merely creating standard rules of grammar, arguably they were also creating a new language. The third and perhaps greatest legacy of Crowther and the other missionaries' translation work was that it turned them into frontline creators of a new ethnic nation.

'I kept my ears open to every word'

Crowther supplemented his vocabulary with constant diligence and research, and said: 'I kept my ears open to every word to catch what I had not then secured, with which I had expected to enrich and enlarge my … vocabulary.'[16] The languages spoken in the '*Aku*' areas had assonance, syllables, and pronunciations that had no equivalents in European languages or script. Recognising that he was translating into tonal African languages, Crowther made orthographic observations and deployed accents in order to denote differences in pronunciation and tone. He made such annotations with words like 'Esu'[17] and 'Osun' (which are pronounced 'Aeh-Shu' and 'Oh-Shun', respectively). As Crowther translated, he was also creating a new language, and its rules of syntax.

Due to the multiple names used to describe the people of Oduduwan descent, the German CMS missionary Sigismund Koelle called on 'The Missionaries of the country [Sierra Leone] … to search after the proper national name of the whole Aku country.'[18] Koelle's plea for the discovery and resuscitation of the original indigenous name for all Oduduwan people was based on the mistaken assumption that such a name existed. Horton admitted that 'there is no National Name by which all the [Oduduwan] tribes

---

16   Ade-Ajayi, 1958, p. 308.

17   For ease of pronunciation and reading (and due to the difficulty of amending characters with the correct annotations), this book spells Esu as 'Eshu'.

18   Ogharaerumi, 1986, p. 49.

speaking the same language but differently governed is known'.[19] Ironically, the name eventually chosen to describe them was not created by Oduduwans, but instead by Muslim foreigners. Since Oyo was located at the northern frontier of Oduduwa-land, it was the closest Oduduwan kingdom to the Hausa States, and also the most well known to them. As far back as the 1600s, Hausa Muslims had used the term 'Yariba' to describe Oyo and its people. This word survived for hundreds of years and became popular in the 1820s when European explorers such as Hugh Clapperton, the Lander brothers, Edward Bowdich, and others who visited West Africa and Hausaland, heard the term from Hausa-speaking informants they met. When Clapperton travelled through Oyo in the 1820s, he spoke of being in 'a district of Eyeo [Oyo], which is called Yarriba by the Arabs and people of Houssa' [Hausa].[20]

'THE YORUBA COUNTRY'

As CMS agents and the attentive Crowther probably read the journals of explorers such as Clapperton, the word 'Yariba' became popular among European writers who transcribed it with varied spellings such as 'Yarba', 'Yarraba', 'Yarriba', and 'Yaruba'. However, it took time for it to grow on Crowther. As a young adult, he spoke of 'my Eyo [Oyo] country'.[21] After living in Sierra Leone for over 20 years, Crowther stopped referring to his homeland as 'Eyo'. During the 1841 Niger Mission he repeatedly used 'Yaruba' to refer to Oyo, and in 1843 he published *A Vocabulary of the Yoruba Language*. In 1850, Crowther helped to translate and publish the first ever book written in Yoruba using Latin script: the book of Romans. In 1852 he further popularised 'Yoruba' as an Anglicised transliteration of the Hausa term when he published *A Grammar of the Yoruba Language* in which he noted: 'Yarriba, or Yaruba, is likewise the Haussa pronunciation' and revised his position by stating that

19   Horton, 1868, p. 159.
20   Clapperton, 1829, p. 4
21   Page, 1908, p. 9.

'*Yoruba* would be more correct'.[22] Hence, a new ethnic descriptor was born. Since then, Yoruba has been the name by which people from the Oduduwan kingdoms and their languages have been known. Crowther's text was seminal not only for popularising the phrase Yoruba, but also because in its preface entitled 'Early Traditions of the Yorubans', he wrote the first history of Oyo ever written by an Oyo native. A nineteenth-century observer present in Sierra Leone unequivocally gave the CMS the blame and credit for popularising the term Yoruba by claiming in 1868 that 'The Church Missionary Society has designated [Oduduwa-land] the "Yoruba Country".'[23]

However, the word 'Yoruba' was a controversial term that Oduduwans from outside Oyo vehemently rejected as it was regarded as an ethnonym only for Oyo. Before the nineteenth century the word 'Yoruba' was rarely used in reference to any of the Oduduwan people except those from Oyo. Non-Oyo people refused to be conflated with the Oyos. Observers at Sierra Leone noted that 'most of the tribes such as the Egbas and the Egbadoes, have objected to their being called Yorubas'.[24]

'Don't call me by that name, I am not a Yoruban'

Koelle also recognised the problematic ethnic tension that the word Yoruba generated among non-Oyos. He said:

> the name being thus incorrect, can never be received by the different tribes as a name for their whole nation. If, e.g. you call an Idsebuan [an Ijebu] or a Yagban [an Egba] a Yoruban, he will always tell you, 'Don't call me by that name, I am not a Yoruban'.[25]

Due to such resistance, attempts to use 'Yoruba' to supplant prior ethnic descriptors did not initially succeed. The use of the word 'Yoruba' to describe all Oduduwans was so contentious that in 1854, Koelle bluntly called for the term to be abandoned:

---

22   Crowther, 1852, p. i.
23   Horton, 1868, p. 159.
24   Ibid., p. 159.
25   Ogharaerumi, 1986, p. 49.

For the past few years they have very erroneously made use of the name 'Yoruba' in reference to the whole nation, supposing that the Yoruban is the most powerful Aku tribe. But this appellation is liable to far greater objections than that of 'Aku', and ought to be forthwith abandoned; for it is, in the first place, unhistorical, having never been used of the whole Aku nation by anybody, except for the last few years conventionally by the Missionaries.[26]

'YORUBA PROPER'

The reasons for the resistance to the adoption of the name Yoruba were obvious. Crowther's Bible translation was based on his native Oyo dialect which he and other missionaries referred to as 'Yoruba proper'.[27] Crowther saw his job as being 'to connect the Yoruba with its kindred dialects'.[28] By doing so, Crowther and the other translators created the impression that Oyo was the cultural and linguistic standard bearer of the Oduduwan people, thereby giving Oyo's dialect a sheen of authenticity as the 'parent' version of the languages spoken by all Oduduwans. However, Crowther's translation was not an instant hit and faced opposition. Those from other parts of Oduduwa-land did not consider Oyo to be a 'kindred dialect'. In 1868 Egba chiefs objected to Crowther's translation (which is perhaps understandable as the Egbas were vassals to Oyo during Oyo's era of imperial conquest). Such objection to the translation and to being referred to as 'Yoruba' demonstrated that the controversy regarding the translation transcended the mechanical recitation of words into a different language. It also represented a cultural battle about group identity. Moreover, Crowther's translation and recording of Oduduwan languages in writing changed their structure, and created differences between the language that the Bible was translated into and conversational language. Many words were spelled in an experimental or idiosyncratic way that did not always replicate the tonal pronunciation of their spoken version.

---

26 Ibid., 1986, p. 49.
27 Johnson, 1921, p. 14.
28 Crowther, 1852, p. 2.

This made reading early editions of the Yoruba Bible a cumbersome exercise. An American Baptist missionary who used Crowther's translations complained that:

> I used to be surprised, and sometimes vexed, when the people could not understand a sentence which I knew to be correct so far as regards words and idiom. It requires much practice to master the tones, and a man who has no ear for music will hardly do it at all.[29]

'The loss of these is greater to me than anything else'

It took 34 years for Crowther to finish translating the entire Bible into Yoruba. The process was lengthy due to the painstaking work required, constant revisions, and personal calamities. Crowther's house burned down in 1862 and the Crowther family lost almost all of their possessions. In a letter to the CMS Secretary Henry Venn, Crowther grieved not about the loss of his material possessions, but about the fire's destruction of linguistic documents and notes that aided his translation work:

> the manuscripts of nearly all the remaining books of the Pentateuch which I would have prepared for the press this quarter was destroyed. My collections of words and proverbs in Yoruba, of eleven years' constant observations, since the publication of the last edition of my Yoruba vocabulary, were also completely destroyed. The loss of these is greater to me than anything else, in so much as it cannot be recovered, nor can I easily recall to memory all the collections I had made during my travels ... Now all are gone like a dream.[30]

However, such delays occasioned by disaster, and the vast amount of work to be done, brought others into the translation work. These included other African clergymen who were born in Freetown to

---

29 Bowen, 1857, p. 133.
30 Ade-Ajayi, 1958, p. 308.

Yoruba parents (such as James White, Samuel Pearce, and William Morgan – whose parents were from Ijesha). Crowther's second son Dandeson and his future son-in-law Thomas Babington Macaulay translated the books of the prophets. The involvement of translators from other parts of Oduduwa-land diversified the vocabulary of the Yoruba Bible beyond the initial Oyo translation and made it more acceptable. Subsequent drafts incorporated Egba and other vocabulary from the coastal areas to Oduduwa-land's southern frontier. After more than three decades of painstaking work, the entire Yoruba Bible was translated and published in 1884. It was so voluminous that it was printed in four large volumes, and was not one book until 1900. It was an impressive body of work and the Yoruba Bible was the first edition of the Bible to be translated by an African into an indigenous African language. The influence of Crowther's Yoruba Bible and linguistic work was not limited to his own kinfolk.

Crowther tried to replicate his unification of Yoruba dialects with the Igbo language. He started studying and recording Igbo words and phrases during the 1841 Niger Mission, and by 1860 Crowther had compiled enough Igbo words for him to publish the first Igbo book ever written in the Latin alphabet: *Isoama-Ibo Primer*. Although he was listed as the book's sole author, Crowther later admitted that he co-authored the book with an Igbo: 'I produced the first primer, with help of the late Simon Jonas, an intelligent interpreter of the Isuama tribe.'[31] The Yoruba Bible and the *Isuama-Ibo Primer* provided the stairway to the Union Igbo Bible which had a similar effect on Igbo ethnic identity that the Yoruba Bible had for Yorubas. Crowther also wrote a Nupe language primer in 1864.

THE CLASH OF RELIGIONS

The translation work of missionaries such as Crowther was a means to an end. Linguistic research and translation was a tool for

---

31   Crowther, 1882, p. vi.

Christian evangelisation. In order to proclaim the superiority of Christianity over the pre-colonial African religions they sought to abolish, the missionaries at times engaged in a curious cherry-picking exercise. While they rejected the validity of the pre-colonial African religions, oddly they validated the names of some of the pre-colonial deities. Crowther astutely recognised that introducing Christianity to West Africans, along with its new cast of supernatural agents and interlocutors such as angels, prophets, Jesus Christ, and the Virgin Mary, would be less bewildering if he incorporated deities that West Africans already believed in. Thus, for example, the name he gave the Christian God in the Yoruba Bible (Olorun) was identical to that of the pre-colonial 'owner of heaven' and supreme being that Yorubas believed in before Christianity arrived. In contrast to other Muslims to their north (such as the Hausa, Fulani, and Nupe), Yoruba Muslims also refer to God as Olorun, and the first Yoruba translation of the Koran which was published in 1906 referred to Allah by the name Olorun.[32] Even after the Yoruba Koran was revised in 1924 to reference Allah, Yorubas still verbally referred to Allah as Olorun and mention Allah only when reading the Koran.

In churches, several of the superlative praise names and phrases used to describe the pre-colonial Olorun were transferred and applied to the Christian God. For example, 'Almighty' was translated as Olodumare, and 'Lord' as Oluwa. The Igbo Bible also gave the Christian God the same name as the pre-colonial Igbo supreme being (Chineke). Such linguistic continuity and convergence between the old and new religions facilitated conversion to Christianity.

However, some pre-colonial deities and spirits became casualties of this continuity in translation. The missionaries and Bible translators recast the role of some pre-colonial deities and spirits by presenting them as creations of the devil or agents working in his legion. Their intent was to present Christianity as the superior moral and authentic religion that could defeat the forces of evil represented by the

---

32 Western education and literacy was so interwoven with Christianity that a Christian (Reverend Cole) produced the first translation of the Koran in Yoruba.

pre-colonial deities and spirits. By doing so, missionaries and Bible translators ironically admitted the existence of the animist deities and spirits they so vilified. Crowther was responsible for the most impactful and notorious example of this recasting of pre-colonial deities. In 1843, he translated the pre-colonial trickster deity, Eshu as 'devil, Satan, demon, adversary, fiend'[33] and also transported this translation of Eshu as the devil to the Yoruba Bible. In the Igbo Bible, the shadowy Ekwensu was also equated with the devil.

Rather than reject the existence of pre-colonial African deities and spirits by portraying them as fabrications akin to Dracula and the Tooth Fairy, African Christian missionaries like Crowther instead re-portrayed them in new roles as evil supernatural renegades in Satan's service. Such recasting is very evident in contemporary African Pentecostal churches. Pentecostalism is much closer to pre-colonial beliefs than many Pentecostal Christians and their pastors realise or are prepared to admit. By portraying pre-colonial religions as inveterate opponents that must be continually fought, Pentecostal churches admit the existence of pre-colonial deities and spirits and invite them into their sanctuaries. They simply require their congregation to abstain from worshipping them. Hence, Pentecostal church services are replete with demonstrations of, and references to, spirit possession and exorcisms, self-professed prophets who claim to have the power to cure diseases and perform miracles, ancestral curses, and malignant supernatural forces that are not referenced anywhere in the Bible. Such mixing of old and new religions is not unique to Christianity and is also found among some Muslims. For example, two British army officers who in the 1800s served in the area that subsequently became northern Nigeria noticed the extent to which several Muslims they met accepted and practised animist religious beliefs. Lt-Colonel Augustus Mockler-Ferryman noted that: 'Neither is superstition wanting in the Mohammedan, who adorns himself with charms of all kinds to ward off disasters and to bring good luck, and who has a considerable amount of faith in the pagan fetishes.'[34] Lieutenant Seymour

---

33 Crowther, 1843 (Part II), p. 72.
34 Mockler-Ferryman, 1898, p. 255

Vandeleur served with hundreds of Hausa Muslim soldiers and wrote that:

> Most of them were plentifully adorned with charms and amulets, to keep off bullets and avert disaster. These consisted of little leather cases containing a piece of paper with a verse from the Koran, also pieces of wood, or shells fastened together by a bit of boot-lace, and were hung either round the neck or on the sword-belt, and sometimes fastened round their arm with the wrist-knife which is so common in this country.[35]

'I saw a lady gorgeously dressed'

One may wonder why Crowther dedicated his life to propagating the religion of a foreign conqueror. The remarkable circumstances of his life that catapulted him from a slave in 1822, to a clergyman in 1843, a missionary to the lands in which he was enslaved in 1845, and the first Black bishop in 1864, were so remarkable that even the most cynical would suspect that divine intervention propelled such events. A Black African bishop who dressed and spoke English like a Victorian gentleman, and who was well versed in Greek and Latin, was a celebrity in the nineteenth century when theories of Black intellectual inferiority were prevalent. He travelled to England ten times in his life, was in constant demand there as a speaker, and he delivered speeches at venues such as Cambridge University. When Crowther visited England in 1851, he visited Windsor Castle with the Prime Minister Lord Russell around 4:30 pm on 18 November 1851. Crowther described the scene before him as follows:

> While we were waiting in a drawing-room I could not help looking round at the magnificence of the room glittering with gold, the carpet, chairs, etc., all brilliant. While in this state of mind the door was opened, and I saw a lady gorgeously dressed, with a long train, step gracefully in. I thought she was the Queen.

---

35 Vandeleur, 1898, p. 198.

I rose at once, and was ready to kneel and pay my obeisance; but she simply bowed to us, said not a word, took something from the mantelpiece, and retired. After she left Lord Russell told me that she was one of the Ladies-in-waiting. 'Well,' I said to myself, 'if a Lady-in-waiting is so superbly dressed, what will be that of the Queen herself!'[36]

After this encounter, Crowther met Queen Victoria's husband Prince Albert in a separate upper drawing room where the two discussed events in West Africa with Prime Minister Russell. As they conversed, another guest whom Crowther described as 'simply dressed' entered the room and joined them. As she entered:

the Prince looking behind him, introduced her to Lord Russell, but in so quick a way that I could not catch the sound. This lady and the Prince turned towards the map to find out Abeokuta and Sierra Leone, where the slaves are liberated ... [I] was conversing freely and answering every question put to me about the way slaves are entrapped in their homes, or caught as captives in war. On inquiry I gave them the history of how I was caught and sold, to which all of them listened with breathless attention.[37]

When a candle blew out and stopped illuminating the maps and books they were reviewing, Crowther heard Prince Albert say to the woman who had joined them: 'Will your Majesty kindly bring us a candle from the mantelpiece?' Crowther was stupefied as he suddenly realised that the 'simply dressed' woman who joined them was Queen Victoria:

On hearing this I became aware of the person before whom I was all the time. I trembled from head to foot, and could not open my mouth to answer the questions that followed. Lord Russell and the Prince told me not to be frightened, and the smiles on the face of the good Queen assured me that she was not angry at

36 Page, 1908, pp. 103–4.
37 Ibid., pp. 104–5.

the liberty I took in speaking so freely before her, and so my fears subsided.[38]

Queen Victoria was relaxed enough in Crowther's company that she asked him to say the Lord's Prayer in Yoruba. After hearing it, the queen said that Yoruba was 'a soft and melodious language'.[39]

UNDER THE ROCK THAT GOD MADE

Despite the remarkable events of Crowther's life, and meeting the second longest reigning British monarch of all time, perhaps the most momentous event of his life occurred in his homeland. In 1845, after over 25 years in exile and separation from his family, Crowther had returned to Yorubaland to begin preaching at a town that the missionaries called 'Understone'. In his journals Crowther wrote the town's name as 'Abbeh Okuta'.[40] As refugees fled the civil wars and devastation that followed Oyo's collapse, around 1830 some of the refugees sought refuge at a location about 75 miles north of Lagos under an overhanging rock called Olumo Rock (Olumo translates as 'God made it'). They founded a new city there which they named Abeokuta (literally: 'Under the Rock' or 'Under the Stone'). Every morning Crowther gathered crowds under a tree and preached to them in Yoruba. What happened during Crowther's time in Abekouta is best described in his own words (from his journal entry of 21 August 1846) without editing by the author:

The text for today in the Christian Almanac is 'Thou Art the helper of the fatherless.' My mother, from whom I was torn away about five and twenty years ago, came with my brother in quest of me. When she saw me she trembled. She could not believe her own eyes. We grasped one another, looking at one another in silence and great astonishment, while the big tears rolled down her emaciated cheeks. She trembled as she held me by the hand

---

38 Ibid., p. 105.
39 Ibid., p.106.
40 Schon and Crowther, 1842, p. 318.

and called me by the familiar names which I well remember I used to be called by my grandmother, who has since died in slavery. We could not say much, but sat still, casting many an affectionate look towards each other, a look which violence and oppression had long checked, and affection which 25 years had not extinguished. My two sisters, who were captured with me, and their children are all residing with my mother. I cannot describe my feelings. I had given up, and now, after a separation of twenty five years, without any plans or devices of mine, we were brought together again.[41]

Despite the joyous reunion of mother and son after a quarter of a century, Crowther's family had suffered more than him while he was in Sierra Leone. After being kidnapped and enslaved, his mother Afala and his sisters managed to regain their freedom. However, his mother and one of his sisters were once again captured and re-enslaved. While his sister's husband managed to free her by paying a ransom, his elderly mother was sold in a slave market. While travelling on an errand for her mistress, she was again kidnapped and sold, until her daughter managed to save enough to buy her freedom for £4 and 10 s.

After being a clergyman for five years, Crowther finally conducted the first baptism of his career at Abeokuta on 5 February 1848. The first person he baptised was his own mother – Afala (who had formerly been a priestess of the deity Obatala). The new Christian baptismal name she took could not have been more appropriate: Hannah. In the Bible, Hannah was the mother of the biblical prophet Samuel.

Although Crowther was born, lived, and died before Nigeria's creation, the effects of his translation work still resonates today. The linguistic unification it created played a foundational role in creating Yoruba nationalism (even though ironically, Crowther and other Christian Yorubas adopted the term Yoruba from Muslim Hausas). Crowther's Yoruba Bible also served as an inspiration for the trans-

---

41   Page, 1908, pp. 95–6.

lation of the Bible into other indigenous African languages, and by 1925 the entire Bible had also been translated into Igbo, Efik, and Hausa, and portions of it into 45 other Nigerian languages.[42] Crowther's translation transcended its immediate purpose of providing a written religious instructional guide, and he also supervised the production of about 50 books and pamphlets on Nigerian languages.[43] His journals are treasure troves about the pre-colonial cultures and religions of several Nigerian ethnic groups. The orthography of the Yoruba language he created was the catalyst for the generation of educational and secular writing in Nigeria. In 1859, Crowther's son-in-law Reverend Thomas Babington Macaulay[44] (the husband of his daughter Abigail) founded Nigeria's first secondary school on the outskirts of Lagos: the CMS Grammar School. One of the school's pupils was Crowther's grandson Herbert, who set in motion the nationalist chain of events that eventually led to Nigeria's independence in 1960.

---

42   Coleman, 1971, p. 102.
43   Paracka Jr, 2001, p. 56.
44   Macaulay was a Sierra Leone-born and British trained clergyman.

13

The Sisterhood

Accounts of pre-colonial West Africa usually revolve around the actions of men. Yet women were usually present in, or more integral to, the seminal events in pre-colonial Africa than is acknowledged. This chapter will bring several important but usually overlooked pre-colonial women into the foreground. These women were just as ambitious, successful, and at times as cruel as the men of their time.

'CONQUER OR DIE' – THE DAHOMEY AMAZONS

Although exaggerated and glamourised for a film audience, the *Dora Milaje* female warriors in *Black Panther* and women soldiers in *The Woman King* are based on Dahomey's elite corps of female soldiers. While foreigners nicknamed them the 'Dahomey Amazons', within Dahomey they were called *Mino* ('our mothers'). The *Mino* were like a female equivalent of 'The Unsullied' from *Game of Thrones*, and had simultaneous roles as a military special forces unit, the King of Dahomey's bodyguards, and also had to take a lifelong oath of celibacy. They fought in the military alongside male soldiers, and vowed to 'conquer or die' during combat. Their duties also included executing condemned female criminals.

'I know them to be furious in battle'

The male and female corps of Dahomey's army mirrored each other and every male soldier had a woman counterpart within the *Mino* who was referred to as his 'mother'. The *Mino* were highly trained and highly rated. They were armed with muskets and cutlasses, and wore uniforms similar to the male soldiers – consisting of knee-length sleeveless tunics with blue and white stripes, and a white ribbon tied around their foreheads. Their disciplinary stand-ards were severe. Those who lost their weapons during combat or wasted ammunition without inflicting casualties on the enemy were punished. The residents of the Yoruba town of Abeokuta to Daho-mey's east were more familiar with the *Mino* than they wanted to be; as they were often on the receiving end of Dahomey's military invasions. Europeans' exotic fascination with the *Mino* led much fantasy and legend to grow around them. Stories of their ferocity and martial prowess are legion. Some rated them as faster at reload-ing their muskets and braver than male soldiers. An American Christian missionary who saw the aftermath of the devastation they could wreak on the battlefield said that:

> The Dahomy [*sic*] Amazons are said to have a perfect passion for the service, notwithstanding they are bound to perpetual celibacy and chastity, under the penalty of death. I know them to be furious in battle … They have a separate organization under generals and other officers of their own sex, and are deeply attached to the king.[1]

'women taken in adultery or too shrewish to live with their husbands'

Although the British explorer Sir Richard Burton claimed that 'Most of them are women taken in adultery or too shrewish to live with their husbands',[2] the King of Dahomey did not conscript an all-fe-male military force consisting of adulterous and nagging women. There were practical reasons for the *Mino*'s existence. Although modern rulers such as Colonel Muammar Ghaddafi of Libya had female bodyguards, in some pre-colonial African societies it was not unusual for women to be given military or law enforcement duties. In seventeenth-century Whydah (Dahomey's southern neighbour) the king sometimes sent his wives to conduct raids and punish offenders. Royal wives were excellent candidates for such

---

1 Bowen, 1857, p. 149.
2 Burton, 1863, p. 121.

duties because they were unlikely to encounter resistance. In many pre-colonial African societies, touching the king's wife was a capital crime punishable by death. A Dutch trader who visited Whydah in the early eighteenth century observed that 'all Persons being forbidden on pain of Death to touch the [king's] Wives, they are enabled to execute his Commands without the least interruption'.[3]

'the king's fingers'

This created incentives to increase the number of royal wives and to deploy them to military service. Female bodyguards may also have been a practical necessity for Dahomey's king since men were banned from staying in the interior of the king's palace at night. The *Mino* were technically the king's wives and had the usual royal immunity from physical attack. Yet very few (if any) of them had intimate relations with the king. Their self-description as 'the king's fingers' more accurately conveyed their status as an instrument of his will. They lived with the king in his palace, and had to live celibate lives devoted to him. Their special royal status made fraternising with them extremely dangerous. Having intimate relations with them was a crime punishable by death. When several of them became pregnant in the 1800s, eight of the men who impregnated them were executed.[4] Despite their special status as a Secret Service-type protector of the head of state, many of the *Mino* were originally foreign prisoners of war that Dahomey captured during its frequent wars and slave raids. Once taken to Dahomey, they were trained to fight from childhood. The enduring effectiveness of their indoctrination in Dahomey and their loyalty to its king was remarkable. In the nineteenth century, one of the *Mino* (a native of the Yoruba kingdom of Ketu who had been captured as a young girl and raised and trained in Dahomey) fought for Dahomey in a war against Ketu – against her own people. She was ironically captured as a prisoner of war for a second time, this time in her ancestral homeland in Ketu. When her parents found and recognised her,

---

3 Bosman, 1705, p. 367.
4 Burton, 1864, p. 277.

they tried to free her. However, she refused to rejoin her family and instead asked to return to Dahomey.[5]

'the whole of the native trade is in the hands of the women'

The military was not the only traditionally 'male' profession that pre-colonial African women participated in. In modern Nigerian discourse, the term 'market woman' is usually used as an invective to describe a woman who trades in the market because she is too uneducated and unsophisticated for other vocations. Yet in the pre-colonial era, businesswomen were held in high esteem and commerce was a stereotypical vocation for women. As late as the early twentieth century, a Christian missionary in Igboland said that:

> the whole of the native trade is in the hands of the women and by them largely the markets are controlled ... marketing is the central feature in the life of every Ibo [sic] woman, and to be successful in trade is the signal for generous congratulation. By this a woman's value is calculated; it affects her own position and comfort; a man considers it in the choice of a wife, and a husband's favour is bestowed or withheld largely according to the degree of his wife's success in the market.[6]

Women's businesses gave them not just social esteem, but also political influence. Each market had a titled female leader (called *omu* among the Igbo and *iyaloja* among the Yoruba). In Igboland the *omu* wore a ceremonial crown consecrated by Nri priests, and sat on a special chair in an area reserved for her. The *omu* and her committee set the price of goods sold in the market, established its rules, and also convened courts to arrest and try offenders who broke the market's rules. The *omu*'s role extended beyond economic matters, and she exercised powers tantamount to that of a queen. The *omu* and her committee were the leaders of the women in their community, and also acted as a council for transmitting women's grievances to men.

---

5 Bowen, 1857, p. 149.
6 Basden, 1921, p. 194.

'[an] extraordinary woman endowed with so many natural gifts and with an uncommon intelligence'

The name 'Tinubu' is perhaps the most famous name in Nigeria at present. It is the surname of Nigeria's current President Bola Ahmed Tinubu. Yet, a woman bearing that name acquired legendary status more than 100 years before President Tinubu was born.

While working in Lagos in the 1800s, the Sardinian Consul Giambattista Scala wrote about meeting an 'extraordinary woman endowed with so many natural gifts and with an uncommon intelligence'.[7] The woman that Scala referred to was the most famous female pre-colonial Nigerian business tycoon. She lived through the most tumultuous era of Yoruba history, including Afonja's coup, Oyo's collapse, the Sokoto Caliphate's extension into Ilorin, Britain's invasion and conquest of Lagos, the abolition of the slave trade, and the cut-throat battle for Lagos' throne. Yet she prospered in the midst of these tectonic events (some of which she was directly involved in).

Efunroye Osintinubu (known as 'Madam Tinubu') was born sometime between 1805 and 1810 in the Gbagura district of Ojokodo (currently in Ogun State) to a family of traders. She learned to trade as a youngster, and was a servant (some say slave) to a chief. She was so charming that the chief grew to love her as if she was his own daughter. Her charisma allowed her to negotiate herself out of servitude, and she opened her own business. Although Tinubu was uneducated, by 1850 she had become one of the wealthiest traders in Lagos and had varied business interests from trading ivory, palm oil, salt, pepper, and tobacco. By the 1860s, she had over 350 employees, in addition to approximately 60 domestic servants attached to her personal household. She also had a secretary named Charles B. Jones who was her personal scribe that drafted her letters to business partners.

Her success was not entirely due to her business acumen and intelligence. When the African-American Charles Delany (the

---

7   Smith and Packman, 2000, p. 30.

grandchild of slaves of Gola and Mandinka ethnicity) visited Abeokuta, Tinubu invited him to her house in 1862. Delany referred to her as 'the Princess Tinubu'.[8] His terminology was not mere flattery. Tinubu's excellent political skills enabled her to marry into the Lagos royal family, and to become close to three kings of Lagos who ruled Lagos on five different occasions between them.

'a wonderfully harmonious example of African beauty'

Tinubu's relationship with the Lagos royalty began in 1833 when the deposed former King of Lagos *Oba* Adele Ajosun visited Abeokuta while in exile and met Tinubu there. Giambattista Scala said that she was:

> tall, slender and well-proportioned; her bearing was proud, but not lacking in grace and subtlety; she had the art of expressing by various movements of her body and by all her postures an indescribable voluptuousness which few could resist ... her lips were full, her mouth large and her eyebrows very thin: nevertheless these features, combined with two large, black, brilliant eyes which had the fascination of a serpent, and two rows of very white teeth formed a wonderfully harmonious example of African beauty which was immediately pleasing and which continued to hold the beholder's gaze for a long time. It is not therefore surprising that this extraordinary woman ... soon came to lord it over these rough men and to find numerous supporters and admirers throughout the tribes.[9]

Unsurprisingly, Tinubu charmed the exiled *Oba* Adele and the two married in 1833. The couple lived in Badagry, just outside Lagos. The newlywed's fortunes dramatically changed when the King of Benin *Oba* Osemwende exercised one of his latent, rarely used powers. Osemwende was the grandfather of the famous *Oba* Ovonramwen (the King of Benin when Britain invaded Benin in 1897).

---

8   Hodgkin, 1960, p. 277.
9   Smith and Packman, 2000, pp. 29–30.

After becoming dissatisfied with the unpopular rule of his vassal, the King of Lagos Ojulari, in 1834 Osemwende sent Ojulari a symbolic message in the form of a skull and a sword. Ojulari understood the message's meaning. He had to abdicate Lagos' throne by committing suicide. Since Ojulari died childless, his suicide paved the way for Tinubu's husband Adele to return as King of Lagos in 1835 after 14 years in exile. Tinubu became the Queen of Lagos and used her royal access to enlarge her business empire and commercial contacts. After Adele died in 1837, Tinubu retained her influence within the royal family, and ensured the continuation of her husband's lineage, by helping his son Oluwole to succeed him as the next king. The widowed Tinubu married the leader of the new king's army, a warrior named Yesufu Bada. Marriages always seemed to diversify and enlarge Tinibu's business interests. Her marriage to the soldier Yesufu Bada introduced her to the weapons trade and she became a weapons dealer with her own private army. She later married for at least the third time, to a prominent Arabic scholar from Borno named Momoh Bukar.[10]

Oba Oluwole died in a freak accident in 1841 after a lightning strike detonated gunpowder stored at his palace. The explosion ripped Oluwole's body into so many pieces that he was identified only because of the royal beads attached to his body. Scala also said that later in Tinubu's life, 'the ravages of time and the vicissitudes of a stormy life had diminished ... her seductive charms'.[11] If this was so, the deaths of her husband and stepson within four years of each other did not end Tinubu's influence in the Lagos royal family. Although kings around her were deposed, died in freak accidents, or were at each other's throats, Tinubu seemed to have a Teflon coating that left her untouched. She always survived and landed on her feet.

In modern Nigerian politics, the term 'godfather' is usually used to describe a wealthy political benefactor who does not contest for political office, but instead uses his wealth to fund the election

---

10 Some sources claim that Adele was her second husband, and that her first marriage was to a man named Abburaka or Abubakar.

11 Smith and Packman, 2000, p. 29.

campaigns and political careers of client politicians, in exchange for favours when the client is elected into office. The client is usually expected to do the godfather's bidding. There are two mistaken assumptions about the political godfather syndrome. Firstly, that the godfather is always a man, and secondly that it is a modern phenomenon. More than 150 years before modern Nigerians became aware of the godfather syndrome and before Madam Tinubu's namesake Bola Tinubu became a political godfather in the twenty-first century, Madam Tinubu practised the art. After Oluwole's spectacular death, Tinubu supported the candidacy of her brother-in-law Akitoye (the brother of her dead husband Adele) over that of his nephew Kosoko (the brother of former *Oba* Ojulari, who the King of Benin forced to commit suicide in 1834).

As the wife of a former king, stepmother of a second king, and sister-in-law of the reigning King Akitoye, Tinubu was an economic force and a power behind the royal throne. Tinubu's relationships with successive kings was not a case of one-way patronage from kings to her. In exchange for royal patronage, business concessions, and introductions, she supported the kings in succession disputes, and provided them with economic and military support.

Unsurprisingly, Tinubu's wealth and political power put her on a collision course with British businesses that wanted to trade in Lagos. The choice of Tinubu's ally Akitoye over his nephew Kosoko was the tipping point in a royal succession dispute that had been brewing for decades, and created a pretext for Britain to invade Lagos and begin its colonial conquest of Nigeria. British authorities exiled Tinubu from Lagos after accusing her of plotting to depose King Dosunmu (one of Akitoye's successors) and assassinate Britain's consul in Lagos, Benjamin Campbell. These were the ostensible reasons, but if Tinubu really plotted to kill a representative of the British government, exile was a remarkably lenient punishment. Those who harmed or threatened harm to British citizens usually suffered an irreversible fate far worse than exile. Tinubu's real crime was that she was an economic obstacle and rival of British traders who were seeking to penetrate and trade in Lagos and the inland areas. Her role as an intermediary 'middleman' meant that

British traders had to go through her and could not trade directly with inland traders without negotiating with, and paying, her as a go-between. She also had powerful enemies and owed over £5000 (nearly £500,000 in today's money) to British businesses, and had to mortgage some of her land in Lagos to cover debt she owed to the wealthy businessman James Labulo Davies (who was born in Sierra Leone to emancipated Yoruba slaves).

'a woman of acute judgment and manly courage'

Yet exile did not dim the ever-adaptable Tinubu's star. She moved to Abeokuta and continued her businesses and political manoeuvring there. Drama always seemed to follow her. Reverend Thomas King (who assisted Bishop Ajayi Crowther with translating the Bible into Yoruba) described Tinubu as 'a woman of acute judgment and manly courage'.[12] While she was at Abeokuta, Dahomey invaded in 1864, and she helped to repel the invasion by providing guns and ammunition from her weapons business to Abeokuta's soldiers. As gratitude for her role in defending them, in 1864 Abeokuta's people gave Tinubu the chieftaincy title of *iyalode* ('first lady' or 'queen of the market'). The *iyalode* title is esteemed and still remains with members of the contemporary Tinubu family. Alhaja Abibatu Mogaji (the mother of Nigeria's current President Bola Tinubu) was the *iyalode* and after she died in 2013, the title passed to her granddaughter (Tinubu's daughter) Folashade Tinubu-Ojo.

Madam Tinubu's irresistible popularity led the British government to allow her to return to Lagos in the 1860s. However, her business empire had a dark side. In the early 1860s, the British Royal Navy officer Lieutenant John Hawley Glover enticed approximately 200 Hausa and Nupe slaves to escape from their masters to join him as escorts and porters as he travelled north from Lagos to Jebba to meet his shipwrecked colleagues (including Ajayi Crowther) there. However, some of the runaway slaves had been in the service of wealthy and politically powerful slave owners such as the King of

12   Shields, 1997, p. 21.

Lagos *Oba* Dosunmu. Someone who Glover's wife described as 'this sharp-sighted lady' and 'a very influential person in this town'[13] (Lagos) also recognised one of the slaves in Glover's company as one of her own, and demanded his return. Madam Tinubu was the woman that Mrs Glover referred to. Tinubu dropped her claim for the return of her slave only after Lieutenant Glover bribed her with clothing fabric. The fact that Tinubu could confront a British navy officer and representative of the British government in such a manner demonstrated the great power and level of near immunity she had acquired. Other slave owners continued to demand the return of their slaves and engaged Glover and the escaped slaves in a gunfight. This conflict between escaped slaves and those who tried to recapture them inadvertently started a domino chain of events that eventually led to the creation of Nigeria's modern-day army and police. Glover was so impressed at how the escaped slaves he recruited conducted themselves under fire during the gun battle (by laying down their loads and kneeling beside them in a circular pattern) that he trained them as a constabulary force nicknamed 'Glover's Hausas'. This 'Glover's Hausas' force eventually evolved into the Nigerian army and its members also formed the first units of what later became the Nigerian Police Force.

A considerable part of Tinubu's wealth came from her slave trading. She was both a slave owner and an intermediary who bought slaves for sale to Brazilian and Portuguese slave traders. She had a fierce determination to preserve her slave-trading business and to oppose those who tried to manumit her slaves. In 1851, Tinubu gave one of her slaves, a twelve-year-old girl named Alabon (whom the British nicknamed 'Rosa'), to Mrs Sandeman (the wife of a British trader in Lagos) as a domestic maid. Since by now it had become illegal for British citizens to engage in the slave trade, British authorities argued that Alabon became free when Tinubu gave her as a 'gift' to Mrs Sandeman, and even obtained a certificate of freedom for her. Yet two years later, Tinubu recaptured Alabon and argued that the girl was still her property. Tinubu also con-

---

13   Glover, 1897, p. 80.

trolled the sexual lives of her slaves. Tinubu and other slave owners often hired out their slaves as lovers to their business and political partners. Yet the slaves could generate serious conflict if they slept with someone that their owner did not approve of. For example, in 1883 Tinubu was so incensed when a man slept with one of her female slaves without her consent that she seized and detained the man, and refused to release him until his family compensated her. A member of the man's family had to borrow 60 bags of cowries and pawn eight other members of the family before Tinubu agreed to release the offender.

As a slave-trading arms dealer, Tinubu was no Mother Theresa. While revered for standing up to the British government, she also enslaved many of those she was allegedly standing up for. Tinubu's legacy survived her death in 1887. She was buried in Abeokuta and an area of Lagos formerly known as *Ita Tinubu* ('Tinubu's Precint') was renamed Tinubu Square after her. Statues of her were built and still stand in both Tinubu Square and in Abeokuta. Because of her fame many people who were not her children or related to her started answering the Tinubu name (including her stepchildren). This created both a large Tinubu clan and a lineage of Muslims bearing the Tinubu name (from her marriages to two Muslim men). Since Madam Tinubu did not have biological children, Nigeria's current president Bola Tinubu is not her direct blood descendant. He is one of the many adopted Tinubus. However, Wale Tinubu (the CEO of the multi-billion dollar oil company Oando PLC) is a blood member of Madam Tinubu's family. Although Wale refers to President Tinubu as his 'uncle', there is unlikely to be a blood relationship between them. Other members of the Tinubu dynasty include Alfa Saka Tinubu (a wealthy businessman and president of the Yoruba Muslim group Ahmadiyya in the 1930s) and his son Abdul Hamid who studied medicine at the University of Glasgow in the 1920s, and is believed to be the first Western-educated Muslim doctor from Nigeria. Saka Tinubu Street in Victoria Island, Lagos, is named after Saka Tinubu.

Because Madam Tinubu was such a larger than life character, it is tempting to mistakenly assume that she was unique. Yet there

were other female businesswomen peers to Tinubu who lived con-
temporaneously in her era. Unlike Tinubu, some of her peers were
blue-blooded members of royal families. The importance of the *omu*
title in Igboland meant that only the most prominent or successful members of society could be appointed to it. The most famous
omu of all time was the granddaughter of the famous obi Osayi of
Aboh. *Omu* Okwei was born in 1872 into royal families on both
her father's and mother's sides. Her paternal grandfather was the
King of Ossomari and negotiated trade treaties with the British
in the 1850s, while her father Osuna Afubeho was a famed and
wealthy warrior who owned a fleet of war canoes manned by several
hundred slaves.

At age nine she was sent to live with her maternal aunt in Igalaland as an apprentice for four years. While there she learned to
speak Igala. She twice married men that her family disapproved of.
The first was in 1888, to a trader from Brass named Joseph Allagoa.
Even though the marriage was short-lived (just over a year) and
left Okwei alone looking after her young child and mother, she
struck business deals with her ex husband's friends and business
colleagues to supply them with foodstuffs and poultry in exchange
for European goods which she resold in local markets. She married
again in 1895, to Opene of Aboh (who already had a wife). Her
family again objected because he was not considered a suitable
enough spouse for a woman of royal birth like Okwei. She became
his second wife and moved to Onitsha (a big trading town) to join
him. She expanded her business in Onitsha to trading in cotton and
tobacco and became a distributor and agent for the Royal Niger
Company (the chartered company which the British government
authorised to operate in Nigeria on its behalf). She also maintained cordial relationships with her business partners by adopting
beautiful young girls, raising them, then in adulthood either gave
them as wives or mistresses to important local and European businessmen. The children born to the foreign businessmen enlarged
her family when their fathers went home. Despite never attend-
ing school, Okwei had the foresight to give her children the best
education possible at the time. Her son Francis Allagoa (from her

first marriage) worked as a district interpreter in the colonial civil service, and became a court registrar. In 1935 he succeeded his father as King of Nembe, and Francis' son in turn succeeded him. Her son from her second marriage (Peter Opene) worked for the Royal Niger Company at Onitsha and stayed in the job for 30 years.

'she drives a hard bargain'

A British trader at Onitsha in the early 1900s said that 'she drives a hard bargain and has the pull in being able to make her own market and at her own price without competition'.[14] Okwei did not remain stagnant and evolved her business in response to changing social conditions. For example, as land litigation increased, she started lending money to litigants and farmers at exorbitant rates of interest as high as 60–90 per cent. In return, the debtors pledged their land and fishing rights to her, and she used them and the interest on money she loaned to reinvest in her business. Another remarkable aspect of her business was that despite not being educated, her sons kept meticulous books of account for her. Although she absorbed modern influences in her business, she did not do so in her personal life. She refused her children's appeals for her to convert to Christianity, practised traditional animist religion all her life, and encouraged her community to continue to observe indigenous traditional practices in order to preserve them from being lost. Despite not being an Onitsha indigene, her influence was such that she became a friend and adviser to the King of Onitsha *Obi* Okosi I. By the time she died, she owned 24 houses in Onitsha alone.

The third member of the triumvirate of famous Nigerian businesswomen who lived alongside each other in the nineteenth century was a product of the 'secondary jihads' that spread outside Hausaland and toppled its neighbouring kingdoms. It is impossible to tell her story without chronicling the conspiratorial chain of events that led to her birth. Nupe was a kingdom which neighboured Oyo (to its south-west) and the Sokoto Caliphate (to its

---

14   Ekejiuba, 1967, p. 646.

north). Its kings claimed descent from an ancient patriarch named Tsoede, who was a fugitive son born to a Nupe princess and an Igala king. To escape persecution from his jealous Igala half-brothers, Tsoede fled to Nupeland, united its people, and established a new kingdom with him and his successor kings holding the title of *Etsu* Nupe.

THE GREAT SCHOLAR

The religious character of nineteenth-century Nupeland was similar to Oyo. Both had a mixed Muslim and animist population. The manner in which the jihad infiltrated into Nupeland and Oyo was also similar. Both were triggered after itinerant Fulani preachers emigrated there in the midst of royal succession disputes. Muhammad Bangana (alias 'Mallam Dendo') was a Torodbe Fulani from Kebbi in what is now north-west Nigeria. He migrated to Nupeland in the late eighteenth century and worked there as a preacher, soothsayer, and seller of supernatural charms. Dendo became popular in Nupeland in the early ninteenth century due to his alleged divining prowess and ability to cure incurable illnesses. Like Alimi in Oyo, he attracted a large group of followers consisting of Fulani immigrants to Nupeland, Hausa soldiers serving in Nupe's army, and Muslim clerics and traders. Dendo became known as 'Manko' (the great scholar).

Dendo's arrival coincided with a royal succession dispute between two rivals who both claimed Nupe's throne (Jimada, the son of the prior king, and Jimada's uncle Majiya). In a remarkable parallel to events in Oyo, Hausaland, and Borno, Dendo's fame gained him royal access and Majiya hired Dendo as his military and spiritual adviser (similar to how Afonja hired Alimi to help him in Oyo, the Hausa kings hired Dan Fodio, and Borno's king hired al-Kanemi). All three kingdoms were eventually overthrown by the men they hired to help them.

Dendo and Majiya's forces killed Jimada in 1805, and Majiya rewarded Dendo by gifting him two beautiful slave girls who were prisoners of war. Dendo kept one of these slave girls as his concubine, and in the early nineteenth century she gave birth to a daughter named Gogo Habiba. She was the only daughter out of Dendo's nine children, and she grew up in a front-row seat viewing her father's Machiavellian scheming to power.

After some time, Dendo's alliance with Majiya broke down, and Majiya expelled Dendo and the Fulanis from Nupeland. Dendo and his Fulani allies took refuge with Alimi in Ilorin and then switched sides by withdrawing their support for Majiya and instead supporting Idrisu, the son of the dead Jimada whom Dendo had helped to defeat and kill. Fresh from their victorious jihad in Hausaland, the Sokoto Caliphate's battle-hardened army sent reinforcements under Aliyu Jedo around 1810 to help Dendo attack Nupe, overthrew Majiya, and put Idrisu on the throne as *Etsu* Nupe. However, Dendo was the puppet master behind the scenes, and he once again switched sides, withdrew his support for Idrisu, and in 1830 brought Majiya back to rule for a second time. Dendo died in 1833 and Majiya died soon after him. Like Alimi and Afonja in Ilorin, their sons inherited their scheming and competed over Nupe's throne as their fathers did. In 1835 Dendo's son Usman Zaki overthrew Majiya's son Tsado and appointed himself as the new *Etsu* Nupe even though he was Fulani. This ended the Tsoede dynasty and led to Nupe being added as a new emirate in the Sokoto Caliphate.

Despite the constant intrigues, wars, and regicide that her father and brothers instigated and that she witnessed growing up, Gogo Habiba was her own independent economic and political force in Nupeland. Two of her brothers (Usman Zaki and Muhammad 'Masaba' Saba) were the first and second Fulani *Emirs* of Nupe. Although she was the daughter of a slave, Habiba's main business was slave trading. She had her own standing army and led her men on slave raids in the Gwari areas.[15] She traded slaves she captured as far south as Lagos (where her contemporary Madam Tinubu resided). These two powerful women Habiba and Tinubu knew of each other, probably collaborated in their slave-dealing businesses, and in the 1850s Tinubu sent money and presents to Habiba.

---

15   Where former Nigerian president Ibrahim Babangida is from.

Habiba was close to her younger brother Masaba, and when he became the *Emir* of Bida in 1841, she became the power behind his throne. Masaba consulted her on major decisions and those seeking an audience with him had to go through her (similar to how Tinubu was an adviser to, and intermediary with, successive kings of Lagos). Even though Masaba built three houses for her, Habiba was powerful enough to reject all of them as being too small to accommodate her and her large retinue of over 6000 followers and slaves.[16] She eventually accepted a fourth house that Masaba built for her in Nupe's capital city Bida. This fourth house was as large as Masaba's palace, and Habiba also claimed the other three houses she previously rejected. Habiba never had children, but she married one of her employees after she was past child-bearing age. Her life ended tragically after she committed suicide following the breakdown of her relationship with her brother.

FEMALE HUSBANDS AND FEMALE SONS

Pre-colonial West African women's social power was also far more independent than currently portrayed. For example, biological and social genders in pre-colonial Igboland did not always coincide. Heterosexual women could marry each other and be 'female husbands', and women could also be 'sons'. Such gender fluidity simultaneously exposed Igbo society's patriarchy, and also that the patriarchy was flexible, could incorporate women into roles reserved for men, and that men even had to cooperate to assign male gender roles to women.

Woman–woman marriages were a response to three elements of Igbo society; its laws of patrilineal inheritance, esteem of childbirth and fertility, and polygamy. Since only males could inherit the assets and power of their fathers, the legacy of families without a male heir was severely jeopardised. In such circumstances, the family could fill the void created by the absence of a male heir if one of its women married another woman. For example, if a family's patri-

16   Idrees, 1991, p. 6.

arch died without a son, his eldest daughter could succeed him as the head of the family by becoming a 'male daughter', and marrying wives as her father had done. The women in such marriages were heterosexual and there was no sexual intimacy between them. In Igbo culture, payment of bride price transcended gender and was more than a mere marital formality. It also gave the person who paid the bride price exclusive paternity rights to all children born to their wife (even to children born from a wife's adulterous affair). By paying a bride price, a woman could claim the children born by her wife as her own. Thus, children born to the female couple (usually fathered by a male of their choice) were deemed to be 'fathered' by the woman who paid the bride price – not the biological father. In this way, her descendants could continue their lineage and inheriting the family's assets. Such marriages also often arose when a woman was infertile or was married to an infertile man. Although these were creative adaptations for women to gain rights that were available only to men, in some cases women entered such unions by choice rather than necessity.

In pre-colonial Igbo culture, polygamy carried economic and social esteem that made both men and women support it. Since bride dowries were very expensive, only wealthy men could afford to have many wives. Polygamy thus became a way for rich men to flaunt their wealth. Polygamy also elevated the status of the first wife. Once her husband married another woman, she would become the 'first lady' of the household with her own separate house in the family compound. She also acquired the right to command the other 'junior wives', who had to obey her as if she was their mother. Being the senior wife also relieved her of certain domestic duties which she could delegate to the junior wives. If her husband was wealthy, being his senior wife also meant that she would automatically be given the female equivalent of any aristocratic title conferred on him. These factors meant that some wives often initiated the process of their husband marrying a second wife (and at times she even raised the dowry). The high-status symbol of polygamy meant that it was not an exclusive right for men only. Like rich men, some wealthy women also married multiple wives in order to increase their clout within society. Some wealthy women who had husbands even entered into polygamous marriages with multiple women.

Not only did pre-colonial women contradict society's biological and social gender roles and navigate social relationships to elevate themselves, but in some places women were indispensable parts of the government. Although women such as *Omu* Okwei of Ossomari and Gogo Habiba in Bida acquired their political powers due to being born into royal families, in some areas it was inverted. In other areas, women held royal status because of their gender. Even in societies where only men were eligible to be the monarch, women held special *de jure* powers and were fundamental parts of their society's constitution and government. Sometimes women held special positions in the state's religion; such as the *inna* of the Hausa State of Gobir who wielded massive political and religious powers second only to the King of Gobir, and was Gobir's temporary ruler when the king was absent (during which time she would wear male attire). In the pre-jihad Hausa States of Zaria and Birnin-Gwari, two positions in the government were reserved for women. In some societies, women exercised huge political power if they were perceived to possess supernatural power. For example, the British army officer Lt-Colonel Augustus Mockler-Ferryman claimed that 'an old pagan priestess (a captive from the Borgus) was maintained at the court of Ilorin and virtually ruled the kingdom'.[17]

The position of queen mother was a vital office in many pre-colonial African societies. While in Benin and Borno the king's mother had her own palace, royal court, and attendants, in other places the woman who held the title of queen mother was not actually the king's biological mother or relative. Queen mother was instead a title and the woman who held the role was a fundamental part of the state's constitutional structure. For example, the Bura and Pabir people of north-east Nigeria recognised a queen mother who had the title of *maigira*.[18] Rather than being born into the role, the king and his court chose the *maigira*. She could not be from the same generation as the king and had to be over 30 years old. Once

---

17   Mockler-Ferryman, 1898, p .255.
18   Compounded from the words *mai* (ruler) and *gira* (woman).

appointed, she had to remain celibate for the rest of her life. This did not forbid her from marrying or from remaining married, as long as she did not have sex with her husband. The king and queen mother were crowned together; with the queen mother being given the role as the official custodian of the king's insignia of office. She was not a mere treasurer of sacred objects. Part of the king's coronation involved him learning the lessons of rulership from the queen mother.

DAUGHTER OF THE LEARNED

Nana Asma'u and her work are not as well known as they should be because she has been in the shadow of her far more famous father and brother. She had the misfortune of being the daughter of the first leader of the Sokoto Caliphate, the sister of its second leader, and the niece of its first *waziri*. Nana was named after one of the Prophet Mohammed's sister-in-laws who also helped him. Nana and her twin brother Hassan were born in 1793 to Usman Dan Fodio's first wife Maimunatu. Nana's parents were first cousins[19] and the twins were among Dan Fodio's 40 children. After the twins' mother died when they were young children, their stepmothers raised them in a family of scholars, in which Nana was surrounded by educated women (including her stepmothers Aisha and Hauwa, paternal grandmother Hauwa, sisters Fatima, Hadijah, and Maryam, and sister-in-law Aisha). She unsurprisingly took up the family vocation. Although her father imposed restrictions on the freedom of women in his family (such as forbidding them from being unveiled, going to the market, or leaving the compound), he encouraged women's education and admonished men who refused to allow their wives to be educated. Nana started learning the Koran by heart as soon as she could speak, and later became a *hafiza* (a woman who has memorised the entire Koran). However, Nana experienced a tumultuous childhood. She was only eleven years old when the jihad that propelled her father to power

---

19 Usman Dan Fodio's father and Maimuna's mother were siblings.

started, and in 1817, she suffered the double heartbreaks of losing her father and twin brother Hassan in the same year when she was only 24 years old.

'The Way of the Pious'

However, Nana blossomed after their deaths. She wrote her first work (a poem called *The Way of the Pious*) in 1820 and followed up with over 60 more written works during the rest of her life. Nana had brilliant linguistic skills. She spoke four languages (her native Fulfulde, Arabic, Hausa, and the Tamachek language of the Tuaregs), and wrote in all of them except Tamachek. Even though Arabic was the official language of scholarship in her era, she wrote over half of her work in Fulfulde. Her polyglot skills and preoccupation with scholarship and writing led her to meet and correspond with other scholars across West Africa, including some as far away as Mauritania.

If not for Nana, we may not know as much as we currently do about the Dan Fodio family. Almost a third of her work consisted of poems and other works about her family members. Not only did her writing expose the personal relationships that built the Caliphate, but her careful keeping of her family's records preserved their legacy. After her father died, she became his posthumous curator by collating, copying, and organising his documents. Her older half-brother Bello (who was 14 years older than her) tutored her as her writing became more sophisticated. Nana and Bello were very close. Bello's mother Hauwa was one of those who raised Nana after her mother Maimuna died. In 1807, when Nana was 14, she married Bello's best friend Gidado,[20] and in turn Bello's wife Aisha was her best friend whom she had known since childhood. These two power couples would later play massive roles in governing and stabilising the Sokoto Caliphate. When Bello succeeded his father as the *sarkin musulmi* in 1817, Nana became one of his advisers.

---

20 Gidado was almost 17 years older than Nana.

'The Sisterhood'

Nana also bequeathed a legacy of women's education in northern Nigeria by founding an association of itinerant women teachers which toured the countryside to educate women. Nana originally called her students *yan'uwa* ('friends' or 'sisters'). Today they are called *Yan Taru* ('Those Who Congregate Together' or 'The Sisterhood'). *Yan Taru* began informally by meeting in Nana's bedroom. After Nana trained an initial corps of teachers called *jaji*, those teachers in turn taught others. The *jaji* teachers wore a distinctive uniform, including a straw hat (called *malfa*) with a red ribbon tied around its rim (which was their official insignia of office), and left no part of their bodies uncovered except their faces. The *malfa* hat originated in the pre-jihad Hausa State of Gobir that Nana's family overthrew. The *malfa* was part of the official regalia of the King of Gobir's sister – who held the title of *inna*. The *inna* was Gobir's most powerful woman official and had a role that simultaneously made her the leader of Gobir's women and the chief priestess in the *Bori* religious rituals. While it was counter-intuitive that Muslim women working for the government that overthrew the *inna* would then adopt the uniform of someone they regarded as the leader of a pagan cult, the continuity of uniform helped to transfer the *inna*'s authority and esteem to *Yan Taru*'s teachers.

Yan Taru's importance transcended educational and religious instruction. It arose at a time of instability in the Caliphate. Not all of Hausaland immediately fell in line behind the jihad leaders, and the jihad incorporated many non-Muslims and Hausa rebels into the Caliphate. Hence, *Yan Taru* helped to stabilise the Caliphate using 'soft power' to pre-empt potential rebellions, by educating many women who may have been ambivalent or hostile towards the Caliphate, and the mothers, wives, daughters, and sisters of those who may have rebelled against it.

Although Nana is presumed to be an outlier and the most outstanding woman scholar of her time, she was not unique. After she died in 1864, her sister Maryam succeeded her as *Yan Taru*'s leader. Maryam was the daughter of Dan Fodio's concubine Mariya, and became a famed poet and teacher. She married twice: firstly, to a member of Gidado's family, and secondly to the *Emir* of Kano Ibrahim Dabo. *Yan Taru* still exists and is still led by Nana's family descendants.

Pre-colonial West African women were not just powerless daughters, mothers, and wives. They were integral members of their society's military, business, political, and educational sectors. However, tectonic events such as the jihad in northern Nigeria, Christianisation of the south, and colonial rule divested them of powers and influence they previously held. These events overlaid a new moral, economic, and political order. The stories of female achievement in this chapter are not intended to gloss over the patriarchal societies that these women lived in, nor does it seek to portray the women as innocents who always acted benevolently. At times, the powerful women in this chapter exploited their power to give their children and family members an advantage over others – just as men did. Yet their gender did not impede their successes. They were successful people who incidentally happened to be women.

14
Conclusion

The historical accounts in this book show that there are many common but badly mistaken assumptions about pre-colonial West Africa, and that the pre-colonial era has portents for contemporary Nigeria.

One of Nigerians' longest running mantra-like complaints is that their country is ungovernable due to Britain's folly in creating a multi-ethnic and multi-religious country of bewildering diversity. However, prominent pre-colonial states such as Benin, Kanem-Borno, Oyo, and the Sokoto Caliphate were multi-ethnic and multi-religious, as were many smaller communities. When Reverend James Schon visited the Igbo town of Aboh in the Niger Delta in 1841, he reported that its inhabitants 'belong to various nations'[1] and that the king's slaves included Hausas, Kakandas, and Nupes.

Pre-colonial inter-ethnic relations often focus on sudden tectonic events such as revolutions and wars. However, peaceful inter-ethnic assimilation and co-existence was often the norm in the pre-colonial era. The itinerant Awka blacksmiths, Muslim clerics, Nri priests, Arochukwu oracle agents, and Hausa expatriate traders were vectors of their cultures, languages, and religions to wherever they travelled. Many of them intermarried with their host ethnic groups, and their presence in communities far away from their homelands gives some context for the colourful legends regarding Bayajidda, *Eze* Chima, Eweka, Ododuwa, Tsoede. etc., which portray different ethnic groups as 'brothers' of each other. For example, if one accepts the *Eze* Chima and Oduduwa legends, their logical conclusion is that the vast majority of southern Nigeria's kingdoms are led by descendants of the same family, and that the Yoruba and Benin monarchies are related to the Igbo monarchies at Onitsha and

---

1   Schon and Crowther, 1842, pp. 232–3.

Aboh. The Bayajidda legend similarly links the Hausa and Borno monarchies, and the Nupe monarchy claims descent from the Igala. Inter-ethnic links between far-flung monarchies transcended oral legends. Pre-colonial states had diplomatic relations with each other. For example, the *Alaafin* of Oyo had diplomatic relations with the King of Borgu and the *Etsu* Nupe, and exchanged gifts with both of them (and *Alaafin* Ojigi had a wife from Dahomey).

Despite being addressed by titles that signify unlimited power (such as 'deputy to the gods'), pre-colonial rulers were not autocrats and exercised their powers only in very prescribed ways. Non-royal councils and taboos encumbered most of their powers. Some of them could be deposed or sentenced to death if they abused their powers, and many of them also faced rebellions by their own subjects. Some pre-colonial kingdoms even had democratic features, as most monarchies were elective, and rarely could children automatically succeed their parents. Leaders were usually chosen by kingmakers rather than automatically from the king's children.

THE NATIONAL QUESTION

The system of government that pre-colonial states deployed provides some portents for Nigeria's contemporary political and religious challenges. Post-colonial Nigeria has limped from one political crisis to another and has not found an answer to its omni-present 'national question' of how to ensure peaceful co-existence between its different ethno-regional and religious groups. During the past 60 years, Nigeria has tried to answer its national question by evolving from a British-style parliamentary democracy, to a military dictatorship, and to its current American-style presidential system of government with 36 states. Yet ironically, Nigeria has not tried the system of government that served most of its communities in the pre-colonial era. Pre-colonial rulers delegated substantial powers to sub-regional lieutenants and operated confederal systems of government (which lasted for 800–1000 years in the Hausa States, Kanem-Borno, and Yoruba kingdoms). Nigeria has not replicated a confederal system in any of its post-colonial governments, despite plenty of historical evidence that confederacy is the system of government that Nigerians have most been accustomed to.

As the only country in the world with its population equally split between Christians and Muslims, Nigeria has throughout its history had an incendiary and unresolved debate regarding whether the country is secular or whether Muslim *Sharia* courts should exist. Yet Nigeria's pre-colonial societies were not secular and did not separate religion from the state. Most pre-colonial societies were multi-religious and rulers such as the *Oba* of Benin, *Ooni* of Ife, *Attah* Igala, and *Obi* of Onitsha were regarded as the gods' lieutenants on earth. The *Mai* of Borno and and *sarkin musulmi* at Sokoto were called 'commander of the believers'. These rulers were simultaneously heads of government and heads of religion. Their roles surpassed the English king's role as 'defender of the faith'. Such close affinities between the head of state and religion support the view of some in contemporary Nigeria who view secularism as a foreign, non-native Euro-Christian concept.

The jihad that preceded the establishment of the Sokoto Caliphate was the most seismic event in pre-colonial Nigeria. The jihad continued for several years after Usman Dan Fodio died and its effects probably surpassed his plans and expectations. Although it was initially targeted at Hausaland, it also triggered 'secondary jihads' outside Hausaland which destroyed or overthrew the three most powerful states near it (Kanem-Borno, Nupe, and Oyo), and led to the collapse of their foundational ruling dynasties (some of which had been ruling for 800–1000 years). Its shockwaves are still felt in contemporary Nigeria, and it spread far beyond Hausaland and extended into at least four different West African countries (Nigeria, Niger, Cameroon, and Burkina Faso). The south-east and Niger Delta were the only regions of pre-colonial Nigeria untouched by the jihad.

The jihad also caused Hausa history to mirror Yoruba history by transferring the Hausa political capital from Daura to Sokoto (akin to how the Yoruba political capital moved from Ife to Oyo). The jihad's aftermath helped to create a sense of northern Nigerian identity and unity that has been remarkably resilient. Many external and social forces have been thrown at the Sokoto Caliphate but it deflected most of them and did not break. *Emirs* and the Caliphate survived British conquest, and repeated fracturing of its territory between 1967 and 1995. A British academic who lived in northern Nigeria concluded that 'The Northern Region had a special ethos all its own and a pride in its identity.'[2]

The outcome of historical events has influenced how we recall them. Usman Dan Fodio is regarded as a hero and Afonja as a traitor. Yet had the Hausa kings suppressed the jihad, they would have written alternate histories that portrayed Usman Dan Fodio as an insurrectionist. Had Afonja succeeded, he would have been lionised as a hero that secured Ilorin's independence from the domineering Oyo. The victors rewrote the narrative of events to suit their own interests, and the task of retracing Hausa and Borno history is impeded because the victors destroyed their predecessors' records and artefacts in order to erase the history of those they deemed unworthy. Thus, the history now known is pieced together from what survived. There is far more known history about northern Nigeria than southern Nigeria because the north had a greater tradition of writing, a larger library of documents, and also because British colonial officers regarded them as more civilised and interesting to write about than southerners (many of whom the British regarded as 'for the most part degraded savages, worshippers of devils, and participators in horrible fetiche [*sic*] rites' living in a 'mass of dark humanity').[3]

THE GREAT WATER

Nigeria's existence is viewed as an extraordinary outcome that would not have occurred but for Britain's intervention. Without British involvement, Nigeria would certainly not exist in the form in which it does today. However, an embryonic Nigerian economic union (but not a Nigerian political union) had already developed prior to Britain creating Nigeria.

---

2   Dent, 1995, p. 131.
3   Mockler-Ferryman, 1898, p. 487.

Pre-colonial communities did not live in disconnected islands without interacting with each other. The river from which Nigeria's name derives contributed a great deal to pre-colonial inter-ethnic and inter-regional economic cooperation between its peoples. Arabs called it *Bahr Sudan* ('Black Sea'), while indigenes who lived close to it called it reverential names such as 'The Great River' or the 'The Great Water'. *Kwora* was its most popular name until the mid-1850s. The River Niger is often taken for granted as a mere topographic feature. However, it provided a pre-colonial marine commercial highway that created business connections between distant parts of the area that later became Nigeria. Pre-colonial merchants shipped tonnes of goods on giant 40-feet-long canoes up and down the river, and markets operated at strategic points alongside the river (at places such as Aboh, Asaba, Idah, and Onitsha). As in modern Nigeria, these markets were inter-ethnic melting pots. Inter-regional commerce led some ethnic groups to be present in unexpected places. Thus, traders from the Niger Delta travelled up the River Niger to its confluence with the Benue River where they met and traded with Ebira, Igala, and Yoruba people, Yorubas bought horses for the Oyo army from Borno and Hausa suppliers, Ebira and Hausa traders travelled down the river as far south as Asaba and Aboh, and Hausa elephant hunters were in Igboland as late as the early twentieth century. Hausa was the language of commerce and was spoken even in the Niger Delta.

This inter-ethnic and inter-regional trade enabled common currencies to emerge. Cowrie shells were the most generally accepted pre-colonial currency. They were not indigenous and were obtained from places as far away as Sri Lanka, the Maldives, Zanzibar, and other locations on India's coastline. Mali and Songhai used cowries as early as the fourteenth century and Benin used them before the Portuguese arrived there in the fifteenth century. Cowries were also used as currency in areas as dispersed as Dahomey, south-east and south-west Nigeria, and Hausaland. Cowries were popular and widely used because their size and shape made them easy to carry and count, and impossible to counterfeit. They were also durable and could be exchanged or stored for years without breaking.

Some areas had their own additional currencies. South-east Nigeria had at least three currencies in addition to cowries. These included brass rods among the Efik people in the Cross River area, and manillas (bracelet-shaped pieces of brass or copper), which were used in the Niger Delta as early as the sixteenth century and also by southern Igbos and Ibibios. Igbos also used a third currency called *umumu* (small arrow-shaped pieces of iron). The Idoma and Tiv of Nigeria's Middle Belt region also used this currency (and called it *akika* and *ibia*, respectively), and it has been found as far away as Katagum (in modern-day Bauchi State of northern Nigeria), and in the Jos area in Plateau State.

More than at any other time in its post-independence history, Nigeria's current political map resembles the pre-colonial era. Nigerian inter-regional relations made a 180 degree turn during the colonial era, followed by a 360-degree turn in the post-colonial era. In 1914, Britain fused multiple pre-colonial territories together to create Nigeria. After Nigerian independence in 1960, Nigerians fragmented their country into smaller and smaller territorial units, and in the 33 years between 1963 and 1996, created 36 separate sub-national states within Nigeria (see Map 4). Since 1999, Nigeria's 36 states have been grouped into six geo-political zones that have tremendous cultural and political resonance. The six zones correspond approximately to six pre-colonial cultural zones that existed before British rule. The north-west zone is composed mostly of areas that were part of the Sokoto Caliphate. The north-east zone includes areas that were part of the Kanem-Borno Empire. The south-west zone consists of areas that were part of the Yoruba kingdoms, the south-south zone includes the Benin kingdom, and the south-east zone consists almost entirely of Igbo-speaking areas. The north-central zone is the most diverse and consists of numerous ethnic groups in Nigeria's Middle Belt, including those that resisted incorporation into the Kanem-Borno Empire and/or Sokoto Caliphate.

With hindsight, perhaps these six zones should have been the basis for six different nations to emerge from British colonial rule, rather than one huge Nigerian state. Alternatively, perhaps

Nigeria's emergence was unavoidable. Although the invention of modern transportation diminished much of its importance, the River Niger's magnetic economic attraction made it almost inevitable that at some point, the river would be a fulcrum around which a state or other union based on economic cooperation would arise and revolve. Britain realised this before others (including Nigerians themselves) did and capitalised on it. Political restructuring and modernisation has not erased the effects of Nigeria's pre-colonial past. That past has operated as an 'invisible hand' that has influenced Nigeria's trajectory. Perhaps the pre-colonial era is not only a forgotten era, but is also present but invisible.

Illustrations

Benin sculpture of an ancient King of Benin with his attendants and soldiers (at the British Museum). (Author)

Benin sculpture believed to be Benin Queen Mother Idia (at the British Museum). (Author)

Benin sculpture of a Portuguese visitor to Benin (at the British Museum). (Author)

Hausa letter written by Usman Dan Fodio in *Ajami* script. (From Charles Henry Robinson, *Hausaland, or Fifteen Hundred Miles through the Central Soudan*. Sampson Low, Marston and Company: London, 1900)

Alake of Egbaland and his officials. (From R.E. Dennett,
Nigerian Studies: or The Religious and Political System of the Yoruba.
Macmillan & Co Limited, London, 1910)

Bishop Samuel Ajayi Crowther and members of his clergy in the 1800s.
(From Jesse Page, *The Black Bishop: Samuel Adjai Crowther.* Hodder &
Stoughton, London, 1892)

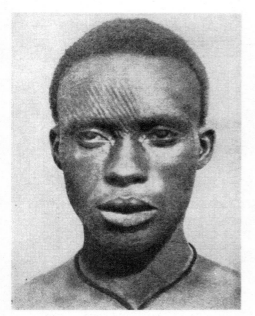

Igbo man with facial tribal scars. (From G.T. Basden, *Among the Ibos of Nigeria: An Account of the Curious and Interesting Habits, Customs, and Beliefs of a Little Known African People by One Who Has for Many Years Lived amongst Them on Close and Intimate Terms.* J.B. Lippincott Co., Philadelphia, 1921)

Dandeson Crowther (son of Bishop Samuel Ajayi Crowther). (From Jesse Page, *The Black Bishop: Samuel Adjai Crowther.* Hodder & Stoughton, London, 1892)

An Igbo woman's hairstyle. (From G.T. Basden, *Among the Ibos of Nigeria: An Account of the Curious and Interesting Habits, Customs, and Beliefs of a Little Known African People by One Who Has for Many Years Lived amongst Them on Close and Intimate Terms.* J.B. Lippincott Co., Philadelphia, 1921)

Members of an Igbo masquerade. (From G.T. Basden, *Among the Ibos of Nigeria: An Account of the Curious and Interesting Habits, Customs, and Beliefs of a Little Known African People by One Who Has for Many Years Lived amongst Them on Close and Intimate Terms.* J.B. Lippincott Co., Philadelphia, 1921)

Mohammed al-Kanemi. (From Major Dixon Denham, and Captain Hugh Clapperton and Dr Walter Oudney, *Narrative of Travels and Discoveries in Northern and Central Africa, in the Years 1822, 1823, and 1824 (With an Appendix)*. John Murray, London, 1826)

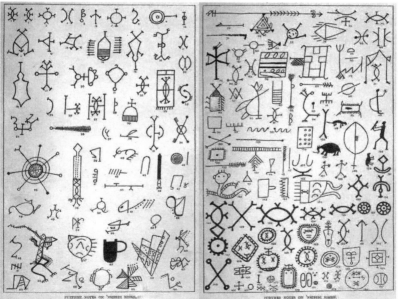

Nsibidi images. (From Elphinstone Dayrell, 'Further Notes on Nsibidi Signs with Their Meanings from the Ikom District, Southern Nigeria'. *The Journal of the Royal Anthropological Institute of Great Britain and Ireland*, Vol. 41 (July–December 1911), pp. 521–40)

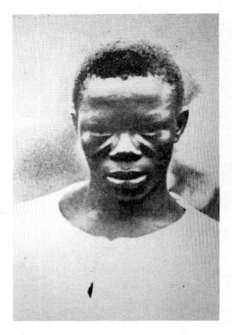

A Nupe boy with facial tribal marks – late 1800s. (From, Charles Henry Robinson, *Nigeria: Our Latest Protectorate*. Horace Marshall and Son, London, 1900)

Oba Ovonramwen, the last King of Benin before British rule. (From, H. Ling Roth, *Great Benin, Its Customs, Art and Horrors*. Routledge & Kegan Paul Ltd, London, 1903)

A group of women and children from Opobo in the late 1800s. (From Jesse Page, *The Black Bishop: Samuel Adjai Crowther.* Hodder & Stoughton, London, 1892)

Three Fulani men – late 1800s. (From, Charles Henry Robinson, *Hausaland, or Fifteen Hundred Miles through the Central Soudan.* Sampson Low, Marston and Company, London, 1900)

A group of Yoruba women in the late 1800s. (From Lt-Colonel A.F. Mock-ler-Ferryman, *British Nigeria: A Geographical and Historical Description of the British Possessions adjacent to the Niger River, West Africa.* Cassell and Co., London, 1902)

Bibliography

Abdulwahab, Abdulkadir. 'The Contribution of Hausa or Fulani Scholars to the Development of Islam in Ilorin Metropolis'. BA Honours Dissertation in Islamic Studies, Department of Islamic Studies, Faculty of Arts and Islamic Studies, Usmanu Danfodiyo University, Sokoto, October 2015.

Ade-Ajayi, J.F. 'Christian Missions and the Making of Nigeria: 1841–1891'. PhD thesis, University of London, July 1958.

Agiri, B.A. 'Early Oyo History Reconsidered'. *History in Africa*, Vol. 2 (1975), pp. 1–16.

Akinjogbin, I.A. 'Dahomey and Its Neighbours, 1708–1818'. PhD thesis, University of London, 1963.

Akinola, G.A. 'The Origin of the Eweka Dynasty of Benin: A Study in the Use and Abuse of Oral Traditions'. *Journal of the Historical Society of Nigeria*, Vol. 8, No. 3 (December 1976), pp. 21–36.

Akpolokpolo, Omo n'Oba n'Edo and Uku. 'Opening Ceremony Address by Omo n'Oba n'Edo, Uku Akpolokpolo, Erediauwa, CFR, Oba of Benin'. *The Benin Centenary, Part 1, African Arts*, Vol. 30, No. 3, Special Issue (Summer 1997), pp. 30–3. UCLA James S. Coleman African Studies Center.

Arnett, E.J. *The Rise of the Sokoto Fulani. Being a Paraphrase and in Some Parts a Translation of the Infaku'l maisuri of Sultan Mohammed Bello*. Kano Emirate Printing Department, Kano: 1922.

Atwood, Roger. 'The NOK of Nigeria'. *Archaeology*, Vol. 64, No. 4 (July/August 2011), pp. 34–8.

Azikiwe, Ben N. 'Fragments of Onitsha History'. *The Journal of Negro History*, Vol. 15, No. 4 (October 1930), pp. 474–97.

Baikie, William Balfour. *Narrative of an Exploring Voyage up the Rivers Kwo'ra and Bi'nue (Commonly Known as the Niger and Tsadda) in 1854*. John Murray: London, 1856.

Bascom, William. 'The Sanctions of Ifa Divination'. *The Journal of the Royal Anthropological Institute of Great Britain and Ireland*, Vol. 71, No. 1/2 (1941), pp. 43–54.

—— 'Review of the Oyo Empire c. 1600–c. 1836: A West African Imperialism in the Era of the Atlantic Slave, by Robin Law'. *African Economic History*, No. 6 (Autumn 1978), pp. 175–8.

Basden, George Thomas. *Among the Ibos of Nigeria: An Account of the Curious & Interesting Habits, Customs, & Beliefs of a Little Known African People by One Who Has for Many Years Lived Amongst Them on Close and Intimate Terms*. J.B. Lipincott Company: Philadelphia, 1921.

BBC. 'The Story of Africa: The Great Empires of Mali and Songhay', 2001. www.bbc.co.uk/sounds/play/p03njw99 (accessed 28 March 2023).

Bindloss, Harold. *In the Niger Country*. William Blackwood and Sons: Edinburgh and London, 1898.

Bosman, Willem. *A New and Accurate Description of the Coast of Guinea, Divided into the Gold, the Slave, and the Ivory Coasts.* James Knopton and Dan Midwinter: London, 1705.

Bowdich, T. Edward. *Mission from Cape Coast Castle to Ashantee.* John Murray: London, 1819.

Bowen, Reverend T.J. *Central Africa: Adventures and Missionary Labors in Several Countries in the Interior of Africa from 1849 to 1856.* Sheldon, Blakeman and Company: New York, 1857.

——*Grammar and Dictionary of the Yoruba Language with an Introductory Description of the Country and People of Yoruba.* Smithsonian Institution: New York, 1858.

Boyd, Jean. *The Caliph's Sister: Nana Asma'u, 1793–1865, Teacher, Poet, and Islamic Leader.* Frank Cass: London, 1989.

——'Distance Learning from Purdah in Nineteenth-Century Northern Nigeria: The Work of Asma'u Fodiyo'. *Journal of African Cultural Studies*, Vol. 14, No. 1, Islamic Religious Poetry in Africa (June 2001), pp. 7–22.

Bradbury, R.E. 'Chronological Problems in the Study of Benin History'. *Journal of the Historical Society of Nigeria*, Vol. 1, No. 4 (December 1959), pp. 263–87.

Brenner, Louis. 'The Shehus of Kukawa: A History of the al-Kanemi Dynasty of Bornu'. PhD thesis, Columbia University, 1968.

Burdon, J.A. 'The Fulani Emirates of Northern Nigeria'. *The Geographical Journal*, Vol. 24, No. 6 (December 1904), pp. 636–51.

Burns, Alan C. *History of Nigeria.* George Allen & Unwin: London, 1929.

Burton, Richard F. *Abeokuta and the Camaroons Mountains, An Exploration* (Vol. 1). Tinsley Brothers: London, 1863.

——*A Mission to Gelele, King of Dahome* (Vol. 1). Tinsley Brothers: London, 1864.

Church Missionary Intelligencer: A Monthly Journal of Missionary Information.

——Vol. IX. T. Hatchard: London, 1858.

——Vol. I, New Series. Seeley, Jackson and Halliday, Hatchard and Co., J. Nisbet and Co.: London, 1876.

Clapperton. Commander Hugh. *Journal of a Second Expedition into the Interior of Africa: From the Bight of Benin to Soccatoo.* John Murray: London, 1829.

Cohen, Ronald. 'Oedipus Rex and Regina: The Queen Mother in Africa'. *Journal of the International African Institute*, Vol 47, No. 1 (1977), pp. 14–30.

Coleman, James. *Nigeria, Background to Nationalism.* University of California Press, 1971.

Colonial Report – Annual for Northern Nigeria, Report for 1904 (No. 437), 1903. Her Majesty's Stationery Office, 1904.

Cosentino, Donald. 'Who Is That Fellow in the Many-Colored Cap? Transformations of Eshu in Old and New World Mythologies'. *The Journal of American Folklore*, Vol. 100, No. 397 (July–September 1987), pp. 261–75.

Crowder, Michael. *The Story of Nigeria.* Faber & Faber: London, 1973.

Crowther, Reverend Samuel. *A Vocabulary of the Yoruba Language: Part I, English and Yoruba. Part II, Yoruba and English. To which Are Prefixed, the Grammatical Elements of the Yoruba Language.* Church Missionary Society: London, 1843.

——*A Grammar of the Yoruba Language.* Seeleys: London, 1852.

——*Journal of an Expedition up the Niger and Tshadda Rivers Undertaken by Macgregor Laird, Esq. in Connection with the British Government, in 1854.* Church Missionary House: London, 1855.

——*Vocabulary of the Ibo Language*. Society for Promoting Christian Knowledge: London, 1882.

Crowther, Reverend Samuel and Taylor, Reverend John Christopher. *The Gospel on the Banks of the Niger*. Seeley, Jackson, and Halliday: London, 1859.

Dalzel, A. *The History of Dahomy: An Inland Kingdom of Africa: Compiled from Authentic Memoirs*. T. Spilsbury and Son: London, 1793.

Danfulani, Umar Habila Dadem. 'Factors Contributing to the Survival of the Bori Cult in Northern Nigeria'. *Numen*, Vol. 46, No. 4 (1999), pp. 412–47.

Daniel, F. 'Shehu dan Fodio'. *Journal of the Royal African Society*, Vol. 25, No. 99 (April 1926), pp. 278–83.

Danmole, H.O. 'The Ta'lif akhbār al-Qurun min umara' bilad Ilurin': A Critique'. *History in Africa*, Vol. 11 (1984), pp. 57–67.

Dayrell, Elphinstone. 'Further Notes on 'Nsibidi Signs with Their Meanings from the Ikom District, Southern Nigeria'. *The Journal of the Royal Anthropological Institute of Great Britain and Ireland*, Vol. 41 (July–December 1911), pp. 521–40.

Denham, Major Dixon, Clapperton, Captain Hugh, Oudney. Dr Walter. *Narrative of Travels and Discoveries in Northern and Central Africa, in the Years 1822, 1823, and 1824* (With an Appendix). John Murray: London, 1826.

Dennett, Richard Edward. *Nigerian Studies: The Religious and Political System of the Yoruba*. Macmillan and Co.: London, 1910.

——'The Ogboni and Other Secret Societies in Nigeria'. *Journal of the Royal African Society*, Vol. 16, No. 61 (October 1916), pp. 16–29.

Dent, Martin. 'Ethnicity and Territorial Politic in Nigeria', in Graham Smith (ed.), *Federalism: The Multiethnic Challenge*. Longman: New York, 1995, pp. 128–53.

Egharevba, Jacob. *A Short History of Benin*. Ibadan University Press: Ibadan, 1968.

Eisenhofer, Stefan and Egharevba, Jacob. 'The Origins of the Benin Kingship in the Works of Jacob Egharevba'. *History in Africa*, Vol. 22 (1995), pp. 141–63.

Ekejiuba, Felicia. 'Omu Okwei, The Merchant Queen of Ossomari – a Biographical Sketch'. *Journal of the Historical Society of Nigeria*, Vol. 3, No. 4 (June 1967), pp. 633–46.

Ellis, A.B. *The Yoruba Speaking Peoples of the Slave Coast of Africa*. Chapman and Hall: London, 1894.

Equiano, Olaudah. *The Interesting Narrative of the Life of Olaudah Equiano: or Gustavus Vassa, the African*. Self Published: London, 1789.

Fagg, B.E.B. 'The Nok Culture in Prehistory'. *Journal of the Historical Society of Nigeria*, Vol. 1, No. 4 (December 1959), pp. 288–93.

Falola, Toyin. *Colonialism and Violence in Nigeria*. Indiana University Press: Bloomington and Indianapolis, 2009.

Falola, Toyin, Doortmont, Michel R., and Adeyemi, M.C. 'Iwe Itan : A Traditional Yoruba History and Its Author'. *The Journal of African History*, Vol. 30, No. 2 (1989), pp. 301–29.

Farrow, Stephen S. 'Yoruba Paganism, or the Religious Beliefs of the West African Negroes, Particularly of the Yoruba Tribes of Southern Nigeria'. PhD thesis, University of Edinburgh, 1924.

Galway, Henry L. 'Nigeria in the "Nineties"'. *Journal of the Royal African Society*, Vol. 29, No. 115 (April 1930), pp. 221–47.

Gaskell, W. 'The Influence of Europe on Early Benin Art'. *The Connoisseur* (1902), pp. 99–103.

Glover, Lady. *Life of John Hawley Glover*. Smith, Elder & Co.: London, 1897.

The Guardian, 18 March 2016.

Gunsch, Kathryn Wysocki. 'Art and/or Ethnographica?: The Reception of Benin Works from 1897–1935'. *African Arts*, Vol. 46, No. 4 (Winter 2013), pp. 22–31.

Hales, Kevin. 'The Moving Finger: A Rhetorical, Grammatological and Afrinographic Exploration of Nsibidi in Nigeria and Cameroon'. PhD thesis, Ohio University, August 2015.

Hallam, W.K.R. 'The Bayajida Legend in Hausa Folklore'. *The Journal of African History*, Vol. 7, No. 1 (1966), pp. 47–60.

Hinderer, Anna. *Seventeen Years in the Yoruba Country: Memorials of Anna Hinderer (Third Edition)*. Seeley, Jackson, and Halliday: London, 1873.

Hiskett, Mervyn. 'The Nineteenth Century Jihads in West Africa', in J.A. Flint (ed.), *The Cambridge History of Africa. Vol. V: From c. 1790 to c. 1870*. Cambridge University Press: Cambridge, 1976, pp. 125–69.

——*The Sword of Truth: The Life and Times of the Shehu Usuman Dan Fodio*. Northwestern University Press: Evanston, Illinois, 1994.

Hodgkin, Thomas. *Nigerian Perspectives: An Historical Anthology*. Oxford University Press: London, 1960.

Horton, James Africanus Beale. *West African Countries and Peoples, British and Native: With the Requirements Necessary for Establishing That Self Government Recommended by the Committee of the House of Commons, 1865; and a Vindication of the African Race*. W.J. Johnson: London, 1868.

Hunwick, John O. 'West Africa and the Arabic Language'. *Sudanic Africa*, Vol. 15, Language in Africa (2004), pp. 133–44.

Hyam, Ronald. *Elgin and Churchill at the Colonial Office, 1905–08: The Watershed of the Empire – Commonwealth*. Macmillan: London, 1968.

Idrees, A.A. 'Gogo Habiba of Bida: The Rise and Demise of a 19th Century Merchant Princess and Politician'. *African Study Monographs*, Vol. 12, No. 1 (1991), pp. 1–9.

Ijoma, J. Okoro. 'The History of the Igbo-Edo Borderland before 1891'. PhD thesis, University of Birmingham, 1979.

——'Portuguese Activities in West Africa before 1600: The Consequences'. *Transafrican Journal of History*, Vol. 11 (1982), pp. 136–46.

Isichei, Elizabeth. 'Ibo and Christian Beliefs: Some Aspects of a Theological Encounter'. *African Affairs*, Vol. 68, No. 271 (April 1969), pp. 121–34.

——*A History of the Igbo People*. Macmillan: London, 1976.

Jackson, Robert D. 'The Twenty Years War: Invasion and Resistance in Southeastern Nigeria, 1900–1919'. PhD thesis, Harvard University, 1975.

Johnson, Samuel. *The History of the Yorubas: From the Earliest Times to the Beginning of the British Protectorate*. CMS Bookshops: Lagos, 1921.

Johnston, Hugh Anthony Stephens. *The Fulani Empire of Sokoto*. Oxford University Press: London, Ibadan, Nairobi, 1967.

Jones, Gwilym Iwam. *Report of the Position, Status, and Influence of Chiefs and Natural Rulers in the Eastern Region of Nigeria*. Government Printer, Eastern Region: Enugu, 1956.

Kerr, Robert. *A General History and Collection of Voyages and Travels: Arranged in Systematic Order: Forming a Complete History of the Origin and Progress of Navigation, Discovery, and Commerce, by Sea and Land, from the Earliest Ages to the Present Time, Volume VII*. William Blackwood: Edinburgh, 1812.

Kota, Kariya. 'A Revolt in the Early Sokoto Caliphate'. *Journal of African Asian and African Studies*, No. 95 (2018), pp. 221–303.

——'A Letter from Muhammad Al-Amin El-Kanemi to a Fulani Muslim Community in Bornu'. *Journal of Asian and African Studies*, No. 99 (2020), pp. 77–87.

Laird, MacGregor and Oldfield, R.A.K. *Narrative of an Expedition into the Interior of Africa, by the River Niger, in the Steam-Vessels Quorra and Alburkah, in 1832, 1833, and 1834 (Volume 1)*. Richards Bentley: London, 1837.

Lander, Richard. *Records of Captain Clapperton's Last Expedition to Africa*. Henry Colburn and Richard Bentley: London, 1830.

Lander, Richard and John. *Journal of an Expedition to Explore the Course and Termination of the Niger, with a Narrative of a Voyage down That River to Its Termination (Volume I)*. J. & J. Harper: New York, 1832.

——*Journal of an Expedition to Explore the Course and Termination of the Niger, with a Narrative of a Voyage down That River to Its Termination (Volume II)*. Harper & Brothers: New York, 1844.

Last, Murray Denis. *The Sokoto Caliphate*. Green & Co Ltd: London, 1967.

——'Contradictions in Creating a Jihadi Capital: Sokoto in the Nineteenth Century and Its Legacy'. *African Studies Review*, Vol. 56, No. 2 (September 2013), pp. 1–20.

——'From Dissent to Dissidence: The Genesis & Development of Reformist Islamic Groups in Northern Nigeria', in Abdul Raufu Mustapha (ed.), *Sects & Social Disorder: Muslim Identities & Conflict in Northern Nigeria*. Boydell & Brewer, James Currey: Suffolk and New York, 2014, pp. 18–53.

Law, Robin. 'How Truly Traditional Is Our Traditional History? The Case of Samuel Johnson and the Recording of Yoruba Oral Tradition'. *History in Africa*, Vol. 11 (1984), pp. 195–221.

Leith-Ross, S. 'Notes on the Osu System among the Ibo of Owerri Province, Nigeria'. *Journal of the International African Institute*, Vol. 10, No. 2 (April, 1937), pp. 206-20.

Leonard, Major Arthur Glyn. *The Lower Niger and Its Tribes*. Macmillan and Co: London, 1906.

Livingstone, W.P. *Mary Slessor of Calabar: Pioneer Missionary*. Hodder & Stoughton: London, 1916.

Lovejoy, Paul E. 'Concubinage in the Sokoto Caliphate (1804–1903)'. *Slavery & Abolition: A Journal of Slave and Post-Slave Studies*, Vol. 11, No. 2 (1990), pp. 158–89.

Low, Victor Nelson. 'The Border States: A Political History of Three Northwest Nigerian Emirates, ca. 1800–1902'. PhD thesis, University of California, Los Angeles, 1967.

Lucas, Canon J. Olumide. 'The Religion of the Yorubas: Especially in Relation to the Religion of Ancient Egypt – Being in Account of the Religious Beliefs and Practices of the Yoruba Peoples of Southern Nigeria, Especially in Relation to the Religion of Ancient Egypt'. PhD thesis, Durham University, 1942.

Macgregor, J.K. 'Some Notes on Nsibidi'. *The Journal of the Royal Anthropological Institute of Great Britain and Ireland*, Vol. 39 (January–June 1909), pp. 209–19.

May, Daniel J. 'Journey in the Yóruba and Núpe Countries in 1858'. *The Journal of the Royal Geographical Society of London*, Vol. 30 (1860), pp. 212–33.

Meek, C.K. *Law and Authority in a Nigerian Tribe: A Study in Indirect Rule*. Oxford University Press: London, New York, Toronto, 1937.

Meyerowitz, H. and V. 'Bronzes and Terra-Cottas from Ile-Ife'. *The Burlington Magazine for Connoisseurs*, Vol. 75, No. 439 (October 1939), pp. 150–2 and 154–5.

——'Ancient Nigerian Bronzes'. *The Burlington Magazine for Connoisseurs*, Vol. 79, No. 462 (September 1941), pp. 88–93.

Mockler-Ferryman. Lt-Colonel A.F. *British West Africa: Its Rise and Progress*. Swan Sonnenschein and Co.: London, 1898.

Mumin, Meikal. 'The Arabic Script in Africa: Understudied Literacy', in Meikal Mumin and Kees Versteegh (eds), *The Arabic Script in Africa: Studies in the Use of a Writing System*. Brill: London, Boston, 2014, pp. 41–76.

Naylor, Paul. 'Abdullahi Dan Fodio and Muhammad Bello's Debate over the Torobbe-Fulani: Case Study for a New Methodology for Arabic Primary Source Material from West Africa'. *Islamic Africa*, Vol. 9 (2018), pp. 34–54.

Njoku, Onwuka N. 'Magic, Religion and Iron Technology in Precolonial North-Western Igboland'. *Journal of Religion in Africa*, Vol. 21, Fasc. 3 (August, 1991), pp. 194–215.

Norris, Robert. *Memoirs of the Reign of Bossa Ahadee. King of. Dahomy an Inland Country of Guinea*. W. Lowndes: London, 1789.

Ogedengbe, Kingsley Oladipo. 'The Aboh Kingdom of the Lower Niger, c.1650–1900'. PhD thesis, University of Wisconsin, 1971.

Ogharaerumi, Mark Onesosan B. 'The Translation of the Bible into Yoruba, Igbo, and Isekiri Languages of Nigeria, with Special Reference to the Contribution of Mother-Tongue Speakers'. PhD thesis, University of Aberdeen, 1986.

Ojo, Olatunji. '"Heepa" (Hail) Orisa: The Orisa Factor in the Birth of Yoruba Identity'. *Journal of Religion in Africa*, Vol. 39, Fasc. 1 (2009), pp. 30–59.

Okonkwo, Christopher N. 'A Critical Divination: Reading Sula as Ogbanje-Abiku'. *African American Review*, Vol. 38, No. 4 (Winter 2004), pp. 651–68.

Okunogbe, Oyebola. 'Does Exposure to Other Ethnic Regions Promote National Integration? Evidence from Nigeria'. World Bank Group, Development Research Group, Policy Research Working Paper 8606, October 2018.

Orr, C.W. 'The Hausa Race'. *Journal of the Royal African Society*, Vol. 7, No. 27 (April 1908), pp. 278–83.

Osadolor, Osarhieme Benson, M.A. 'The Military System of Benin Kingdom, c.1440–1897'. PhD thesis, University of Hamburg, 2001.

Page, Jesse. *The Black Bishop: Samuel Adjai Crowther*. Hodder & Stoughton: London, 1908.

Palmer, H. Richard. 'The Kano Chronicle'. *The Journal of the Royal Anthropological Institute of Great Britain and Ireland*, Vol. 38 (January–June 1908), pp. 58–98.

Paracka Jr, Daniel Joseph. 'The Athens of West Africa: A History of International Education at Fourah Bay College, Freetown, Sierra Leone (1816–2001)'. PhD thesis, Georgia State University, 2001.

PBS. *Africa's Great Civilisations: The Atlantic Age*. www.pbs.org/video/africas-great-civilizations-atlantic-age-hour-five/ (aired 1 March 2017).

Philips, John Edward, 'Ribats in the Sokoto Caliphate: Selected Studies, 1804–1903'. PhD thesis, University of California, Los Angeles, 1992.

Posnansky, Merrick. 'New Light on Benin Archeology and Technology'. *Transactions of the Historical Society of Ghana*, Vol. 16, No. 1 (June 1975), pp. 117–23.

Ratté, Mary Lou. 'Imperial Looting and the Case of Benin'. Master of Arts Dissertation in History, University of Massachusetts, Amherst, 1972.

Rawson, Geoffrey. *Life of Admiral Sir Harry Rawson*. Edward Arnold: London, 1914.

Read, Charles Hercules and Dalton, Ormonde Maddock. 'Works of Art from Benin City'. *The Journal of the Anthropological Institute of Great Britain and Ireland*, Vol. 27 (1898), pp. 362–82.

——*Antiquities from the City of Benin and from Other Parts of West Africa in the British Museum*. Trustees of the British Museum: London, 1899.

Reichmuth, Stefan. 'Imam Umaru's Account of the Origins of the Ilorin Emirate: A Manuscript in the Heinz Sölken Collection, Frankfurt'. *Sudanic Africa*, Vol. 4, Special Issue on Kano (1993), pp. 155–73.

Reis, Joao Jose. 'Slave Rebellion in Brazil: The African Muslim Uprisings in Bahia, 1835'. PhD thesis, University of Minnesota, December 1982.

Richardson, Robert. *The Story of the Niger*. T. Nelson and Sons: London, 1888.

Robinson, Charles Henry. *Nigeria: Our Latest Protectorate*. Horace Marshall and Son: London, 1900.

Roth, Felix N. 'A Diary of a Surgeon with the Benin Punitive Expedition'. *Journal of the Manchester Geographical Society*, Vol. 14 (1898), pp. 208–21.

Roth, H. Ling. *Great Benin, Its Customs, Art and Horrors*. Routledge & Kegan Paul: London, 1903.

Rudkin, Captain W.E. 'In British West Africa. The Operations in the Agbor District, Southern Nigeria, June to August, 1906, Consequent Upon the Murder of Mr. O. S. Crewe-Read, District Commissioner'. *United Service Magazine*, Vol. 35 (April to September 1907), William Clowes & Sons: London, 1907.

Ryder, A.F.C. 'Missionary Activity in the Kingdom of Warri to the Early Nineteenth Century'. *Journal of the Historical Society of Nigeria*, Vol. 2, No. 1 (December 1960), pp. 1–26.

——'The Benin Missions'. *Journal of the Historical Society of Nigeria*, Vol. 2, No. 2 (December 1961), pp. 231–59.

——'A Reconsideration of the Ife-Benin Relationship'. *Journal of African History*, Vol. vi, I (1965), pp. 25–37.

Sa'ad, Sadi. 'The Dynamics of Political Development in a Multicultural Society: The Case of Ilorin during the 19th and 20th Centuries'. PhD thesis, Department of History, Faculty of Arts, Ahmadu Bello University, Zaria, 2015.

Schon, Reverend James Frederick and Crowther, Samuel. *Journals of the Rev. James Frederick Schön and Mr. Samuel Crowther: Who, with the Sanction of Her Majesty's Government, Accompanied the Expedition up the Niger in 1841 on Behalf of the Church Missionary Society*. Hatchard and Son: London, 1842.

Shaw, Flora L. *A Tropical Dependency: An Outline of the Ancient History of the Western Soudan with an Account of the Modern Settlement of Northern Nigeria*. James Nisbet & Co.: London, 1905.

Shields, Francine. 'Palm Oil & Power: Women in an Era of Economic and Social Transition in 19th Century Yorubaland (South-Western Nigeria)'. PhD thesis, University of Stirling, 1997.

Smith, H.F.C. 'A Neglected Theme of West African History: The Islamic Revolutions of the 19th Century'. *Journal of the Historical Society of Nigeria*, Vol. 2, No. 2 (December 1961), pp. 169–85.

Smith, Robert. 'The Alafin in Exile: A Study of the Igboho Period in Oyo History'. *The Journal of African History*, Vol. 6, No. 1 (1965), pp. 57–77.

Smith, Robert (ed.) and Packman, Brenda (trans.). *Memoirs of Giambattista Scala, Consul of His Italian Majesty in Lagos in Guinea (1862)*. Oxford University Press: Oxford, 2000.

St Croix, F.W. *The Fulani of Northern Nigeria: Some General Notes*. Government Printer: Lagos, 1945.

Starratt, Priscilla Ellen. 'Oral history in Muslim Africa: Al-Maghili Legends in Kano'. PhD thesis, University of Michigan, 1993.

Stevenson, Ian. 'The Belief in Reincarnation among the Igbo of Nigeria'. *Journal of Asian and African Studies*, Vol. XX, No. 1–2 (1985), pp. 13–30.

Sundkler, Bengt and Steed, Christopher. *A History of the Church in Africa*. Cambridge University Press: Cambridge, 2004.

Talbot, Percy Amaury. *In the Shadow of the Bush*. William Heinemann: London, 1912.

Taylor, John Christopher. *Isuama-Ibo Katekism: Translated from Dr Watts's First Catechism*. W.M. Watts: London, 1859.

——*Ijo or Idso Primer*. Church Missionary Society: London, 1862.

The Times, Saturday 25 September 1897.

Thurstan Shaw, Charles. 'The Guinea Zone: General Situation', in M. Elfasi (ed.), *General History of Africa: Africa from the Seventh to the Eleventh Century*. UNESCO: Paris, 1988. pp. 461–87.

Tunis, Irwin Leonard. 'Origins, Chronology and Metallurgy of the Benin Wall Bas-Reliefs'. MPhil thesis, School of Oriental and African Studies, University of London, September 1979.

Ubah, C.N. 'Changing Patterns of Leadership among the Igbo, 1900–1960'. *Trans African Journal of History*, Vol. 16 (1987), pp. 167–84.

Ukpabi, S.C. 'The Archaeology of Iboland'. *African Studies Review*, Vol. 14, No. 2 (September 1971), pp. 336–41.

Vandeleur, Lieutenant Seymour. *Campaigning on the Upper Nile and Niger*. Methuen & Co.: London, 1898.

Willett, Frank. 'Ife and Its Archaeology'. *The Journal of African History*, Vol. 1, No. 2 (1960), pp. 231–48.

Wood, Funlayo E. 'Bush Knowledge in the Concrete Jungle: A Day in the Life of an Urban Babalawo'. *Transition*, No. 125, Religion (2018), pp. 89–103.

Index